PRAISE FOR *VOICE MARKETING*

"*Voice Marketing: Harnessing the Power of Conversational AI to Drive Customer Engagement* is an insightful and informative book that demystifies the world of voice assistants and provides practical strategies for leveraging this emerging technology to drive business growth. The authors' clear and concise writing style makes complex topics easy to understand, making this book a must-read for anyone looking to stay ahead of the curve in the rapidly evolving world of marketing." —**Shelly Palmer**, professor of advanced media in residence at Syracuse University's S.I. Newhouse School of Public Communications, CEO of The Palmer Group, and author of five books, including *Blockchain–Cryptocurrency, NFTs & Smart Contracts*

"This book charts the many possibilities for a completely new form of interaction between customers and brands. Progress in this field will happen very fast, and the rewards for people who master the interface first will be disproportionately large. Reading this book will improve your odds immensely." —**Rory Sutherland**, vice chair, Ogilvy, and author of *Alchemy: The Dark Art and Curious Science of Creating Magic in Brands, Business, and Life*

"As conversational AI moves from being 'nice to have' to 'must have,' *Voice Marketing* is a must-read for those looking to implement conversational AI in their customer experience strategy, offering valuable insights and expertise from industry pioneers. This book provides a comprehensive guide to leveraging this emerging technology to enhance customer engagement and satisfaction." —**Pete Erickson**, founder, Modev and organizer of VOICE & AI: The Generative & Conversational AI Conference

"We interact increasingly with artificial intelligence through voice prompts, and by way of those interactions, we experience a world that we are only starting to see. In their book, *Voice Marketing: Harnessing the Power of Conversational AI to Drive Customer Engagement*, Minsky, Westwater, Westwater, and Fahey do a phenomenal job demystifying where voice marketing is today and how it will fit into consumers' daily interactions with brands." —**Joe Scartz**, chief digital commerce officer, TPN, Omnicom Media Group, Inc

"*Voice Marketing* is the go-to resource for brands to understand what voice marketing is, how it works, and why they need to invest in it today. I love the mix of storytelling with research sprinkled throughout the book. It has everything from case studies to the importance of audio branding and even what role AI will play in the future of voice marketing. A must-read to ensure your brand will be found when consumers call for it." —**Christoph Trappe**, global content strategy consultant, Trappe Digital LLC and host of *The Business Storytelling Show*

"When it comes to voice marketing, so many of us simply learned by doing, even if it meant occasionally messing up our 'wake word' or inadvertently placing an Amazon order. We have learned what our devices sound like, just as we learned to recognize particular sonic branding and needle-drops. In their new book, *Voice Marketing: Harnessing the Power of Conversational AI to Drive Customer Engagement*, Minsky, Westwater, Westwater, and Fahey show us just how much we have left to learn, with great breadth and depth. There is an element of reading the future here too, as the wildly growing worlds of AI and language models are addressed. Throughout the chapters, the importance of how to best serve prospects and customers remains at the forefront." —**Dave Aron**, professor of marketing, Dominican University

"How has AI changed daily life? The digital world is now conversational. There are 500 million Alexa-enabled devices. Apple Siri and Google Assistant are available on billions of smartphones, in cars, and household gadgets. ChatGPT amassed 100 million monthly active users faster than any application is history. Is your brand conversation-ready? The authors have laid out a strategic and practical guide to navigate the shift to conversational customer interactions. Read it to understand how AI is changing the digital landscape. Use it to seize opportunities and avoid common pitfalls." —**Bret Kinsella**, founder & CEO, Voicebot.ai & creator of *The Voicebot Podcast*

VOICE MARKETING

HARNESSING THE POWER OF CONVERSATIONAL AI TO DRIVE CUSTOMER ENGAGEMENT

Laurence Minsky, Susan Westwater, Scot Westwater, and Colleen Fahey

FOREWORD BY PHILIP KOTLER

ROWMAN & LITTLEFIELD
Lanham • Boulder • New York • London

Senior Acquisitions Editor: Natalie Mandziuk
Assistant Acquisitions Editor: Yu Ozaki
Sales and Marketing Inquiries: textbooks@rowman.com

Credits and acknowledgments for material borrowed from other sources, and reproduced with permission, appear on the appropriate pages within the text.

Published by Rowman & Littlefield
An imprint of The Rowman & Littlefield Publishing Group, Inc.
4501 Forbes Boulevard, Suite 200, Lanham, Maryland 20706
www.rowman.com

86-90 Paul Street, London EC2A 4NE

British Library Cataloguing in Publication Information Available

Library of Congress Cataloging-in-Publication Data
Names: Minsky, Laurence, author. | Westwater, Susan, author. | Westwater,
   Scot, author. | Fahey, Colleen, author.
Title: Voice marketing : harnessing the power of conversational AI to drive
   customer engagement / Laurence Minsky, Susan Westwater, Scot Westwater,
   Colleen Fahey.
Description: Lanham : Rowman & Littlefield, [2024] | Includes index.
Identifiers: LCCN 2023019718 (print) | LCCN 2023019719 (ebook) | ISBN
   9781538155394 (cloth) | ISBN 9781538155400 (paperback) | ISBN
   9781538155417 (ebook)
Subjects: LCSH: Word-of-mouth advertising. | Social media—Marketing. |
   Artificial intelligence—Economic aspects. | Customer relations.
Classification: LCC HF5827.95 .M56 2024 (print) | LCC HF5827.95 (ebook) |
   DDC 658.8—dc23/eng/20230630
LC record available at https://lccn.loc.gov/2023019718
LC ebook record available at https://lccn.loc.gov/2023019719

♾️™ The paper used in this publication meets the minimum requirements of American National Standard for Information Sciences—Permanence of Paper for Printed Library Materials, ANSI/NISO Z39.48-1992.

To Mickey Brazeal, in recognition of his lifelong dedication to the advancement of learning in the field of marketing through his teaching and writing.

We celebrate his promotion of knowledge and express our gratitude for his support of our own endeavors, especially for going above and beyond in helping us structure this book.

Contents

Foreword

Philip Kotler, SC Johnson Distinguished Professor of International Marketing, Kellogg School of Management, Northwestern University

When I wrote *Marketing 5.0: Technology for Humanity* with Hermawan Kartajaya and Iwan Setiawan, the common thread among the innovations we described was marketing's big move from extolling a business's offers to accommodating its audiences.

We defined Marketing 5.0 as "the application of technologies to create, communicate, deliver, and enhance value through the customer journey." In focusing on the new tools, platforms, and thinking strategies available to marketers since 2021, it was inevitable that we would note the emerging world of voice-enabled interactions.

This exceptionally human form of customer interaction got a boost from the pandemic, when people had more time and privacy to talk with in-home devices and appliances instead of typing keypads or swiping screens. And these new habits haven't disappeared now that employees have begun to return to their workplaces. The behaviors have stuck around.

Steadily and without fanfare, the world of voice has advanced to the stage in which you may find you're using it yourself without ever having consciously decided to adopt it.

Though less of a media darling than the metaverse and not as buzzy as robotics, voice is more apt to find its way into every corner of the customer journey.

Voice is already at work simplifying the processes of shopping online, helping audiences gather information, encouraging exploration of virtual worlds, easing requests for service, facilitating the sharing of stories across media, and filling even bigger jobs such as providing companionship and medical care.

Voice has also begun to open the internet to include the visually impaired, people with low literacy, sufferers of hand pain or dexterity problems, and members of the neuro-divergent community. In extending the use of voice, voice marketing can add richness to people's lives.

Comparatively little has been written about the potential of voice—and even less about voice-activated marketing, in which marketers have to respond to the infinitely varied requests from their audiences. With no drop-down menus to guide them, customers have complete control. The need for a carpet cleaner might be expressed as "How do I get this stain out of my throw rug?" "My dog pooped on my carpet," or "Where can I buy a dog-friendly floor mat?"

This freedom has led to an important new job called conversation design, just one of the skill sets needed for voice marketing. Many of the other occupations where you'll find evidence of voice expertise are those enumerated in the first table of *Marketing 5.0*: artificial intelligence, natural language processing, sensor technology, robotics, virtual reality, and the Internet of Things.

I was impressed with the chapters that describe how companies and their brands can already benefit from adding voice opportunities to sell their products. I believe that this book offers the best and most concrete in-depth view of voice marketing opportunities.

If you agree with us that "Marketing is the set of human activities directed at facilitating and consummating exchanges," you'll be excited to read the examples of exchanges shared in this book—all facilitated by a simple superpower most of us mastered before the age of five.

Marketing Over Voice Applications

Imagine you are driving in your car and need directions to a restaurant so you ask Siri, Google Assistant, or the in-car assistant for a list of coffee shops, and you hear the answer you need to send you on your way. Simple. From the business perspective though, if you're a coffee shop owner, you want your place to be the one that gets mentioned. Achieving that is not as simple because search tends to be conducted differently on voice assistants than via traditional means, so your optimization strategies need to be different as well. Plus, you might want to enable the voice assistant to take the order so it's ready when the customer arrives.

Now imagine you're at home cooking dinner and your hands are full, but you need to find a certain recipe, so you ask your voice assistant to find it. If you manage a food brand and you want the home chef to include your product in their creation, you might want to develop a voice-activated recipe program. Imagine how many more units you would sell if you were to suggest how to use your products, precisely at the point of need.

Or imagine it's night and you're watching a commercial and decide you want more information about the product or service being advertised, but you are too tired to get up to grab your laptop, so you pull out your phone and, because it's faster to talk than to type, you simply ask Google Assistant, Alexa, or Siri for information, and it responds by answering your request and offering a link to take you to the appropriate web page. For this to work for customers, marketers must optimize their content to be discoverable on these voice assistants. Think of the incremental sales—and the resulting extra profit—that you would be able to generate because you had inserted your brand into the right place at the right time.

In the future, you might even enhance the experience to allow the customer to purchase your product right from their voice assistant.

Finally, imagine a customer ordering an item from your website and wanting to know what stage of the delivery process it is in, so they simply ask their voice assistant, and it speaks up with an immediate update of where the item is and when to expect it. Imagine the relationship marketers can build by providing this level of brand experience. However, for this to work, you will need to have a voice-enabled customer relationship management (CRM) system to fulfill the request.

These examples show the power of marketing your brand through voice assistants, a power that is sure to grow as the capabilities increase. Voice isn't merely a future option marketers might enjoy someday—it's available now—and, as you'll see, smart marketers are already using voice applications and channels to help advance their brands. If you want to join Allstate, Amazon, Butterball, Coca-Cola, Dominos, Google, Marriott, McDonald's, Mercedes-Benz, Reebok, Samsung, Starbucks, and other leading marketers to broaden and deepen your position in the marketplace, now is your chance. As you will see in later chapters, they are using it for new product introductions, short-term promotions, sales support, the actual shopping experience, post-purchase customer services, brand building, and more.

Before we deep dive into voice marketing and explore ways to use it along the various points of the path to purchase to deepen your brand's relationship with its prospects and customers, encourage them to take the next step along the path, keep them engaged, improve their overall brand experiences, and drive incremental sales, it's first important to understand how the world of voice is defined and glimpse some of its key aspects. That's what we'll cover in this chapter. We'll also provide you with two outside guest perspectives to help you understand the full power of voice for your brand.

To start, *voice* is an umbrella term for any interaction that allows a person to control a computer or device by simply talking to it. Rather than typing on a keyboard or tapping and swiping on a screen, you tell the computer or device—even an appliance—what you want, and it responds to your requests, questions, or commands. When it comes to voice, many people might immediately think of a smart speaker such as Amazon Alexa or Google Assistant, but there are many other ways voice technology can be used to engage with a brand to get information, make a purchase, get user instructions, complete a task, and more. The application could be as simple as speaking into your television remote to change the channels or searching for product information by speaking to Siri, Alexa, or Google Assistant on your phone or even talking to a brand's owned assistant on their website or within their mobile app. It can be used in a business enterprise to make the jobs of controlling a presentation, finding a file, and even scheduling meetings easier, faster, and smoother.

In other words, *voice* is a catchall word describing any platform where the user's actual voice, not a keyboard, is the main input that drives the experience. It is also important to recognize—and we will get further into this later in the book—that voice might not be the *only* type of interaction or input during the full course of the experience. For instance, consumers might use a voice application to search for a product to find information about it, but then continue shopping on their computers with keyboards or in store to make their final purchases. A voice experience might be the first touchpoint in a series of interactions with your brand that result in a request for a coupon or other promotional discount, information on where to buy your product or service, help with onboarding and setup, or troubleshooting a problem to avoid a call to customer service.

While consumers and enterprises now have these new applications of voice, the use of voice to control or to elicit a response is not so new. Automated telephone attendants (ATAs) have provided call routing and other customer services through interactive voice recognition platforms (IVRs) since the early 1990s.[1] What's exciting about these new voice applications is the way the experiences are structured and the range of the devices involved, giving them wider applications. In fact, beyond voice calls, these voice interactions can involve everything from water faucets to appliances to light bulbs to an assistant that lives on your mobile phone or in your car. As a result, the use of conversational AI is now a powerful new way for your customers to interact with your brand in their homes using smart speakers, in their cars using their smartphones or the Alexa auto device, or on the go using their headphones or AirPods. This gives them a way to find information on the internet without needing to type, swipe, or look at a screen. Voice technology enables customers to take their brands with them. To echo back to when Steve Jobs launched the iPod over twenty years ago, the voice ecosystem puts thousands of brands within reach, now just a spoken word away.

How Voice Works: A Look at Artificial Intelligence (AI)

While there's a range of devices that audiences can use to engage with voice experiences, the whole process starts with the ability to recognize and process your speech. This is possible through machine learning, which is a subset of AI. Conversational AI refers to the specific technologies that you can talk to, like chatbots or voice assistants. Through the use of speech recognition and natural language processing (NLP), we are able to make it possible for a voice assistant like Siri, Alexa, or Google Assistant to understand, interpret, and generate a response to spoken language.[2]

Achieving reliable and consistent speech recognition and NLP requires a large amount of data that is then used to inform the language models that power it. The range of the data impacts how well those models will be able to handle accents, various pronunciations, cultural language variations, and even industry-specific jargon like medical or legal terminology.

As a marketer, it is important to know the role AI plays in voice experiences and how it powers them, but you can be sure that there are engineers, linguists, programmers, and even AI trainers whose deep expertise fuels the technical development and creation of these technologies (so you're not required to have that deep knowledge). For that reason, in this book, we're not going to go any deeper into those areas because otherwise this book would be called AI marketing, and it's called voice marketing.

A simplified view of how voice recognition works

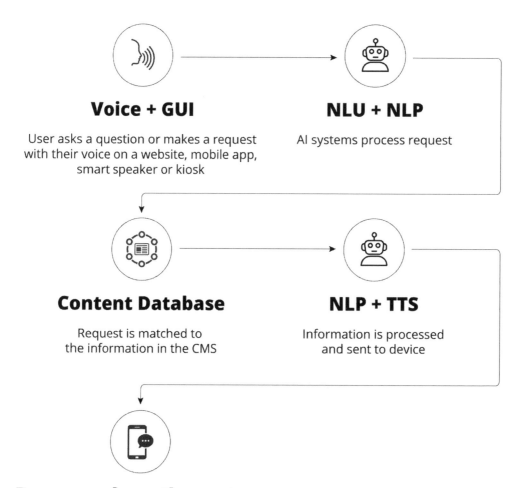

Voice + GUI

User asks a question or makes a request with their voice on a website, mobile app, smart speaker or kiosk

NLU + NLP

AI systems process request

Content Database

Request is matched to the information in the CMS

NLP + TTS

Information is processed and sent to device

Response from the system

User receives content in audio and/or visual formats

Figure 1.1. A simplified schematic of the conversational AI voice recognition and response process.

The Voice Landscape

The voice brand ecosystem is different from others in that, depending on what device and global region you're looking at, you'll find a different category leader. As of this writing, the dominant voice assistant from the perspective of mobile phones is Apple's Siri assistant, but if you look at the smart speaker sector in the United States, Amazon Alexa is the leader in adoption and usage. Google is in the middle. To add another layer of complexity, Apple's Siri still holds a massive mindshare even though the company has not aggressively supported their smart speakers as part of their voice strategy. Of course, since voice is a new medium, there is currently a broad range of different terminology.

Voice Assistants—These are essentially the voice equivalents of the visually based mobile applications that live on your phone, though these allow you to interact and control your device through speech. Voice applications can exist as a stand-alone experience such as an owned assistant that lives on your website or within the ecosystem of assistants that has been created by one of the big tech manufacturers. Of course, each of the manufacturers has a different name for the voice application in its own ecosystem. On Amazon Alexa, these apps are referred to as Skills, Google Assistant has App Actions, Apple calls their approach Siri Shortcuts, and Samsung's Bixby refers to them as Capsules.

Any content or function created by the manufacturer as part of their assistant is referred to as "first party" while anything that's created by an outside development team or an outside sponsor such as your brand is called "third party." It's important to know the difference, because first-party and third-party voice apps are governed, treated, and marketed differently. Finally, because Apple has not opened up development of applications for Siri to third-party developers, it's not possible to create a voice-only application directly for Siri. But there are Siri Shortcuts, which enables Siri to retrieve data directly from iOS applications to provide information to the end user without opening the app. Siri Shortcuts can also provide a way for brands to link their users deeper into their iOS app in response to the person's voice request.

As with any technology, this landscape is constantly changing and evolving. Early in 2022, Google announced it would be sunsetting Google Conversational Actions and removing access to them by developers and users as of June 13, 2023.[3] Amazon also restructured and reduced some of the teams associated with Amazon Alexa late in 2022.[4] This raised some concerns that perhaps voice assistants, especially Amazon Alexa, were not long for the marketplace. The reality is that the voice space is evolving, and some areas that looked promising were not delivering the profitability needed. Amazon still has a robust team supporting Amazon Alexa internally and externally as evidenced by its presence at CES and other trade shows and conferences and also the job openings that are still being posted.

The Kinds of Voice-Enabled Interactions

There are three main categories into which the interaction can fall:

1. **Voice Only:** Experiences that have voice as the only input and output. Amazon Echo Dot and Google Home are generally considered voice only although,

technically, they are not because of their small visual cues (like the light ring on the Echo Dot).

2. **Voice First:** These are instances where voice is the primary input and output, but it is not the only input. Examples here would be Amazon Show and Google Nest Hub.

3. **Voice Enabled:** In these experiences, voice is not the only method for input or output. It might not even be the primary method but has been added or integrated to the experience. The level of integration can range from voice being used for security authentication to voice existing as an option for input, to the ability to launch a full-blown assistant. Examples include voice to text on a mobile app, a website that can be navigated with voice commands, or a kiosk that allows users to type/tap or speak input. Knowing the differences can help you when you're identifying the kinds of experiences you want to provide your user.

The Range of Voice Devices

There are several types of devices commonly used to access these voice experiences. Below is an at-a-glance view of the two top places brands can create a voice experience. Please note that we did not include Samsung Bixby because as of this writing, Capsules and the stand-alone Bixby devices have not been widely adopted.

Kinds of Voice Experiences

Amazon Alexa	Voice Search, Alexa Skills
Google Assistant	Voice Search
Samsung Bixby	Capsules
iOS	Siri Shortcuts, Owned Assistant
Android	Android App Actions, Owned Assistant
Website	Owned Assistant
Smart TV	Owned Assistant
In Car	Owned Assistant

Figure 1.2. An overview of all the ways Voice can be integrated into your technology channels.

- **Smart Speakers:** These are internet-enabled speakers where a user can engage a voice assistant by spoken commands; they are capable of streaming audio content, relaying information, and communicating with other devices. Examples include Google Nest Mini, Apple HomePod, and Amazon Alexa Echo Dot.
- **Mobile:** Smartphones or tablets that integrate the voice assistant natively into the operating system. Apple's Siri, Google Assistant, and Samsung's Bixby are examples of

assistants with native integrations. Amazon's Alexa assistant is also available to mobile users; however, it's not a built-in assistant. Additionally, iOS and Android apps can have an owned assistant integrated, which allows a brand to voice enable their app and provide another way to enhance their experience.

- **Smart Display:** These devices are smart speakers that come with touchscreens. These are the key drivers of the concept of multimodal experiences in which voice works in concert with visual display. Examples of smart displays include Amazon Alexa Show devices and Google Nest Hub.
- **Hearables:** Headphones or in-ear devices that deliver voice experiences without any screen. The examples include Apple AirPods, Amazon Earbuds, Samsung Galaxy Buds, and Google's Pixel Buds.
- **Wearables:** Just like hearables, these devices deliver voice experiences without a screen, but rather than sit in the ear, they're worn as clothing or accessories. Examples of wearables are the Apple Watch, Amazon Echo Frames, and Ray Ban Stories smart glasses.
- **In Auto:** These devices bring voice-driven experiences into automobiles. The top examples include Apple CarPlay, Amazon Alexa Echo Auto, and Google's Android Auto. In addition, there are built-in assistants created by the car manufacturer as part of their infotainment packages such as the Hey Mercedes assistant or the BMW Intelligent Personal Assistant.

While we have limited our list to the six different types of devices representing the ecosystem today, we're sure more will come along, as they are already appearing in home appliances and more.

The Two Types of Voice Experiences

While most consumers think of voice experiences in terms of the device that they're using (most of the time, it's a smartphone or a smart speaker), a marketer needs to go one level deeper to understand that there are two kinds of voice experiences: (1) voice as a product and (2) voice as part of your overall customer experience. While we will explore this concept more deeply in chapter 6, let's take a quick look at the difference.

To start, a voice experience as a product can be stand-alone applications like a game, educational experience, news content, utilities, and even entertainment—in which the voice experience is the end destination. All channels drive to it, and it is at the center of the brand, so the overall voice experience is essentially the product. Brands can use these types of experiences to enhance their images, which you'll explore in some of our case studies.

And the other important use of voice applications (and probably more relevant to marketing and product teams) is thinking about it as part of your total customer experience, which can improve the quality of the interactions your customers have with your brand.

To help enhance your customer experience, think of where you can use voice applications within your customers' journey. For some brands, it will make strategic sense to offer voice content during the awareness phase—optimizing your web content for voice search can go a long way to help ensure your website is provided as the answer to a voice request.

For others, it will make more sense to offer it in the consideration or purchase phase. And finally, for many brands, it will make sense to offer it along the entire path to purchase including the retention phase.

Voice and the Marketing Funnel

Because there are different places in the customer journey where voice can enhance your overall marketing reach, you can use it to improve your ROI both directly and indirectly:

- **Indirect ROI:** One way to use voice that can indirectly boost your brand's ROI is to improve your customer experience by answering frequently asked questions—the actual (not theoretical) questions that your customers have about your product, service, or stores. These FAQs should answer the questions that your audience has asked at each phase of the customer journey from their initial information seeking period to product onboarding or troubleshooting to support your customer after the purchase. While FAQs probably won't directly result in a purchase or in increased revenue, they help move your customer along the desired marketing path. Two other examples in which voice could be used to create useful, branded voice experiences are lifestyle content that prospects might access during the awareness phase and how-to information for post-purchase onboarding. But there are many additional voice experiences you can create that are appropriate for your audience at the top, middle, and bottom of the funnel that we will explore in later chapters.
- **Direct ROI:** Then at the bottom of the funnel, you can more directly impact ROI through a voice application by providing product information, store locators, direct ordering and purchasing capabilities, order tracking, services that facilitate the purchase of the product or service, and other steps that help close the sale. In other words, you can use voice with the kinds of actions that often get tracked in multi-touch or last-touch attribution models. We've found it could even be easier to get a budget allocation to start developing a voice strategy when you can tie it directly to immediately improving financial results, so this is where many brands start (and once proven, use the data to grow their voice program from there). Of course, many tactics that contribute directly to the ROI can also help contribute to improving the customer experience, so the division between the two is not as clear as it might seem. And we will look at programs and tactics that can directly contribute to your brand's profits in later chapters.

Why Voice Matters to Your Audience

The first part is simple; it is a place where your customers hang out, so you should hang out there too. As a matter of fact, according to the 2022 Voice Consumer Index research—key industry research conducted annually by Scot and Susan Westwater of our authorship team—63% of Americans currently use some form of voice assistance on their smart speaker or mobile device.[5] Why are people using voice? There are strong reasons for users' attachment to voice, reasons that are driving adoption at unsurpassed rates. First, voice-based devices are simply easier for most people to use, because now they can use natural language to control a computer or device to find the information they're looking for. There are no special commands or visual interfaces to learn. Users just need to make a request and they get a response. It's also much faster to speak than it is to type. After all, the average person can type at 40–65 words per minute while that same person can speak 120–140 words per minute. Plus, it's truly hands free, so users can engage in another task while using it. The ability to multitask appeals to consumers as well as to professionals, such as surgeons. Its appeal goes beyond the ability to manage interactions when a person's hands are busy and unable to swipe, tap, or click; there's also a reduction of friction that just makes many tasks easier. Voice experiences can also deliver a wealth in meaning by conveying the expression or inflection in the tone of the voice that informs the user whether something's humorous, serious, or sensuous, tailoring the communication and deepening the connection with the brand.

Perhaps more importantly, voice is easier, more inclusive, and accessible. It empowers people who have physical limitations or vision impairment, as well as those who have limited or no literacy. If you know how to speak and listen, you can use a voice assistant. In many cases, there is also a lower price to entry for consumers than in previous technology shifts because many people can use voice applications on their existing smartphones or on low-cost smart speakers. Gone are the challenges of setting up a computer and learning how to use a keyboard and/or mouse, and since all of those different pieces of hardware are not necessary, voice lowers the need for computer literacy as well.

Finally, there are entire populations who don't speak English as their primary language who can benefit from voice technology. Many global websites provide information in English and in the United States, with maybe a few pages of Spanish content—but in very few other languages, if any. Many of the advances in speech recognition have focused on adding further languages, dialects, and accents, which increasingly allow marketers to provide their information to the groups that have been previously underserved because of language barriers and will create opportunities to signal closer alliances with key targets. There are even ways to digitally recreate a voice-over that can speak multiple languages such as Spanish, French, and Italian. More on the use of synthetic or digitally recreated voices will be provided in chapter 3.

Combined, all of this provides a big opportunity for you to reach a wider audience and provide more value to more people. In fact, it is estimated that anywhere from 50%–75% of all US homes currently have at least one smart speaker.[6] That translates into about 60 million people. Because people often own more than one smart speaker, there are now about 157 million of these devices in U.S. households.[7] While this estimate includes homes that have multiple devices, it doesn't, however, include the billions of mobile devices worldwide that have the capability to use voice assistance.

The speed at which these devices have been adopted is truly record-breaking. Smart speaker growth is happening faster than any other technological adoption in our history.[8]

The US population has moved firmly into the early majority phase of adoption. That means we've moved beyond the innovators, bleeding edge folks, and even early adopters. Now we're starting to see the vast majority of Americans adopting these devices. Other countries like the UK, Germany, Australia, and a few others are about nine to twelve months behind.

It's Not Just the Young

On top of these record-breaking adoption rates, adoption and usage are not limited to one singular age group. Voice assistants are being used across the spectrum of all adults, including seniors. This fact is exciting because that gives brands a variety of opportunities that you don't normally get when you're looking to market over a new technology, because it opens the possibilities of creating experiences that benefit multiple age groups instead of just the younger ones—and that brings inspiration to many innovators. We cover more about who is using voice in chapter 4. While these adoption figures are impressive, we believe even more people will be adopting the use of voice in the future.

Voice Search

With this rapid growth, voice capabilities have already had a major impact on search behavior. In 2016, for instance, Google announced that 20% of the traffic coming to their mobile app on Android was through voice search.[9] Please keep in mind that was back when voice search was still relatively new—yet we saw many people searching this way. While Google hasn't released updated numbers, we believe that there's a strong probability that seven years later, the number has climbed substantially.

More recently, Microsoft shared the statistic that 25% of desktop searches on Windows 10 were happening through voice.[10] It seems that as people became comfortable and familiar using voice search on their mobile devices, they're trying it on their desktops as well. Another significant data point is that right now 41% of adults use voice search every single day.[11] So whether the search is through a smart speaker, smartphone, desktop, or some other device, consumers are using voice to find information they're seeking.

Finally, according to the most recent version of the Voice Consumer Index research, 92% of voice consumers are now searching the web with their voice and 40% of them do so regularly.[12]

What Makes Voice Compelling to Your Brand?

Voice offers up a whole new way to reach and engage with your entire audience. It's the first new channel since mobile, and as we already mentioned, it has the potential for inclusivity and accessibility that hasn't previously been possible. Like websites, voice assistants are available twenty-four hours a day, seven days a week, 365 days a year. There's no such thing as a holiday or a day off, so they are always there to answer questions and assist your customers. "A custom assistant, in addition to being thought of as an employee, should also be thought of as a companion, a concierge, a personal assistant, etc.," said Jason Fields, chief strategy officer of Voicify (you can learn more about Jason's views in his Guest Perspective in the next chapter). "Unlike human operators, they can also have hundreds upon hundreds of conversations at the same time without needing to scale up resources."

Voice also allows you to create a new emotional dimension for your brand. Your brand can now have an actual sound and quite possibly its own distinct voice. Its persona is now the personality that powers the character your audiences speak to and engage with, creating an even more robust experience and emotional connection with your brand.

Voice also provides a new avenue for creating good customer experiences. As mentioned earlier, voice assistance is available 24/7 and can provide information and help with tasks without requiring users to look up a phone number, wait on hold, or search a website. A good experience from a customer perspective allows them to get what they want when they want it. Let's look at Butterball Turkey, for example. Butterball expanded its Turkey Talk Line to Amazon's Alexa platform. Using the scripts from the call center (and the most frequently answered questions), the company had three of their operators record the answers they would commonly give, ensuring consistency with the phone experience. Home cooks didn't have to put down their utensils, wash their hands, or dial up to engage in live chat over a desktop, laptop, or smartphone to get answers to their turkey questions. Rather, the home cooks simply had to say, "Alexa, ask Butterball . . . " to access the answers they needed. And they could implement the instructions in real time, as well as ask Alexa to repeat the answer should they have missed something.

Voice can also provide another way for your customers to use your product. A great example is the way Comcast now provides the Xfinity remote, which is voice enabled. Extensions like this one can enhance the customer experience without requiring a complete reinvention of the product or the development of entirely new product features. In other words, voice technology gives you an opportunity to build upon what your brand is doing well and provide a new way to deliver it to make it easier for your consumer, differentiating your brand in the short term and, when others copy you, being admired as the leader.

With voice, you're able to provide a consistent and positive experience that allows you to deliver what customers need or expect without compromising quality and providing 24/7 availability without the cost of retaining remote call center staff. Voice does not require you to increase your staff to improve your customer experience. Rather, it uses your content and makes it available to the right person, at the right time, in all the right places and all the right mediums. As a result, you can improve operational efficiency, reducing costs while increasing revenue. Consider this: according to IBM, US companies spend close to 1.3 trillion US dollars annually on customer support through call centers.[13] If you were able to offload 1% of those calls to a voice assistant on your website or within your mobile app, the reduction in calls would save US companies 13 billion dollars per year.

For the first time in years—not since mobile—we have a new channel and a new way to engage with customers. Unlike earlier "new" channels, voice provides you with an opportunity to listen to the actual words that your audience uses and to create content in their language. Rather than guessing at what's relevant to the audience, you can hear them telling you what's truly relevant to them and sharing what they find challenging. Imagine having the "perfect" brand spokesperson. One who always was spot-on with their responses so that those answers were consistent and always reflected your brand's value proposition. One who never went off-script or deviated from the way your organization talked about your brand and your products. How game changing would that be? It's what a well-crafted voice experience can give you. It is the power of voice, and it can improve customer experience and help your audience move along the path to purchase. Think of voice as a way of enabling your brand to offer a personal concierge who is available any time your customer wants or needs them. And that brand spokesperson is one of the most knowledgeable salespersons in the world, who never gets up on the wrong side of the bed in the morning and is always more than happy to help.

Voice can also be a compelling way to provide real-time assistance during the sales process. By being at the ready with information that a prospect needs to make a purchase decision, you can increase sales. While a lot of users are turning to it for audio entertainment, there are also prospects who are asking questions and seeking information and those who are already in the shopping mode. Rather than conducting their research using their fingertips, hunting, and clicking, and tapping, they're using their voices. As a result, you can help move potential customers along from discovery mode to consideration to purchase. If you don't provide that information and your competitor does, you may have a lost an opportunity that few brands can afford to miss, especially in highly competitive markets with tight margins.

Finally, voice can improve branded experiences by being the consistent, tangible embodiment of your brand personality, so prospects can truly engage with it. Voice can, when appropriate, laugh with your customers, support them with an answer to an urgent question, and even express empathy when the physical experience didn't meet expectations. Voice experiences give you the opportunity to not just make sure the words are right, but to get the sound and the tone right as well. You have an opportunity to be consistently mindful of, not just the words, but how they are delivered. These exchanges do not rely on another human to remember a script, emphasize the key points, and deliver it with the tone you want, but instead, they allow your brand to shine by conveying its true essence. And if you work in a highly regulated industry, there's no fear that the conversation will become noncompliant, resulting in a legal issue for you and your team of lawyers, because you're in control of what the script (and the assistant) says.

Think of it this way: word of mouth has always derived its power through the recommendation of a trusted friend. Now what if you were to offer a brand personality that is closer to that of a trusted friend? What if the new word of mouth becomes word of a voice assistant? Voice enables a brand to have one-on-one connections with each of your prospects and customers—after all, the conversation will be individual, requests will be made in the user's own words—and though personalized, voice interactions will enable you to reach many more people, given the scalability it offers.

Sound interesting? Read on to learn how to take full advantage of voice within your marketing program. In the next chapter, we're going to look at branding in a world that doesn't need sight. You'll learn more about audio branding in chapter 3 and about who is using voice in the next one. And by the end of the book, you should be able to develop an effective voice marketing strategy as well as understand the steps you need to take to execute it. This is not a book that deals with coding for applications, as there are experts in that area. Your job is to create and execute a compelling marketing strategy, and this book will get you there. In the meantime, we have some contributions from outside experts who can help set some more of the groundwork you need to be successful. Enjoy!

GUEST PERSPECTIVE 1

The Marketing Industry Is Up Next for AI Disruption

Paul Roetzer

Voice falls within the world of artificial intelligence (AI), so before we continue to look at voice alone, we felt it was important to look at AI in its entirety. And who better to look at it than Paul Roetzer, the founder of AI Marketing Institute, an online resource that helps marketers build a competitive advantage with AI by providing expert content, online education, interactive tools, and strategic consulting. Paul is also the author of The Marketing Performance Blueprint *(2014) and* The Marketing Agency Blueprint *(2012), and he is the creator of the Marketing Artificial Intelligence Conference (MAICON) and the AI Academy for Marketers. As a speaker, Paul makes artificial intelligence approachable and actionable and helps change agents drive transformation through marketing talent, technology, and strategy. Finally, he has consulted for hundreds of organizations, ranging from small startups to Fortune 500 companies. Here's what Paul had to say:*

Artificial intelligence (AI) is the science of making machines smart, like us. It's a broad term that refers to both the process and result of teaching machines to do intelligent tasks. AI-powered machines use algorithms—coded series of steps—to do tasks that used to be exclusively done by humans. These machines can read, write, hear, speak, see, move, and predict outcomes like humans do. And you encounter them every day, whether you know it or not.

AI algorithms exist to read emails and help write responses (Gmail). They can hear your questions and speak back to you with an accurate answer (Alexa). They can see objects in the road and move to avoid them (Tesla's Autopilot). They can predict which products or movies you'll like based on what you watched in the past (Amazon Prime, Netflix).

AI can do all of this because of machine learning, which is when we teach computers to teach themselves without explicit programming. We train the machine on an initial set of data; it then applies what it learns to new data.

Here's where the magic happens. Because the machine doesn't just do what it's told, it's free to find its own path to a goal, and often does. Sophisticated AI often achieves results in ways that humans don't expect and can't predict. On top of it all, the machine then learns from the outcome. It learns what works and what doesn't, then adjusts its approach next time to do better. The result is that AI-powered machines improve over time. For instance, Gmail's AI suggests short snippets of text for you to use in email responses; now, it predicts the next word you're going to write in real time.

Make no mistake; there's plenty that AI can't do despite what science fiction would have you believe. Real-world AI is what we would call "artificial narrow intelligence" or ANI. These are machines that specialize in one or more narrow tasks set by humans. They learn and produce results humans don't always expect, but they don't have agency. They can't decide to rebel, stop working, or work on a goal other than the one that their humans set for them. No other type of AI exists. There are no self-aware machines or super intelligent robots.

But our real-world AI has progressed in exciting ways only recently. AI used to be limited. The first AI research started in the 1950s, and it's been hyped as world changing for almost as long. Yet it fell short of expectations multiple times. Over a series of "AI winters," funding dried up, and research stalled for decades. Glimmers of hope for AI's promise came from Wall Street's adoption of basic AI in the 1980s and 1990s. Then, it consisted of basic algorithms, limited automation, and simple recommendation functions. But it wasn't until the last decade that a confluence of factors made AI as powerful, important, and game-changing as it had been projected for decades.

What changed? Why is this time different? There are a few reasons:

1. **Advances in AI**. Fundamental breakthroughs in machine learning and deep learning (an advanced type of machine learning) occurred in the early 2010s that put AI back on the map and unlocked the technology's true potential.
2. **An explosion of computational power**. Technology finally caught up to aspirations. Limited computational power stunted AI researchers in past decades. They didn't have the firepower to realize their visions of artificially intelligent machines. Our era is different. We now have processors powerful enough to perform sophisticated machine learning and deep learning functions. These processors are also cheap enough for widespread use. The result is we have exponentially better hardware to power AI.
3. **Increased investment**. The previous two factors spurred a third: massive investment in AI technology and talent. Big tech companies have gone all in on AI, baking the technology into their platforms and products through acquisitions of companies and talent. Facebook, Amazon, Apple, Microsoft, and Alphabet (Google's parent company) collectively acquired at least 14 AI startups in the same year.[a] Tech giants also have snapped up much of the AI talent currently available, leading to shortages across the sector.[b] Investors are following suit. The Brookings Institution, a think tank, estimates AI companies in the United States alone attracted $40 billion in investment in 2019.[c] The result is a major acceleration of AI innovation and adoption across industries.

Today, AI has grown into its potential thanks to these factors. It now powers entire industries and brings futuristic capabilities to real-world technology. Semiautonomous driving is commercially available in cars, with fully self-driving cars deployed in test environments. Facial recognition used by internet giants is already at or better than human level. Hedge funds and trading platforms run 100% by artificial intelligence now exist. Voice recognition and natural language generation are powering our digital assistants. There's no question: this time it truly is different. And as the use of AI spreads, it is beginning to seep into every industry on Earth, transforming how we do business in the process.

The marketing industry is up next for disruption. McKinsey Global Institute, for instance, estimates that AI and other advanced analytics could have up to a $5.9 trillion annual impact on marketing and sales alone. It's not hard to see why. AI can already do (or augment) many tasks that marketers spend large amounts of time and money to do today. In marketing, AI can:

- Research and write content.
- Create ads, optimize targeting, and manage paid budgets.
- Write and test email subject lines, optimize email send times, and improve deliverability.
- Nurture and qualify leads.

- Create social media posts and monitor conversations about brands, products, and trends.
- Do keyword research, identify search opportunities, and do sophisticated SEO work.
- Provide one-to-one personalized product, content, and service recommendations.
- Much, much more.

And the list is growing daily as new companies and applications centered on AI look to automate or improve manual tasks in marketing and sales. In fact, AI can do or augment so many things than marketers can that we estimate 80% of what marketers do will be intelligently automated to some degree within three to five years. But this isn't cause for alarm. While AI will make some traditional marketing roles obsolete, it will primarily enhance today's marketing jobs and unlock entirely new roles. In the process, it will improve our effectiveness and career satisfaction.

Consider how much time your marketing team spends every month reviewing analytics, creating performance reports, building data visualizations, scheduling social media updates, determining blog post topics, copywriting, curating content, building strategies, and allocating resources. Now, imagine if AI performed most of these activities, and a marketer's primary role was to curate and enhance AI recommendations and content, rather than doing everything from scratch. It's already happening today. In Marketing AI Institute's *2021 State of Marketing AI Report*, we teamed up with Drift to survey more than 400 marketers about their understanding and adoption of AI.

The majority said AI was very important or critically important to their success in the coming year. What's more, 80% of them believe AI will intelligently automate more than a quarter of their tasks in the next five years. More than a third of marketers surveyed say they're already piloting AI technologies. The reason for this is simple: AI solves many traditional marketing challenges that have been holding marketers back and accelerates revenue in the process.

As the number of connected consumers and devices expands, the amount of data produced exponentially increases. Meanwhile, marketers' ability to filter through the noise and turn data into actionable intelligence remains limited by biases, beliefs, education, experiences, knowledge, and brainpower. After all, we humans have a finite ability to process information, build strategies, create content at scale, and achieve performance potential.

Despite advances in marketing automation—and the billions of dollars currently pouring into marketing technology companies—much of the technology that marketers rely on today to plan, execute, and evaluate marketing campaigns is elementary. But AI has the power to change all of that. Forward-thinking marketers using AI are already able to do more with less, run personalized campaigns of unprecedented complexity, and transform companies and careers with new ways of doing machine-intelligent marketing. The future isn't just coming; it's here.

[a] Paul Sawers, "13 Acquisitions Highlight Big Tech's AI Talent Grab in 2020," VentureBeat, published December 25, 2020, https://venturebeat.com/2020/12/25/13-acquisitions-highlight-big-techs-ai-talent-grab-in-2020/.
[b] David Jarvis, "The AI Talent Shortage Isn't Over Yet," Deloitte Insights, published September 30, 2020, https://www2.deloitte.com/us/en/insights/industry/technology/ai-talent-challenges-shortage.html.
[c] Zachary Arnold, "What Investment Trends Reveal about the Global AI Landscape," Brookings, published September 29, 2020, https://www.brookings.edu/techstream/what-investment-trends-reveal-about-the-global-ai-landscape.

GUEST PERSPECTIVE 2

The Google Voice Landscape

Danny Bernstein

The authorship team of this book believes the time is now to start developing and testing your voice mar-keting strategies, as it's only a matter of time that voice will be as popular—if not more—than clanking away on a keyboard to interact with the internet. Our collective view was partly informed by our conver-sations with Danny Bernstein, the former managing director of Global Partnerships, Google Assistant & Research at Google and is now with Microsoft. Rather than paraphrase what he had to say, we asked him to provide his thoughts directly to you. While at Google, his team was responsible for product-enabling partnerships that drive the adoption of Search, Google Now, and Sign-In by consumers, developers, and global partners. Danny joined Google via the company's acquisition of Meebo in June 2012 and has played a leading part in growing the Google Assistant product and platform (despite Siri's and Alexa's prior leadership) by forming and directing key early-stage strategies for partnerships and ecosystem product development. Google Assistant now has the largest user base and highest customer satisfaction of any digital personal assistant product. Now that you know Danny, here are his thoughts:

In 1952, Bell Labs designed a voice recognition device, named "The Audrey," which was able to distinguish and understand spoken digits between zero and nine with more than 90% accuracy.[a] A few years later, in 1961, IBM debuted a voice recognition device, "The Shoebox," which recognized sixteen unique spoken words.[b] In the same decade as "The Shoebox," the futuristic television show *Star Trek* depicted a voice assistant, "The Computer," which was able to comprehend and express information verbally, performing automated tasks and sharing information with its space-faring crew. Fast-forward to 2008 when voice technology was just beginning to become more mainstream in both fact and fiction. Google's voice search brought speech recognition technology to millions of users on mobile devices the same year as the movie *Iron Man* showcased the natural-language user interface computer system JARVIS—an always-on, ambient virtual personal assistant whose concept delighted sci-fi fans and technology enthusiasts equally. The year 2008 seems like epochs ago as the gap between reality and fiction continues to narrow for voice technology—helped by the introduc-tion of ambient and contextual computing showing up in more and more ways in our daily lives.

Now more than ever, people are getting help by simply asking their devices, "Do I need a coat today?" or "Tell Joan that I'm running late," without needing to give detailed context. People are increasingly expecting their digital assistants to understand their preferences and environment and bring proactive support to them, particularly in voice applications. We often say that voice is about actions. While typing queries are more information seeking in nature, we see that voice queries tend to be more action seeking. For example, consumers expect their devices to order their afternoon coffee without giving specific instructions, context, or location.

So what does this shift in consumer behavior mean for companies and brands? There are many organizations out there ready to jump on the opportunity and go all in to bring voice to con-sumers as part of their growth and service strategy. We see many brands in such verticals as media streaming, food ordering, productivity, communication, and fitness as early adopters who have found success being the first movers on voice. Some of these pioneering brands are seeing results like increases in monthly or daily active users, product adoption, and customer lifetime value as the result of introducing voice into the user journeys. Brands that use voice as a channel today will be well suited to be at the forefront of reaching the next generation of consumers.

That doesn't mean that opportunities to explore voice more incrementally should be overlooked. A great place to start is by thinking about ways your brand can integrate and work with voice platforms. Ask yourself: "How could voice work for my brand? What could we do that would differentiate us in this space? How would voice or leveraging ambient interfaces allow us to do things better?" Analyzing your organization's needs and asking these questions is a good place to start.

Even if adopting voice and ambient computing seems more like a long-term bet, it's worth testing how it can work for your brand and to learn how you can leverage this unique technology. Today we are seeing voice behaviors manifest in so many different areas far beyond thermostats and timers. Helped by AI and cloud computing, we are increasingly seeing brands that are finding ways to meet consumers with voice in applications like call centers, real-time dispatching, and more. Now more than ever, consumers are looking to brands to bring them versatility, creativity, innovation, and helpfulness to their product experience and daily lives. The brands that explore, collaborate, and partner with voice platforms will truly reap the benefits of being on the forefront of this large-scale technology.

[a] Eboch, M.M. *How Do Virtual Assistants Work?* (Capstone Press, 2020).
[b] IBM100, "Pioneering Speech Recognition," Accessed June 14, 2023, https://www.ibm.com/ibm/history/ibm100/us/en/icons/speechreco/transform/

 ## EXTENDED CASE STUDY

Nike and Reebok New Product Introductions

It's no secret that to really stand out in the sneaker industry, brands must embrace innovation, generating enough hype to attract the attention. It's not enough to just do a "product drop"—a popular marketing strategy among makers of sneakers and streetwear for driving demand for exclusive, limited-edition merchandise. Now, brands must find interesting and innovative ways to execute those drops. One new way uses voice AI. Both Nike and Reebok found that leveraging voice assistants could provide the unique experience they needed to deliver effective product drops.[a]

When launching a self-lacing sneaker that is so futuristic that people can't stop talking about a sneaker scene from *Back to the Future II*, the motivated marketer will want the product release to be as innovative the shoe is.[b] Equally important is to make sure the audience knows that, while this "next generation" sneaker appears to be from the realm of hoverboards and time travel, it's also an authentic basketball sneaker designed for the next generation of NBA superstars.

Nike faced that challenge with their Adapt BBs, and they decided to team up with Google, RAIN, and R/GA to launch "the most futuristic shoe in the most futuristic way, ever" so a fan could have a chance to get a pair before everyone else did.[c] The result was the first ever voice-activated shoe drop—a live, in-game shopping experience where anyone watching the game could shop for the exclusive shoe simply by asking Google Assistant.

To bring this kind of experience to market, Nike had to reimagine the traditional drop. They partnered with Google and Turner to introduce the Adapt BBs to the world, but instead of running a thumping TV commercial, they leveraged the only entertainment this audience watches live: the game itself. And instead of the other commercials, Nike hyped the voice-powered shoe release through social and digital out-of-home takeovers, priming fans to interact with Google Assistant.[d] NBA stars Jayson Tatum and Kyle Kuzma answered fan questions in custom videos on the platform, then debuted the shoes during the game itself on TNT. The shoes' prominent coverage included a courtside segment, on-screen messages to get people talking with Google Assistant, and a halftime show takeover where commentator Ernie Johnson announced to fans that they could buy the shoes right then and there if they asked Google Assistant how to get a pair.

"The most unique element was that it was a voice-activated sale during a live broadcast," said RAIN client strategy director Dale LaRue in an interview with Voicebot. "It's the first time anyone's seen that voice could actually unlock content in real-time."[e]

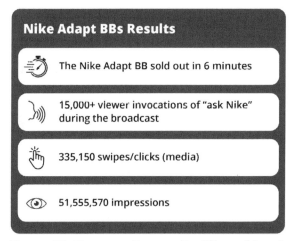

Figure 1.3. Here are the results Nike achieved, according to RAIN, the agency who developed the experience.[f]

Source: RAIN Agency

The shoe sold out in six minutes, lighting up a new way for fans to shop for what their favorite athletes are wearing. In addition, the event earned the R/GA, RAIN, and Nike team three Bronze Cannes Lions in Creative eCommerce, Excellence in Brand Integration, and Sponsorships and Use of Integrated Media.

Reebok also turned to voice assistants as part of its "Sport the Unexpected" campaign to help support the drop of its Club C sneaker that was its first shoe coming out of its collaboration with the female rapper Cardi B.[g] Fans were able to enter a contest to win a pair of the "Crystal Coated" Club C limited-edition sneakers by saying "Open Reebok Sneaker Drop" to either popular virtual assistant.[h] Once entered, entrants could even check their status by asking either assistant "Ask Reebok Sneaker Drop if I won" on September 7 between 10 a.m. and 12 p.m. ET.[i] A total of fifty pairs of the sneaker were given away, making the limited-edition sneaker feel that much more exclusive.[j]

If Nike and Reebok can create excitement and buzz by using voice to introduce such visually oriented products and to promote instant shopping, your brand can too. To borrow a phrase, just do it!

[a] Oliver McAteer, "Reebok Drops Limited Edition Sneakers on Amazon and Google Home," Campaign US, published August 27, 2019, accessed January 14, 2022, https://www.campaignlive.com/article/reebok-drops-limited-edition-sneakers-amazon-google-home/1594682.

[b] Ashley Carman, "Hands-On with Nike's Self-Lacing, App-Controlled Sneaker of the Future," The Verge, published January 15, 2019, accessed January 14, 2022, https://www.theverge.com/2019/1/15/18167388/nike-self-lacing-shoes-adapt-bb-smart-bluetooth-app-features-battery-life-price-release-date.

[c] RAIN, "Selling Out Sneakers through Voice," published July 2019, accessed January 14, 2022, https://rain.agency/nike.

[d] Dale LaRue, "The First Voice-Activated Sneaker Drop," RAIN, published July 2019, accessed January 14, 2022, https://rain.agency/raindrops/the-first-voice-activated-sneaker-drop.

[e] Eric Hal Schwartz, "Nike Voice Sale for Sneaker Launch Runs Away with Cannes Lions Awards," Voicebot.ai, published July 1, 2019, accessed January 14, 2022, https://voicebot.ai/2019/07/01/nike-voice-sale-of-sneakers-runs-away-with-cannes-lions-awards/.

[f] Turkington, Eric, RAIN, personal email, January 3, 2022.

[g] Robert Williams, "Reebok Drops Cardi B Sneakers on Alexa, Google Assistant," Marketing Dive, published August 27, 2019, accessed January 14, 2022, https://www.marketingdive.com/news/reebok-drops-cardi-b-sneakers-on-alexa-google-assistant/561762/.

[h] Kelly Johnston, "50 People Will Win Reebok Limited Edition Sneakers via Amazon Alexa and Google Home," Voicebot.ai, published August 26, 2019, accessed January 14, 2022, https://voicebot.ai/2019/08/26/50-people-will-win-reebok-limited-edition-sneakers-via-amazon-alexa-and-google-home/.

[i] PR Newswire, "Reebok Drops Limited Edition Club C through First-of-Its-Kind Skill Via Amazon and Google Home," published August 26, 2019, accessed January 14, 2022, https://www.prnewswire.com/news-releases/reebok-drops-limited-edition-club-c-through-first-of-its-kind-skill-via-amazon-and-google-home-300906855.html.

[j] License Global, "Reebok Debuts Cardi B Collab on Amazon Alexa, Google Assistant," published August 27, 2019, accessed January 14, 2022, https://www.licenseglobal.com/apparel/reebok-debuts-cardi-b-collab-amazon-alexa-google-assistant.

Branding in a Voice-First World

Talk to five branding experts and it's likely that you'll get five different definitions of branding. They start with the idea that the brand is the visual logo, a literal translation of the branding iron applied to your product, the packaging, the store, office environment (usually on or above the door), letterhead, email signature, and in the upper left corner of a website. This definition of branding—to point out the obvious—doesn't work in all contexts. Think radio and now think voice, where there are no visual cues. But even when people start to talk about brands beyond the literal logo, the conversation still comes back to the visual. For instance, Larry Light, the former chief marketing officer of McDonald's purportedly said, "A brand is more than a trademark. It is a 'trust' mark. A brand is a covenant between the company and the consumer. A trusted brand is a genuine asset."[1] Yes, he is correct that a brand is an asset and a covenant. But he still refers to something visual—a trust mark. It's concrete. But what if your customer can't see or even feel the brand? It could be, for instance, a service, which is something you would experience but would never see nor touch.

Another widely used definition of a brand is the product or service name—but the brand name is meaningless without the product or service itself, the associations beyond the product or service, and the context. Then a third group defines the brand as the product, service, or other entity, but this approach doesn't take the consumer or user into account and the associations they have with the brand; rather, it is provider or marketer centric. And then there is a group that defines brands in relation to the expected outcome. In other words, brand is referred to as a promise or the set of expectations for the outcomes of using it. But this description doesn't take the powerful branding elements such as name, logo, colors, sounds, and scents into account—elements that help set the expectations—and it looks at the product as being one dimensional as the single benefit the product or service provides. In addition, this definition doesn't recognize that brand associations and image can often enhance the experience of using it.

The definition that Laurence Minsky, one of the authors of this book, and Ilan Geva finally endorsed in their book *Global Brand Management* was "what consumers, prospects, and other stakeholders think, feel, and say about the product, service, person, or other entity."[2] Since a marketer can never really know what their prospects and consumers truly feel and think about their brand, you can use former Amazon CEO Jeff Bezos's purported definition: "A brand is what they say about you when you're not in the room" and then assume what people think and feel based on what they say and do, keeping in mind that actions speak louder than words. In other words, in the parlance of public relations specialists, it's your reputation. As a result, a brand can "reduce any of the 'perceived risk' and anxiety of making a selection,"[3] but it can also add to the enjoyment of the experience using or encountering the brand.

More importantly, since your features can be easily and quickly copied or duplicated in today's world, brand—your perceived differentiation—becomes one of your most valuable assets. So, how do you extend your brand within a voice environment? We will explore that question in this chapter. But first we must look at the world of voice a bit more deeply and define what the technologists and futurists in the field mean by a voice-first world, which we defined in chapter 1 as, in short, "instances where voice is the primary input and output, but it is not the only input." An example of a device that uses voice as the primary input and output is the Amazon Echo. Two examples of smart displays that combine voice and visuals would be Amazon Show and Google Nest Hub. But the concept of "voice first" is a little more robust and nuanced than what this definition implies—and it carries implications for your marketing beyond voice applications.

So What Exactly Do We Mean by Voice First?

If you spend any amount of time in or around the voice community, you will probably hear the term *voice first*. And you're probably thinking, "Oh no, not another 'first.'" We had "website first" when strategists claimed that a brand's website should be at the center of all marketing. Next, we had "social first" (we remember when many of our marketing colleagues intoned that Facebook would replace the need for websites), followed by "mobile first" in 2009—which is making mobile users the top priority in a marketing program and designing all digital elements to work on mobile devices.[4] Then it was "content first" (important, too, but it overlooked context and design), and then "user first."

Now we have "voice first." But unlike the other claims of "first," "voice first" means more than a boast that the platform is the most important one. In fact, the voice-technology community recognizes that all platforms and outlets are potentially equally important—placement depends on what you are trying to achieve. Your goal as a marketer is to get the right message in the right place at the right time—and the various voice-first (or voice-only) devices such as Amazon Show and Google Nest Hub provide just a few of the "places" (i.e., platforms) you need to have your message accessible, findable, or deliverable at the right time. But voice first carries one more key implication: by saying "the right message," it's more than just having the right content; it's also having the right delivery format. Based on the platform, the message could be delivered through a combination of words (spoken or printed) and pictures (still or moving), pictures alone, and/or words alone.

In other words, when we refer to voice first, we mean that finally, you need to put the customer first, because their information needs are going to be the fixed point as they encounter the brand in various ways. Your prospects are not going to change their needs based on the modality that they use to interact with the brand. Rather, these needs are based on their location on the path to purchase, as marketers hope that they move from awareness to consideration to purchase to retention. Depending on their location along the path, your prospect will still need to know the category issues, product features and benefits, the key differentiating point, product or service price, warranty, and other attributes as well as usage information (and the available product support) and whether the interaction is in a voice experience, a visual web experience, or an on-site or on-premises experience. But how you deliver the stage-appropriate information provided and the nature of the interactions will change based upon the devices and the modality they are using.

The other thing to know is that the voice-only experience is often the hardest modality to solve. The solution is easier to achieve when voice works in concert with screen-based content such as a video, kiosk, and words on the website or blog, because the visuals assist in delivering your message. In those instances, once you have identified your audience's problems, needs, desires, and frustrations, you can use the additional capabilities of the channel or medium to give the user additional context. With voice-only formats, including radio commercials, you are unable to tap into the visual content for further explanation or expansion of the message. So you must solve the customer's problem in the most basic way possible, which is through words and sounds. On the plus side, audio can take advantage of "the theater of the mind"—provide enough clues and drama to create something more powerful than anything created for the big screen, television, or other visually oriented mediums. In other words, marketers can often paint a more compelling picture through implication than through explanation—and audio is the perfect medium for conveying the implications. Visually oriented communications achieve this feat of conveying the implications through the interplay of the words, music, and pictures, whether static or moving images. On the other hand, audio achieves this through sounds, word choice, music, and timing, creating images in the brain, drawing on the imagination of the listeners—images that can't be conveyed by any concrete visual. Think of old radio dramas such as the one that set off the panic about a Martian invasion, called *War of the Worlds*. Although that classic book by H. G. Wells had been successful and popular, it didn't achieve such a strong reaction until Orson Welles and The Mercury Theatre on the Air staged a dramatization of it on Halloween 1938, which many listeners who missed the beginning of the broadcast thought was a real invasion.[5]

Another aspect of the voice-first approach relates to the way a user will engage with a device or hardware. As more and more products offer a voice-enabled option, it is expected that voice will become the first method of activation or engagement because of how much easier it is to speak versus type or swipe. Just think: It's much easier to pull out a phone and speak than it is to open the phone, tap on a mobile application, and then type in information.

But while the user may employ voice as their first point of accessing the brand, we cannot forget that they are in charge and will choose how they want to continue the engagement. The 2022 Voice Consumer Index research conducted by members of the authorship team found that while 82% of respondents indicated that they would visit a product's website and 75% said they would use a brands mobile app to learn more about a product, nearly 70% indicated an interest in continuing with a voice experience to learn more about a product.[6]

So marketers need to make sure that they can deliver the information in all the ways that a user might choose. Marketers can't assume that people are going to always continue the experience with voice (although they might), but if we solve for voice only as the first step, we know that we've addressed their main concern at the first touchpoint, making it easier to translate the message to the other mediums. And if we are being consistent across all the channels as the experience progressively develops, the user will still have a positive experience that moves them forward on their path to purchase regardless of how they choose to move forward with your brand.

Our definition of voice first stems from the concept of "customer first," which means putting the needs of your audience first. Remember, despite what you see from many engineering-focused firms, your content shouldn't come from what you want to tell them; rather it should be derived from they want or need to know. In other words, it's not what you want them to buy; it is what they want to purchase. Nothing new or controversial here. But this concept is especially pertinent in voice environments because it primarily uses a pull, not push, strategy. It's a conversation, not a monologue or manifesto. Even during a multimodal speaker experience (which accounts for less than 20% of smart speaker devices), users do not have a primary navigation menu to guide them. The only content that users can encounter are the answers that Alexa, Google Assistant, Siri, or another assistant serve up in response to the specific questions or requests they make.

Outside of smart speakers, which are designed to be voice first, there's also the integration of voice technology and conversational assistants into mobile applications and even desktop experiences. The successful uses of voice conversational AI in these devices will still have an audience-first approach and a need to deliver against the user's request quickly and efficiently.

As the result, marketers need to fully adopt a customer-first mindset if they want to realize a successful voice experiences. While marketers might claim to place the customer first, oftentimes, they do not. Instead, they broadcast self-serving messages. Just look at all the irrelevant information you encounter in other channels. This can be served up—even in many different types of digital ads—because it takes advantage of the audience's attention to other content that interests them. In fact, we have found many "feature–benefit" enthralled marketers still using this approach, particularly within business-to-business advertising. But with voice applications, you don't have the advantage of the user's passive attention. If you're creating voice or audio content that no one is actively seeking, nobody will hear it, and you are not going to achieve your goals or any return on your marketing investment (ROI), as it won't be seen (or heard) even if it is the most beautiful, funny, wonderful, and elegantly worded messaging on the planet.

Where Your Brand Can Play

Since a particular difference between a voice experience and a web search is that there is no menu, a brand is completely at the mercy of its customers' interests and needs to fit itself into those interests in the ways customers want them to. That makes a customer-first approach essential in this world. You must let the customers' questions and requests lead you, and you also must figure out where it's appropriate for your brand to interject itself. For example, if you are in the health-care category, you obviously don't want to be answering questions about the weather or baseball scores.

Often the first step a brand must take is to identify areas of interest to your customers and would-be customers where it is appropriate for the brand to speak on a particular subject. A brand does this by looking for the intersections where the business's needs and objectives overlap with the customers' needs for solving a problem or fulfilling a desire. In an excellent example of this, the Tide voice skill on Alexa offers advice on the general category of stain removal by promising to help you "Tackle tough stains, understand how to use your machine and care for hard-to-wash fabrics."

If you focus on finding those pertinent intersections, you are going to realize some impressive wins, generating a compelling ROI story that you can take to the other parts of the organization to further leverage voice's power on behalf of your company. Of course, these rules do not only apply to voice applications—they should apply to all your marketing and all your content efforts—but this approach can be overlooked or ignored in the other marketing media. In the world of voice marketing, unless the customer requests your content, your brand is completely invisible and inaudible.

Experiment, Observe, Adjust, and Learn

One final caveat: Because of the newness of voice activation as a medium, the rules, techniques, and best practices are still being discovered. Think back to the start of the web—as opposed to today when marketers have more than thirty years of results to refer to—marketers can't always accurately predict how customers are going to interact with your brands or how they will choose to frame their questions or requests. This is where audience research comes in. Talking to existing and prospective customers not only gives you a better idea of what problems they're trying to solve but more importantly the questions (and word choices) they use throughout the path to purchase. While these insights help inform your initial approach, it is nearly impossible to account for all of the ways your audience will ask for this information. Therefore, you must expect to experience more trial and error, experimentation, and iterations. Voice-activated marketing forces marketers to truly get back to the basics and seek to identify and understand the audience, their needs, and your brand's place in their lives and then figuring out where those things intersect with customer needs to create something that's useful and usable for your customer. Once you do, the voice solutions become more obvious and easier to envision.

Branding in a Voice-First World

In a voice-first world, many of the creative metaphors used in branding become an actual reality. Audiences, for instance, can now have a literal conversation with a brand or its spokesperson and can develop a relationship with them. For instance, the common brand foundational terms of "voice" and "tone" move from being a figurative explanation of the words to use in the branding guide to literal the sounds, words, and attitudes the brand emotes over voice. In addition, a true brand personality becomes a necessity for differentiating the product, service, or other entity from its competitors', because it is literally being experienced when a person is using their voice to interact with your brand. If you have a brand character on packaging, for example, how does it sound and how does it engage with the individuals? This was a challenge General Mills had to solve when it created a voice app for its Lucky Charms brand that had their mascot Lucky the Leprechaun taking users in an interactive adventure across his world to "help save magic,"[7] which we'll explore in more detail in the extended case study for this chapter. MoonPie also faced a similar challenge when they created the MoonPie MoonMate, a virtual roommate that in addition to providing a range of recipes that featured its product, engaged users with "jokes, philosophical comments, and slightly off-kilter compliments."[8]

When consumers are engaging with a voice interface, you can't rely on visual cues—even if you have a multimodal experience with a screen. In some cases, when there is a smart speaker with a screen, the visuals become part of the supporting cast and are there to reinforce the brand or information, not be the primary way to convey it. In other cases, such as a voice assistant built into a mobile app, the user might ask a question with their voice and get a resulting app screen with their answer on it—not a spoken response. As a result, a brand using voice needs to fully establish itself through the words it selects; the way it speaks, including its pronunciation, word emphasis, and speed—is it chill or excited?—and how it sounds, including whether it's male, female, nonbinary, an animal, a robot, or something else. These brand characters can be recorded via a voice-over session with professional voice talent or be digitally created using synthetic voices. There's more about the considerations for synthetic and digital voices in chapter 3.

Finally, the emotional context of the conversation becomes another factor to get right because conversations are dynamic. In short, your brand isn't just showing and telling who it is through the visuals, but instead, it is literally talking in the way that embodies its core values, without mentioning them. In a voice experience or any conversational experience, no one ever wants a monologue about your brand and what makes it great. Even when a customer asks a smart speaker to tell them about a brand, they don't want a long-winded answer that drones on and on.

As one of our content strategy colleagues explained, with voice, you can't rely on visuals to bail you out if your message isn't clear. Even when there are multimodal experiences with voice, the screen is there to assist, not drive the experience. After all, with multimodel experiences, people are often accessing the visuals on a smartphone screen, not a smart speaker with a larger display (at least for now). We also know that just because a screen is available, it doesn't always mean it will be used, which means you must make sure that the dialogue is clear enough that it can stand alone—without the support of a screen to explain the details. As a result, it's important to think through every step that you are trying to explain or every piece of information you are trying to give when you are developing a voice application, and this requires a delicate balancing act between brand building and providing useful information.

You don't want your brand to get in the way of comprehension, but you also want to make sure your brand is present. This is another way the brand personality becomes incredibly significant, because it will guide the word choices that bring the persona of the voice assistant to life.

But the persona of the voice assistant should not always match that of the brand spokesperson or brand icon, especially while the world of voice is still developing. Brands have invested heavily in creating and evolving their mascots, like the Michelin Man, Tony the Tiger, or Mr. Clean, and until you've tested the many ways people make their requests and are sure that your skill won't be out of character or frustrating to the audience, keep your prized characters in supporting roles or leave them out of your voice experience altogether. For example, when General Mills created the Lucky Charms voice experience that we mentioned earlier, they made sure that the voice of the Lucky character matched the voice that is used in all of their television and audio content. However, they also came up with the idea of including the role of a separate narrator who then was able to help navigate between the different personalities that were a part of the story and the interactive experience.

Along similar lines, you wouldn't necessarily want your brand spokesperson to handle customer experience issues, troubleshooting, or even the onboarding process, as you probably wouldn't want to talk to Lucky the Leprechaun to discover the product's nutritional information. The same thinking might be applicable to your business. After all, a brand personality should be able to flex to handle the voice of a brand character and a spokesperson for more serious conversational situations. Think of an adult you know. They might speak to their child in a different voice than the way they speak to a friend or an employer. Brand managers who have moved beyond the outdated "matching suite of luggage" approach to branding recognize this ability and need. It makes the overall brand personality more robust. So while the concept of brand voice seems simple at first, it can become complex because of the nuances you need to consider and potential contexts of the experience. Meanwhile, your brand voice needs to feel coherent within a voice experience with the way it comes across in print, on broadcast, in store, on premise, within the product, and anywhere else someone might interact with it.

In addition to the overall brand personality and voice, you need to figure out the tone options—the nuances that are appropriate for the context of what is happening. For example, you probably wouldn't want an overly chipper or whimsical brand persona to be the tone of your bank brand's customer service voice experience. Rather, you might want a tone that is more empathetic and understanding. Likewise, you might want a tone that is more helpful when the customer is locked out of their account and has to reset their password. In other words, it's important to understand the context and nature of the task and then develop the dialogue and responses accordingly to align with that context.

Another aspect of a voice experience is that there isn't necessarily a menu or navigation bar to be viewed, which means there are two ways that a user can find out what they can do: (1) they can explore the voice application through trial and error, or (2) the marketer can guide them through it either outside of the experience through marketing materials such as advertising, onboarding emails, and a host of other touchpoints or within the experience using well designed prompts. One caveat with prompts: If you require too much guidance or too many confirmations from the user, the conversation will become less natural and potentially more frustrating for them.

To help you create a great conversational experience, there are some incredible books about conversation design, which we have included in the reference section of this book. Our mission is to help you understand how to use voice applications for building your brand and business to enhance your marketing ROI. Technology implementation, however, comes after you determine what you need to do and what you want to provide. We recommend that you then engage voice strategists, conversational design specialists, and voice developers during the content creation and technology implementation stages, just as you would hire specialists for coding your website or producing your videos.

Audio Branding + Content = Your Brand

As mentioned above, the brand voice must be consistent and genuine across all the platforms and channels, or it will create a disconnect that will make your user pause and question the brand—and that consistency comes from having a robust brand foundation. The good news: You don't have to reinvent your brand. But you can use this moment to conduct a brand audit to ensure you are being consistent—within the flexibility of tone to accommodate the context of the encounter—across your marketing channels and touchpoints. What do customers say about you when you are not in the room? Is your mission, vision, purpose, values, and key message appropriate for today—and for the future?

Then you need to come back to your senses (and those of your prospects and customers). How is your brand being brought to life—and why? Look beyond the visual. How does it feel, taste, smell and, of course, sound? Most branding experts spend all their time on the visual aspects of the brand—it's important—but you also need to understand and convey the atmospherics, as the father of modern marketing, Phil Kotler, calls them, which make the brand more robust. For the voice arena, this means understanding and bringing to life the audio branding elements—music and sounds as well as the spoken voice.

Although we focused quite a bit on language and words and dialogue, that doesn't mean those are the only things that make up successful voice experiences. In addition to having well-structured, appropriate dialogue, you also need to think through and develop the other audio aspects that convey and reinforce the brand promise and persona. You must develop a comprehensive audio language because these elements can also serve as a way-finding system in an environment without visuals. What sound effects and music and audio cues will help your user know when it's time for them to speak and when they should listen?

While it's possible to create voice experiences that do not have a connection to audio branding, the audio branding discipline helps to build your brand as well as build a better audio experience. Plus, the audio branding language and the related elements you create can be used across your other sound-enabled environments from broadcast and online commercials to radio to on-hold systems and ringtones to products (think of the signals your headphones and earbuds make) to even your visually oriented digital experiences. What audio branding entails is what we will be exploring more deeply in the next chapter.

By now, you're probably wondering about what content you need to get started for your voice experience. The good news is the first place you should look is at your existing content. Take an inventory of it to see what can be easily converted to a voice environment (and then determine how your audience might search for it with a spoken request). The audit is an opportunity for you to be able to understand what content is working and what content is not working across all your platforms and touchpoints of your marketing ecosystem so you can adjust them accordingly. Not just for your voice experience. If you are looking at your customer service scripts, for instance, and you find the most successful call-handling scripts have a particular pattern, you can use that insight in the creation of your dialogue for your voice assistant. If you also find that there are other pieces of content that aren't doing such a great job, you can adjust them or find out what will make them more successful, optimizing your content for all your touchpoints. After all, it's your branding elements, plus the actual useable content, multiplied by how those are conveyed that creates your brand perceptions. We will explore content development considerations in future chapters. But first, let's hear from a marketing leader on how voice will disrupt brand marketing and how brands will advance voice and then from a voice expert on your options.

 GUEST PERSPECTIVE 1

Why Brands Have a Crucial Role to Play in Our Voice-Activated Digital Future

David Roth

We think brands should start investigating voice now for use in their marketing efforts. And we are not alone. One proponent of voice for marketing purposes is David Roth, who is the CEO of The Store WPP, EMEA and Asia and the chairman of BrandZ and BAV Group. Within his many roles, David leads WPP's BrandZ, the world's largest brand equity study. He is a leading authority on digital, artificial intelligence, and voice recognition in retail. His books and studies include The History of Retail in 100 Objects, The Third Era of Digital Retailing, *and* Smart Shopping—How Artificial Intelligence Is Transforming the Retail Conversation. *In addition, David has been featured on the BBC, CCTV China, Phoenix TV China, CNBC, Yale, and CKGSB as well as at Cambridge Universities and the World Economic Forum, Davos. Here are his thoughts on the place of brands in voice:*

Technology has been reshaping our lives for decades now. Like it or not, it's the new form of human progress. I see voice as one of the most profound technological disruptive forces. To tell you why, let me talk about twins.

There's a phenomenon that's occasionally reported by some of the 100 million sets of twins around the world. Even when separated by miles or even continents, they simply sense their twin's emotions and feelings. "Twin telepathy" is the stuff of fascinating stories, not established science.

But what if twin telepathy were real and it applied to us all? What if each of us had a twin who knew everything about us or almost everything—not just what we're doing right now, but also what we've been doing, what we're likely to do next, and how we feel about it. Someone who knows even before we do what we need and maybe even does it for us in anticipation.

This is the not-too-distant future. And there are already early signs of what's to come. The convergence of ever-greater and even-cheaper computing power, connected devices, edge computing, and artificial intelligence will, over the next few years, create data versions of ourselves that will be able to make decisions and purchases on our behalf. Using huge amounts of our personal data combined with data from tens of millions of others, we have the potential to create a digital version of an ideal butler, a Jeeves who anticipates our every need. Our very own "digital twin." The democratization of a "butler for all." And we will communicate with this twin using the most ubiquitous, natural, and low tech of all interfaces—our voice.

Voice is fast emerging as the dominant computing interface, and "conversational AI" is what will power our future interactions with our devices, home appliances, cars, and the products and services with which we engage. To put it in a nutshell, everything will have a layer of AI in it and all AI will be conversational. You don't get bigger than that.

Because of its ease of use, convenience, and eventual ubiquity, AI-voice interaction will undoubtedly reshape communication, brand building, buying behavior, and consumer shopping journeys. In the context of this, voice will transform the way we engage with brands on multidimensional levels. Its impact on marketing and brand building will be profound. The rules of shopper marketing in a voice world will change profoundly as will the way it helps brands grow their shareholder value. And this is why everyone, from the new recruit to the chairman of the board, needs to understand voice as this value exchange plays out.

A Shake-Up for Brands

The opportunity and challenges for businesses are going to be as immense as they are profound. In 2019 in China, the Alibaba 11.11 Global Shopping Festival (Single's Day) brought voice to center stage for the first time. More than a million voice orders were placed and paid for using the Tmall Genie smart speaker, as consumers snapped up and paid via voice, among other things, 1.4 million tons of rice and 76 tons of liquid detergent in just twenty-four hours. These numbers are big, but in terms of sophistication, voice ordering is still in its early days. So how long will it take for the concept of a digital twin to become a reality?

Progress will come, broadly speaking, in three stages. While these three stages represent profound technology and capability inflection points, the shifts between them will be almost imperceptible to consumers, who will simply notice clunky Q&As gradually giving way to sensible and increasingly sophisticated, useful, entertaining, frictionless, and intuitive conversations. But behind the scenes many forces, technology trends, and innovations will be hard at work. We will move from the current stage of voice recognition and basic conversations to enable the voice assistant to interpret colloquial speech and multiple accents. We will see a ramping up of AI, which, in combination with NLP, will do away with robotic command-and-response interactions.

More natural-feeling conversations will happen, and voice assistants will offer tailored suggestions and make ever-more-informed recommendations. "Contextual remembering" will mean assistants pick up where they left off and take previous discussions into account, in much the same way as two people meeting for subsequent times don't need to go through the same "getting to know you" conversations on each occasion. When the voice-recognition element of the technology pales in comparison with the role of artificial intelligence, voice assistants will be able to recognize detailed nuance in speech patterns. They'll be able to measure not just actions but the intentions, detect emotional states and even potential health problems. This third stage—and with it, the birth of my digital twin—is still some years away, but the twin is already gestating.

The reality will be that voice will become people's primary means of interacting with the digital world and the way consumers will interact with brands. This will be the new era of true "conversational commerce." The rules of shopper marketing in a voice world will change profoundly. As consumers increasingly embrace this technology, smart brands must explore how to be part of the conversation.

Twelve Implications

What are the implications that everyone involved in the business of brand building must know? Here are some:

1. **Voice is stickier:** Recognize that consumers will gravitate to brands that give them voice options and then stick with them.
2. **Don't wait—experiment and learn now:** Being an early mover in a voice-activated world is essential given its implications for the way people discover, browse, consider, and make purchase decisions. Early movers will maintain significant long-term advantage.
3. **New search skills will be needed:** Brands that have spent years learning the fine art of search optimization for a screen-based web will need to appreciate that a fresh approach is required for sound.
4. **Need to understand and navigate your way through two critical voice paths—"explicit" and "implicit":**

   - Explicit is when you ask your device a question that names a brand or specific product, something like "Take me to Target," that prompts a private one-on-one conversation between you and the brand.
   - Implicit is more about a specific product category or something with a much more general intent. "Where can I find the best deal on AA batteries?"

The combination of skills in both is the pathway to success.

5. **Voice needs to be multimodal:** Your voice strategy needs to be multimodal (i.e., voice for asking a question—especially search—but with the optionality of a screen for the answer). Keep in mind that, on average, we can talk three times faster than we can type, but we can read two times faster than we can listen.[a]
6. **Voice will help you win "the nano" moments of shopping:** In the increasing "nano" moments of shopping where more decisions are being made via the smartphone, voice interactions will be a critical component to win.

7. **In stores, voice also offers huge potential to enhance the physical shopping experience:** Think product selection, information, and physical navigation of the space.

8. **Because online commerce will move to conversational commerce, shopping experiences will become far more human-like, contextual, and personal:** And this means that voice can be used across the length of the commerce journey to purchase and brand advocacy.

9. **Voice is the next frontier in extending lasting brand relationships:** The growth and development of voice should not just be about getting to the "buy" command quicker. Executed well, its role is to strengthen a brand's relationship with its customers. Brands that define their voice and adapt to a voice-controlled digital universe will create deeper relationships with consumers through more bespoke personalization. After all, personalization drives brand love.

10. **It's your next generation of market research:** In many ways, voice technology can deliver next-generation market research to brands, because it is as much about listening to consumers as it is about talking. The rich seam of data that voice interactions generate will serve as a round-the-clock always on focus group, with their permission, of course, without the one-way mirror. The aggregated data generated by natural conversations, when crunched by AI tools, promises to be transformational.

11. **New skills will be required:** This may mean creating new roles within the company or consulting outside it, but new skills will be needed to harness the immense power of conversational commerce—as voice represents nothing less than a fundamentally new way of speaking and engaging with customers. The sound, tone, intonation, and nuance of a voice assistant will have a very powerful impact on the listener's perception of a brand.

12. **There will be a new moral maze:** As AI-voice develops, the potential to collect and collate more than just words will arrive because our way of communicating will move from command to conversation. This conversation will be freighted with personal information that when cross-referenced and contextualized becomes a vast amount of intimate data. Whether this technology becomes an all-listening, rather than all-seeing, version of Big Brother or a confidante of utter discretion and loyalty, which will be predictive and make autonomous decisions on our behalf, will depend on how seriously we take the issue of trust now, rather than further down the road when it might be too late to build. Remember that Jeeves was always on Wooster's side.

[a] Bjorn Carey, "Smartphone Speech Recognition Can Write Text Messages Three Times Faster than Human Typing," Stanford News, published August 24, 2016, accessed January 19, 2023, https://news.stanford.edu/2016/08/24/stanford-study-speech-recognition-faster-texting/.

GUEST PERSPECTIVE 2

Deviating from General Purpose Assistants: Custom Intelligent Voice Assistants

Jason Fields

There are two ways to progress with a voice strategy—work within the ecosystems of Amazon, Apple, or Google or create your own voice assistant. But what are the benefits and the considerations of creating a custom voice assistant? To find out, we turned to Jason Fields, the chief strategy officer at Voicify, one of the original SaaS conversational AI platforms. Before his time with Voicify, Jason spent twenty years as an executive in digital agencies, focusing on customer experience and digital transformation strategy. He also spent seven years as an adjunct professor at Emerson College teaching in their IMC master's program. He has a BA in Communication from the University of Massachusetts Amherst and an MA in Media Studies from New School University. Jason lives in the Pacific Northwest with his wife, Kristina, and their dog, Harley. Here's what Jason has to say:

Amazon Alexa and Google Assistant have been a powerful accelerator of conversational AI. With smart speakers in hundreds of millions of homes and a billion more people interacting with voice assistants on mobile devices, it's safe to say the future is bright for this trend. While the tech giants have the resources and reach to advance technology like conversational AI far past a niche market, so far, the general-purpose assistants have primarily been limited to novelty use cases. According to Amazon, meditation tools, gag apps, and party games dominate the list of top Alexa apps. It's worth mentioning that this pivot follows a predictable pattern. Nearly every previous channel has experienced the same trend of novelty to purpose. Popular early websites ranged from a single video feed of an aquarium to simply translating your name into Hawaiian.[a]

While such diversions are worthy of a few hours of fun with friends, what's currently missing are branded voice applications providing real business value and meaningful customer experiences. Enterprise brands do not top the charts within the walled-garden voice ecosystem for three well-known reasons:

- Discoverability
- Retention
- Monetization/ROI

By usage, the most popular voice apps in the walled-garden ecosystems continue to be simple, single-turn interactions such as asking a question, checking the weather, or setting a timer. In fact, among the top eighteen, making a purchase is last on the list. Contrast this with the top reasons enterprise organizations have decided to adopt voice technology, and a stark misalignment appears. In a 2022 survey of 400 decision-makers,[b] 87% are looking for improved productivity, 77% want new business opportunities, and 62% want to increase revenue. In another recent survey,[c] when asked how voice assistants drive value, 83% said convenience and speed, 77% said improved customer support, and 74% said brand identity and experience.

The employment of a custom assistant at the enterprise level addresses the challenges and goals and does so almost passively. The paradigm of "employing a custom assistant" creates such a natural way of framing the opportunity that brands can apply existing ways of thinking through roles and responsibilities for human personnel against a "virtual employee" (perhaps writing a job description for a custom assistant is a good starting point for companies). A custom assistant seamlessly addresses the challenges of discoverability, retention, and monetization/ROI through a simple action: deployment to owned channels or endpoints.

- Discoverability—when deployed to an owned ecosystem, the custom assistant is presented holistically through design and experience integration.
- Retention—the custom assistant is consistently available, likely in an ever-expanding manner of capabilities and presence.
- Monetization/ROI—like an employee, a custom assistant will be tasked with specifications of the desired experience and systems knowledge driving revenue or efficiency, or both.

The Endpoint Matters

The term *endpoint* is defined as the final stage of a period or process. Applying this concept to conversational AI, the endpoint is the location where the assistant is deployed. While this is logical from the perspective of the brands that publish assistants, from another, perhaps far more important point of view, this is the starting point since it is the point at which the user (customer, employee, prospect) engages with the assistant. Regardless of perspective, the term *endpoint* is where the assistant lives.

Originally, there was only one real choice for most organizations looking to deploy a voice assistant, and at Voicify we call it the leased model. In the leased model, offered by the big tech platforms like Alexa and Google Assistant, brands were attracted to the efficiency of piggybacking on the market penetration of those platforms, receiving help from the coupling of software and hardware: the endpoints of speakers, screens, mobiles, and TVs. Yet those endpoints aren't where their customers are; it's where Amazon's and Google's customers are. One might argue that customers of Amazon and Google are also everyone else's customers, but conversational AI isn't a very good awareness play since discoverability is such a big problem. And most organizations that spend the effort to create an intelligent voice assistant have more substantive goals than merely showing up. For that reason, a custom assistant, in addition to being thought of as an employee, should also be thought of as a companion, a concierge, a personal assistant, etc.

Brands with the most successful voice assistants are thinking more broadly about endpoint options. As maturity in the space deepens, the question shifts from "What's the quickest, easiest way to deploy a voice assistant?" to "Once deployed, where would a voice assistant provide the most impact for our customers and our business?"

For most brands deploying their custom assistant to their website, native mobile applications are a natural first step. A custom assistant can ease navigation and goal attainment friction while offering a secondary user interface and a more natural solution for accessibility.

While web and mobile are table stakes for most businesses, each industry will have secondary considerations. Food service may deploy to drive-throughs and telephony systems. Consumer goods may focus on in-store kiosks, virtual stores in the metaverse, or even the products themselves. The shipping industry can embed a custom assistant in hardware at the employee level within operations. Sports and entertainment may choose to deploy to social or gaming platforms.

Certainly, customer support is a ubiquitous use case for all businesses. By deploying to the web, mobile, telephony, and SMS, the brand can bring problem resolution and the self-service experience to many channels, powered by the same conversational AI. Keep in mind that in the context of customer service/support, the goal often isn't (and I argue should rarely be) to downsize a customer support team. Rather, by handling the most common of customer needs, a brand is freeing up its human resources to solve complex problems and offer a white glove experience in service of retention.

What Custom Assistants Bring to the Enterprise

At the highest level, all custom voice assistants share common attributes that help distinguish them from first-wave walled-garden voice apps and help explain why they are so critical to the future of conversational AI.

Value Creation

As the voice market has matured, use cases for the technology have transcended mere novelty. Value creation, the most fundamental reason enterprise brands are excited about voice, is also the most salient design imperative for a custom voice assistant. Fortunately, when voice becomes a seamless layer of a brand's end-to-end customer experience, it can move the needle on meaningful metrics like increasing revenue, decreasing cost, and improving customer satisfaction.

Tight Integration

Custom voice assistants are easier to integrate because they are completely owned at every layer. Organizations have total freedom to connect them to legacy technology or any other platform via webhooks and APIs. This freedom and flexibility allow brands to weave voice into their products and services in far more seamless, meaningful, and valuable ways than orphaned and atomic, first-wave voice applications.

Brand Alignment

A custom voice assistant isn't another experience that a user needs to go and find. Custom voice assistants are a seamless layer of the brand's overall customer experience, whether as a product extension or any other part of the customer's journey with the brand.

Needs Focused

One of the top considerations driving the design of the walled-garden ecosystem is the need to handle every possible question a user might ask. The resulting experience is breathtakingly wide but incredibly shallow. This need to be all things to all users amplifies the complexity of the discoverability challenges inherent to screenless experiences. If a user asks to talk to "wolverine," are they talking about the animal? The movie? Or the shoe brand? Custom assistants solve the discoverability problem by narrowing the scope of a potential user's needs to a specific domain and including custom handlers for any edge cases. Also, custom voice assistants typically go much deeper into the information they are designed to handle. The result is a far more elegant and seamless experience.

Privacy and Data Protection

By owning the data and experience at every level, organizations that choose a custom voice assistant strategy are free to create and adhere to their privacy and data protection policies. While this may seem like a small detail, in an era of increasing regulation and spiraling costs related to a breach, not to mention the loss of trust and brand affinity, for many organizations, it is the best rationale for eschewing the old strategy for deploying voice apps.

Data Access

Unfettered access to information is another benefit of owning the data associated with a branded voice experience. The walled-garden ecosystem doesn't allow access to all the data that helps brands understand the value of their voice efforts. With complete access, it's possible to see how long users engage, where they drop, and what they are asking for that is not provided. Organizations can use this information to perfect conversation design over time, increasing the value of a custom voice assistant.

Decreasing Cost of Ownership

While it may be correct to say that it's long been possible to design, build, and deploy custom voice assistants, it's not always been an economically viable choice for most organizations. Recent innovations are putting significant downward pressure on the cost of creating and owning custom voice assistants. For instance, Voicify brings the core capabilities of conversational AI (wake words, ASR, NLU, personalization, TTS, effects management, multichannel distribution, management UI, analytics, machine learning, and integrations) into a single platform, negating the burden of tech teams to provision and assemble them separately. For most brands, this translates to a ten times reduction in cost and effort.

While conversational AI is simpler to execute and deploy today than it was five years ago, it still is a sophisticated capability that is most effectively used by enterprise-scale organizations. We now operate in a world where the enterprise can execute a custom assistant without being limited to a leased endpoint model where rules and regulations aren't congruent with their own. And soon, we will see technology companies that serve the mid-market (e.g., Yelp, Angie's List) or service platforms (e.g., DoorDash, Toast, Square) develop a custom assistant for scale, able to serve their subscribers' customers in a personal and meaningful manner with subscriber-level context. In short, conversational AI and the custom assistant is the holder of a powerful user interface that has been at the center of human communication for millennia: our voice.

[a] Brian McCullough, "How the Internet Happened: From Netscape to the iPhone" (New York, NY: Liveright, 2018), chapter 4, paragraph 4.
[b] Derek Top, "Opus Research Report: '2022 State of Voice Technology,'" published February 10, 2022, accessed January 23, 2023, https://opusresearch.net/wordpress/2022/02/10/opus-research-report-2022-state-of-voice-technology/.
[c] Derek Top, "Opus Research Report: 'The Business Value of Customized Voice Assistants,'" published February 26, 2021, accessed January 23, 2023, https://opusresearch.net/wordpress/2021/02/26/opus-research-report-the-business-value-of-customized-voice-assistants/.

EXTENDED CASE STUDY

General Mills Lucky Charms Brand Building

Lucky Charms cereal from General Mills has a very long history of being a market leader. When Lucky the Leprechaun made his debut in 1964, it was one of the most expensive advertising launches of its time, with the critter being featured in full-color ads in the Sunday comics, in comic books, and on animated television commercials.[a] Aiming to continue its leadership nearly fifty-four years later and to drive its association with St. Patrick's Day (the brand's official anniversary date), Lucky Charms needed to bring its brand story to life in a modern and engaging way for families.

With an increasing number of families using voice assistants in their homes, Lucky Charms saw a great opportunity to bring its beloved brand icon, Lucky, right to these families through Alexa's voice and their own imaginations. Working with the interactive production studio Xandra and Amazon, Lucky Charms first created "The Story of Lucky Charms," one of the first storytelling Amazon Alexa Skills produced by a consumer-packaged goods company. The result was an interactive story-building experience.[b]

Through "The Story of Lucky Charms," Lucky and his magical friends took families on an immersive choose-your-own adventure. The story kicks off by asking users to choose which rainbow they want to travel through to take them to the magic portal. The interactive adventure continues with their choices determining who they meet and how they make their way through Lucky's magical world. With several paths to choose from, the options were limitless—enough so that the creators claimed you would never hear the same story twice.

Supported with an integrated campaign that leveraged paid, owned, and earned channels, The Story of Lucky Charms Alexa Skill enjoyed high engagement and high ratings (4.5/5 stars, 150+ reviews in the first two months).[c] In addition to using paid and organic social media posts, Lucky Charms used Spotify Audio Ads to drive traffic to the voice application.

Jessica TeBrake, assistant manager, Brand Experience at General Mills, is quoted in a blog post on the company's website as saying, "We're getting back to our roots of storytelling. Voice has become such a big part of how people experience content, so we wanted to dial up our opportunity to tell stories with audio and voice."[d]

Building upon the success of the Amazon Alexa Skill, Lucky Charms launched a second voice experience, Lucky Charms Magical Mission, a few months later. This time the interactive voice experience was available on both Amazon Alexa– and Google Assistant–enabled devices. In this experience, fans explore Lucky's world through the eight charm lands to help Lucky restore the magic that has been disappearing. After the introductory chapter, fans can pick which charm land they want to visit, and as they complete each mission, they can choose to visit the remaining lands.

Featuring ten audio chapters that run between two to three minutes each, the story features the voice of Lucky the Leprechaun and several original characters, including a narrator. By using a narrator to provide instructions and guidance to users, Lucky Charms was able to keep its brand spokesperson doing what he does best: spreading the magical cheer of Lucky Charms. To further expand the reach of the story, Lucky Charms also made the ten chapters available as podcasts on Spotify, Google Podcasts, and Apple Podcasts. To access Lucky Charms Magical Mission, you can go to https://www.amazon.com/General-Mills-Charms-Magical-Mission/dp/B08FTGHLFH.

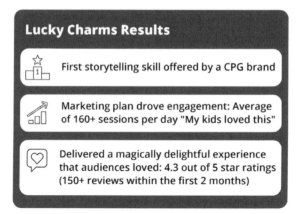

Figure 2.1. The results General Mills achieved through their Lucky Charms Magical Mission voice application.

Lucky Charms found success with its forays into voice by creating engaging experiences that expanded upon its brand icons, giving its audiences a way to join Lucky the Leprechaun in his world. By breaking story content into interactive experiences, Lucky Charms was able to tell a complete story that fit the short attention span of its audience. Having a robust, cross-channel marketing support plan with clear calls to action drove traffic to delightful voice experiences whose immersive and fun nature kept them coming back to engage with Lucky and his magical friends. This secret of success—having an engaging story with the marketing—is a lesson for all marketers who want to find success in the new world of voice.

[a] General Mills, "The History of Lucky Charms," published March 17, 2014, accessed December 28, 2021, https://blog.generalmills.com/2014/03/lucky-charms/.
[b] Amazon, "Lucky Charms Case Study," published April 2020, accessed December 28, 2021, https://build.amazon alexadev.com/rs/365-EFI-026/images/Xandra_LuckyCharms_Final05082020.pdf.
[c] Eric Schwartz, "New Voice App Takes Kids on Lucky Charms Branded Audio Adventure," Voicebot.ai, published September 16, 2020, accessed December 28, 2021, https://voicebot.ai/2020/09/16/new-voice-app-take-kids-on-lucky-charms-branded-audio-adventure/.
[d] Hanna Johnson, "Chase Lucky for His Pot of Gold This St. Patrick's Day," General Mills, published February 10, 2020, accessed December 28, 2021, https://blog.generalmills.com/2020/02/chase-lucky-for-his-pot-of-gold-this-st-patricks-day/.

Audio Branding and Its Importance

When two members of the authorship team, Laurence Minsky and Colleen Fahey, wrote *Audio Branding: Using Sound to Build Your Brand*, they knew that each brand needed a cohesive sonic universe to stand out and become more competitive. They didn't suspect that the world was about to present an even more urgent reason to build a sonic brand. At that time, voice search was still in its early infancy.

Now it's a rambunctious tween, growing like a weed.

And with it, consumer behavior has begun to shift. Podcast listenership has exploded,[1] many forms of radio have seen gains in audiences,[2] and more people shop using their voices.[3] People also entertain themselves increasingly through music and games that they launch with their voices. The quarantine only hastened the adoption of voice-enabled apps because people stayed home seven days a week. As the new behaviors become permanent, we see a significant increase in voice usage. In December 2020, according to an eMarketer survey, more than half of US adults said they had never shopped for goods via voice AI and had no interest in trying voice shopping. In fact, just 9% of US adults had ever shopped via voice, and only 2% had done so regularly.[4] Fast-forward to 2021, when brands had become more strategic in their use of voice. Research conducted by PYMNTS found that more than 41% would be more likely to do business with a company that would let them use voice commands to manage money or payments.[5] Similarly, the Voice Consumer Index 2021 uncovered that 41% of US adults had made at least one buy using voice technology.[6] In 2022, that number increased by 8% to 49% of all US adults having used voice to make at least one purchase.[7]

Marketers who are trying to strengthen brands by using voice technology may be feeling growing pains, though. For one thing, most voice experiences, even when built by brands, for Alexa, Siri, and/or general-purpose assistants tend to sound as if they've been offered by the platform rather than by the brand itself. For another, when a consumer asks one of these platforms about a brand, the answer usually defaults to Wikipedia's description, rather than the one a brand manager would certainly prefer. Some brands that are ahead in many branding ways haven't caught up to the voice-enabled world yet. But the ones that already have a sonic brand soundscape will be far ahead of the rest when they step into that voice-first world. For instance, when Coca-Cola comes out with their own proprietary voice experience, they will have a great head start on brand differentiation—because they have long invested in multisensory branding and even beyond a signature melody, their sonic brand assets include specific ice cube clinks, opening pops, pouring, and fizzing sounds.[8] Using those signals to welcome, transition, and punctuate Coca-Cola's voice app will allow the brand to clearly stake out its own borders in the general-purpose assistant instead of getting lost in any voice platform's vast and undifferentiated sea. With its own tune and sound effects, Coca-Cola will have the power to provide a recognizable and refreshing auditory brand experience for its audio audience. The moral for a marketer? If you want your voice experience to help build your brand, your brand must sound focused and consistent before you leap into tactical matters.

In this chapter, we'll look at the three major components of sonic branding: brand music, the brand's spoken voice, and the tiny brand signals and alerts that guide the user's way through products and experiences. And because the world of podcasting is rising so fast, we'll touch on approaching podcasts with an audio branding hat on. We'll explore the different ways the sounds are used, the methods for arriving at them, and the discipline involved in maintaining them. All of this has impact on your voice marketing, because your sonic brand lays the foundation for a recognizable, ownable, and brand-building voice experience.

A Definition of Audio Branding

The easiest way to understand audio branding, also called sonic branding, is to compare sonic brand systems with visual branding systems. In the visual world, a brand stands out via its color palette, typefaces, and logo design that it uses with consistency no matter where you encounter it—whether on the side of a building or in the tiniest mobile app. The principles are the same for sonic branding systems. The tune, tempo, sonic logo, and in some cases, spoken voice (or voice-over) generally remain consistent, though the sound might be deployed in a particular way to open a big meeting or might be carefully adapted as a micro-melody for when a product is turned on and off. Both visual and ideally, sonic identity systems are ruled by the all-important Brand Style Guide, often referred to as a "Brand Bible."

While this hearing-based branding discipline goes by many names—sonic branding, audio branding, sonic identity, sound branding, and auditory branding, to name a few—the different words all refer to the same idea—the use of sound, music, and voice to set your brand apart. Sonic branding isn't a new field (think of the venerable sonic logos like the

NBC chimes, the BBC news tune, the "Intel Inside" sound, and McDonald's five-note sign-off), but it has recently become a much more visible and pervasive one. An audio brand provides you with a sonic vocabulary based on your brand essence and personality, and it gets expressed across each brand experience including branded content, video and audio advertising, on-hold lines, events, and increasingly, your podcasts, TikTok videos, and voice experiences. This breadth can't be achieved with a cookie-cutter approach; a brand needs to flexibly adapt the core musical idea to the needs of the audience. The brand's sonic vocabulary must be used to enhance and differentiate the audience's experience at each branded touchpoint within the unique system of sounds created for the brand. In creating an Amazon Alexa Skill, the brand's soundscape might be used to welcome the user, signal the end of an answer, and communicate a transition. For a piece of content, it might be adapted to underscore the dramatic narrative and tell the audience how to feel. For an on-hold experience, the brand's music might be designed to provide interesting sonic variety with which to shorten the perceived wait time.

Though your sonic brand's functions differ from experience to experience, your sonic identity will be identifiable as your own via your music's tune, texture, tempo, and rhythms; your specific sounds for alerts and signals; and your recognizable brand voice or voices. In the end, all contact points share the same sonic DNA and sound as though they come from the same family. That's reassuring to the audience because consistency has a way of building brand trust.[9] Sonic branding systems become long-term brand assets that last and can gradually evolve as the brand refocuses its positioning—without sacrificing the precious brand equity that has been built. And by owning your sonic branding elements, marketers can save on time finding the one-off sonic elements and on licensing fees.[10]

The Proof Is in the Attention

A 2020 study by Ipsos found that audio cues were more likely to catch attention than any type of visual cues.[11] Brand assets give marketers a full set of tools for helping establish mental "real estate" in customers' minds. But until now, which assets rank strongest in driving brand creative effectiveness (e.g., logos, colors, taglines, celebrities, characters, sonic cues) has not been well understood. That's why the Ipsos "Power of You" study, which measured the relative impact of brand cues on ad performance, was so revealing. For one commonsense thing, it showed that branded assets, both visual and auditory, outranked borrowed interest.[12] Brand assets that leverage the power of the brand, such as brand mascots and sonic brand cues, deliver more performance than assets that are borrowed from a wider culture, such as celebrities and popular songs. Does Tony the Tiger or the Michelin Man rank above famous celebrities? Well, ads that use brand characters rank very high (right below branded music), at 6.1 times more likely to be high performing, suggesting that just as with branded music, marketers should consider reinvesting their celebrity money on building their own brands' celebrities. The Ipsos study suggests that "You," the brand, is better served by supercharging your own sensory and storytelling cues and tops it off by revealing that sound is currently a wastefully untapped asset for most brands.

Impact of brand assets on brand attention

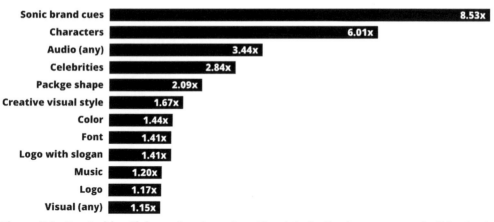

Figure 3.1. Created by Sixieme Son based on the data in the Ipsos reaserch, this chart shows the imapct of specific brand cues against the performance of the ad.

In summary, following are the three recommendations made by Ipsos upon analysis of the survey results:

1. "The presence of brand assets is strongly linked to positive branded attention effects, more so than just directly showing or talking about the brand.
2. Brand assets that leverage the power of 'you,' such as characters and sonic brand cues, are more effective for brands than assets that are leveraged from wider culture, such as celebrities and music.
3. While less frequently used, audio assets are on average more effective than some visual assets, which suggests brands can take the opportunity of audio to improve the branded attention of their video creative over time."[13]

What to Think About Before You Create Your Sonic Brand

Our experience has shown us that some presuppositions that may seem intuitively right can work against the development of a successful sonic brand. This is often due to the understandable idea that you're setting out to create music rather than to design a brand. The aims of each are different and so are the methods. Here are three warnings to keep in mind when creating a sonic brand:

Prepare to sacrifice the sweet and lovely (unless you're a truly sweet and lovely brand). The biggest trap for a brand marketer is to try too hard to be liked. Instant likeability usually means your offering is too familiar and thus, too predictable. The goal of a sonic brand is not to be a beautiful piece of music. Its purpose is the work of branding—attract attention, differentiate from competitors, communicate brand values, stick in the mind, and become associated with the product or service. If the composition is too easy on the ears, it usually means the piece feels too familiar, which runs the danger of being too easy to ignore or forget. Personality and surprise are a brand's best friends. But surprise isn't always liked at first; it might strike the ear as strange, and it might not test at the top of the likeability scale. That's okay and probably to your advantage.

Don't assume a good sonic logo means your work is done. A sonic logo does most of the heavy lifting in the world of sonic brand identities, but it's necessarily short and doesn't provide enough information to future designers of sonic adaptations. For those, you need a longer piece of music. Not much longer; in fact 45 seconds will do, but long enough to establish tempo, rhythms, instrumentation, voices, harmonies, textures, and even the way the musical idea develops.

You can't just ask for music and walk away. If you were commissioning a classical symphony, you might need to step back; the composer probably would need space and time for their thoughts to develop. But in branding, you know the nuances of your brand better than the designer does, so check-ins are necessary. Sometimes you will become even more aware of the brand's nuances as you hear them expressed in a musical vocabulary, and you'll realize you need to go further in communicating the subtleties of the brand. The musical designer needs to rely on your input.

The method we recommend follows a very inclusive and collaborative methodology that involves the brand leader and important brand champions such as agencies, design firms, and key internal departments to voice strong opinions and play an active role in guiding a sonic brand's development. As this chapter unfolds, you'll discover that the collaborative development of a sonic brand, including each of its main components—music, voice, and signals—involves a thorough grounding in the category, followed by divergent thinking and exploration, and finally convergent thinking and refinement. Then, once the core guiding idea has been determined, the final sonic brand DNA needs to be sensitively adapted to real uses in the big, messy world.

How to Determine a Brand's Musical Identity

The brand's promise, personality, and values serve as the main guides in designing the brand's musical identity. But you can't get there directly by just simply stating your core promise and aspirational values and edging toward the door. You need to go through a bit of a journey. To use a blunt and simplistic example, it's not enough to say, "This brand stands for leadership," and think you've communicated the subtleties of that brand's style of leadership or captured the expression of "leadership" that would stand out among the competitors in the brand's sector.

To start with, your team needs to become familiar with the music and sounds used by the brand's competitors to hunt out the musical clichés of the category. You will want your sonic branding partner to weed out and avoid those. You will need to find a way to stand apart from those brands without sacrificing your own brand's essence. You'll need to find a way to create something fresh and differentiated, while preserving any sound or music in which your brand has established hard-won and cherished equity. And your team will need to articulate musically what you mean by the words you're using to describe your brand. That's a real challenge. The firm can tackle this problem by sending their sonic strategists out into the vast cosmos of music to find different ways that one might say what a brand stands for using the beloved nonverbal language of music. How would you convey, for instance, precision or approachability or fun? Each one of those brand values suggests a wide variety of different musical approaches. The team then creates audio "mood boards" of short clips of music that represent each key principle. These would be used to facilitate thoughtful conversations with clients and their marketing partners in a "Listening Committee" workshop to then remove the wrong sounds and explore the musical ideas that have potential.

In exploring *precision*, for instance, some types of "precise" might be perceived (using real examples here) as too cold or others, too sharp edged. In exploring approachability, some musical selections might be seen as too cluttered, too "granola," or too childish for the brand. Other sounds might capture the appropriate rhythm or introduce unexpected but intriguing instrumentation that's worth exploring further. That way, the mood boards help create barriers to creating with the wrong sounds—which saves time—and they help provide inspiration—which leads to fresher ideas. With this input, the composing/music designing process can begin both with safe guardrails and inspiring starting points.

As an example of how mood boards can open up a discussion of new dimensions that hadn't previously been considered, here's something that happened not long ago. The client, their ad agency, and the sonic branding agency were participating in a mood board workshop exploring the general idea of *curiosity* and *openness to discovery*, when a couple of snippets of music in the mood board triggered a sense of *mystery*. The clients, who had just been listening to a focus group with a specific segment of their target, realized that anything mysterious might trigger feelings of fear in them, and might actively discourage this group. The client directed us to rein in our musical expression of curiosity and stay on the lighter side of the surprising-to-mysterious continuum so that their composition and its future interpretations didn't step over the line and unintentionally evoke feelings of dread. That insight might not have been easy to put a finger on without the provocation of the snippets of "darker" music in the mood board.

As marketers, we're all constantly juggling the pole of familiarity/understanding with the pole of novelty/discovery. The right amount of familiarity can hugely support liking and the right amount of novelty can cause anticipation, while at the same time, too much of familiarity can create boredom and too much of the novelty can create confusion. Music has a wonderful elasticity that can help address these tensions, because the audience can easily recognize a familiar piece that's arranged in a fresh way in support of a new experience.

USAA, a Fledgling Sonic Brand with Quick, Measurable Impact

Using the process outlined above, the USAA sonic identity creation began with the competitive analysis, which revealed a preponderance of hyper-masculinity in music aimed at military and ex-military people, as well as a singularly robust competitive environment in the nonmilitary-oriented competition. The US insurance category has boasted some of the oldest continuous musical cues. The State Farm "Like a Good Neighbor" piece was written by Barry Manilow over fifty years ago, "We are Farmers" has been sung consistently for decades, and "Nationwide is on your side" is a longtime, well-known tagline. It was into this competitive atmosphere that USAA planned to launch its first sonic brand as part of a TV campaign that launched at the tail end of 2019.

The sonic identity strove to capture their idea that "We serve the military but we're not the military" and convey the values of optimism, camaraderie, rigor, and authenticity. The brand needed to be strong, distinctive, and recognizable to break through. The idea that emerged for the brand's sonic logo was completely different from anything in the market-place. It featured a call-and-response "US A-A" that was inspired by the military cadences (sometimes called "Jody calls"), which our mood board sessions had uncovered as a warmly remembered part of a military life.

Though the USAA sound had been in the marketplace for less than a year, the audio identity soon attracted attention and positive results. The sonic logo was shown by the Ver-itonic Audio Logo Index to have ranked high on such measures as authentic, inspiring, and trustworthy. It scored higher than the much older Nationwide sound, and it also placed 12 points higher than the McDonald's theme, which had been introduced in 2003.[14] Before the first year was over, the Veritonic Audio Logo Index placed it fifth among audio logos on the measure of "correctly recognized," beating many logos that had been in the market for decades. The sonic logo also has been awarded the AMA's BrandSmart Gold in the cat-egory of Innovation as well as a Transform Award in recognition of "best practices in brand design and strategy." The sonic identity appears very subtly in the company's soothing, new on-hold music for Survivor Relations calls, eliciting the highest ratings ever scored since the measurements were taken. Today, the company has plans to use the audio identity to inform the sounds and alerts within the voice assistant at its launch.

Emerging Importance of Yet Another
Sonic Brand Element—The Human Voice

Music has historically led the charge in sonic branding, but as the number of voice searches grows, savvy brands are beginning to see opportunities for selecting and unifying their spo-ken voice too. Here, we're not talking about "brand voice" in the sense of writing style, but about the literal voice formed by your vocal chords.

Some brands have used the human voice to create their special brand sound in TV and radio advertising. For example, Tom Bodett's enduring voice for Motel 6, which the brand began to use in 1986,[15] and the Geico gecko's long-term voice, show how vocal tone can bring distinctiveness to a brand and can become a powerful brand asset over time. But few brands integrate the voice of their advertising into their voice experiences or the voice of their voice experiences into their advertising. Many voice experience creators are content to use the vanilla voices offered by Amazon for their clients' applications, just as production houses will choose actors with "good pipes" for advertising instead of choosing distinct, fitting, and consistent personalities for the brands.

This suggests that the marketers responsible for the strength of their brands remain deaf to the power of the sound of a spoken voice as a key brand asset. And in this burgeoning world of voice technology, most creators have not come to regard voice experiences as a branding opportunity. Brands had better get started, though, because a brand that boasts a sonic identity, including vocal identity, has a real advantage going into the world of smart devices and voice-led activities. It's a step ahead of the competition—because recognizable music, sounds, and voice are usually the only branding cues a brand gets when people are searching for information on smart speakers.

A Voice for the Brand and Not Just for the Campaign

We have established the premise that brand consistency builds trust. And we know that familiarity breeds liking (also called "favorability"), so it follows that the voice you hear from a brand within its voice experience on a smart speaker, website, or mobile app would ideally be the same voice you hear on your customer service on-hold system, your content, and your advertising tagline. So how do you go about making such a momentous decision as choosing a voice to represent your brand? Here's a process that breaks it down into concrete and manageable stages:

1. Start by briefing your sonic branding partner on your brand's essence and its values. This time the brand's personality is a big part of the conversation.
2. Then do a review of the voices that tend to be used in your category. Sixième Son recently did a competitive analysis for a large bank in Canada and discovered that all their competitors were using businesslike male voices. This led the team to suggest that a warm woman's voice would immediately differentiate them.
3. To imagine the person that would embody a brand, we prefer to start by looking at classic archetypes. Traditional categories include the Sage, the Magician, the Hero, the Creator, the Explorer, the Outlaw, the Jester, the Lover, the Caregiver, the Everyman, the Innocent, and the Ruler. Often, you will find that your brand embodies characteristics of more than one archetype. That's fine. Some believe that the formula should be 70% of the main archetype and 30% of another flavor—for instance, a Ruler who's also an Innocent would be a very different character than a Ruler who's also a Jester. The idea is to begin the process of deeply considering the character who will represent your brand.

   Usually that exploration launches you into a deeper discussion that refines the definition of a more specific character, often called a "brand persona," one that paints a clear picture for copywriters, actors, and conversation designers. Once you've landed upon the characteristics of the voice that represents your brand, you'll be in a better position to decide its gender, accent, and age range; you may even have ideas about pitch and energy level.

   For one client, a very mature, high-quality brand admired in the industry, the team felt that the Sage was the closest archetype for its brand for all the solid qualities it suggests: experienced, trusted, and wise. The team envisioned the Sage in the persona of a mentor. But that representation seemed too stationary for this dynamic company, and it lacked some of the optimistic energy and innovation inherent in the brand. So the character on whom they settled kept some aspects of a mentor but took on characteristics of a coach. Later, a female-oriented organization, looking to convey similar sage-like characteristics through their choice of voice, but not wanting to feel too distant or unapproachable, chose the inspiring persona of the "cool aunt."

Beyond archetypes, a brand may want to incorporate further criteria, such as regionality. For an Emirati airline, relevant differentiation in their English-language announcements was achieved by choosing the voice of a cosmopolitan native of that Emirate instead of the typical British voice. The use of the same person to give announcements in Arabic and English underscored the authentic roots of the brand and made the brand stand apart from its competition.

4. Decide if you intend to use the voice mostly for teaching and narration or whether you will be using it for scripts that require acting ability. If the former, you need a trained voice talent, but for the latter, you must go further; you will want to find actors who understand and can express nuances of emotion and can fully inhabit a character.

5. If you're creating a voice-activated application, you have further questions to answer. The most important one is "How should the voice be generated?" Should it be the recorded voice of a human performer, the digitized voice of a particular human, or a Polly voice that works like an instant voice-over generator (usually the least engaging option but also the least expensive). Often, the right answer is to combine two methods.

A rule of thumb for choosing what type of voice approach to use is "The longer the text, the better it is to use a human." Linguists and programmers are working mightily to make the previous sentence untrue, and they're making great strides. But as of today, the rule still holds.

If you're using a human voice actor, you can start by getting a voice talent agency to help you assemble the demos of acting talent that fit your criteria. If you intend to use a synthesized voice, there are companies that have catalogs of synthesized voices. Just be sure you're getting a voice that captures your brand's persona, isn't overused, and over time, will be identifiable as part of your brand. It's also possible to digitize a specific human voice to use as the chatbot. The voice can be translated into another language and still sound like it's coming from the same individual.

Caution! A smooth, generic, professional-sounding voice is unlikely to achieve the recognition you need. Keep in mind that a voice that has some distinctive quality will be more attention getting and memorable than a blandly professional one. Be sure to consider what kind of characteristic might be a fit for your brand. Is it a raspiness, a slight accent, an interesting lilt, a rhythmic quality, or an unexpected timbre? Michaël Boumendil, founder of Sixième Son, likes to call this non-vanilla vocal quality "the itching powder" because it gets under your skin.

6. Okay, whew! You've chosen your voice; maybe it's a human one, or maybe it's a synthesized or a digitally recreated one. You are planning to use it for a long time across multiple touchpoints. It's time to consider the licensing agreement. You'll probably continue to evolve your voice app as new customer questions show up and new technologies come along, and you'd be unwise to use a new voice each time. It's better to negotiate your rate now, with possible increases built in every few

years. Also, you will need a long license period, and you may want to discuss getting the actors' permission to digitize (also called "concatenate") their voices so you can eventually build text-to-speech scripts.

Here's an illustration using a real example that could become a possible scenario for a brand. The Paris Metro's stops have been announced by the same woman's voice for decades. They were first recorded by Simone Hérault in 1994. People call her voice by her name, "Simone," and enjoy the familiarity of her sound. She continued to record new stops as the Metro extended to new routes. But when she got to be in her seventies, the Metro system realized that this partnership wouldn't last forever and worked with her to digitize her voice. Now her voice double, sometimes called "e-Mone" in the industry, lends her reassuring tones to the stations, mobile phones, and ticket machines. Her voice will be available for new messages and AI voice interactions for years to come.

This method presents a perfect situation for the use of a digitized voice as very short pieces of information are less likely to sound odd or robotic.

The Power of Small Sounds and Signals

Have you ever turned on a highly sophisticated technological device only to hear a tinny, high-pitched ding or bing-bong? That's probably the standard sound that the chip makers have supplied. Now imagine opening up a MacBook Air laptop. Their start-up sound feels like a sunrise, full of hope and optimism. It's less than two seconds long, but it still affects your mood and expectation. After the sound was suppressed on some devices for a few years, it's back on the MacOS Big Sur along with a package of "system sounds [that] are all-new and even more pleasing to the ear. The new system alerts were created using snippets of the originals, so they sound familiar." In finding a balance between the familiar and the novel, they've used a true best practice. The company asserts that new sounds don't come out of nowhere, but are "familiar to the Mac, but remastered and more refined," said Alan Dye, Apple's vice president of human interface design.[16] Apple proves it understands that an exquisite product design doesn't stop at the visual and tactile level. A purposefully designed sound must be part of the customer experience.

Bad Sound Can Cheapen a Device, Appliance, or Vehicle

A story you hear over and over goes something like this. When the long-awaited new device is finally near completion, the more brand-aware engineers often turn to marketing to ask what kind of sounds they should use. At that point, the marketing team is caught flat-footed and normally turns to a standard solution. If the company had a sonic identity, though, they'd have a place to begin. In other cases, the engineering team doesn't even consult with marketing but simply uses the beeps and buzzes provided by the chip manufacturer with no idea that competitors may be using the same sounds or that users might find them uncomfortable, annoying, and even anxiety provoking.

One farsighted manufacturer of audio electronics decided to do it differently and despite not having a sonic brand, created a premium range of sounds for the signals in their high-end headphones. The company looked for a sound that would underscore the brand promise that they put their impeccable technology to use to support their users in bringing out their best selves. The proposed anchoring concept became "the organic halo." With the meaning of "organic" (suggesting nonsynthetic, human to human, and genuine) united to the meaning of "halo" (that conveyed radiating, sharing energy, and expanding), the creative team was grounded and extraordinarily inspired.

Nine different executions emerged from the guiding idea. Four that made it to the last round were "airy," "sharp and round," "laser in light form," and "vibration." The cross-functional team ranked the choices according to a rubric that considered three factors:

1. Communication of the brand
2. Ability to differentiate from competition
3. Customer experience

In the end, the idea that won allowed customers to physically feel the depth and range of the product's exceptional sonic characteristics as well as to comprehend the breadth and precision of its sound quality via the on/off signals, the Bluetooth connecting and connected sounds, the low-battery alert, and a small handful of other important mini-communications. The brand also comes through as 100% distinctive and thorough in its approach. The lead sonic UX designer at Sixième Son comments that this holistic approach works, but only partially, in the automotive sector where the sound design of any given signal can be influenced by over 100 people, including mandatory regulatory and safety experts.

Creating Voice Experiences That Stand Out

Voice experiences, too, can communicate the brand, differentiate from the competition, and enhance the user experience through strategic use of sound. But many voice-driven apps suffer from the lack of strategic sound design. They don't use either a specific voice to represent the brand or unique, tailored music to help draw the auditory boundaries around the experience. They forgo the chance to signal to a visitor that they've left the generic platform and have arrived in the brand's unique environment.

One organization that approached the sonic design of their voice experience mindfully was the Open Voice Network, as they are dedicated to promoting high standards within the community of professionals working in the voice ecosystem and feel the obligation to model exemplary behavior for the whole arena. The Open Voice Network is an international group working to make AI-enabled voice assistance worthy of user trust. Their multinational team of volunteer professionals is endeavoring to create global standards for privacy, programming, and accessibility. Inclusivity is one of their guiding values. Additionally, they don't wish to be perceived as an organization from the United States, where they started, but as the global network they have quickly evolved into.

Their sonic branding process began with a brief for the music because that would set the tone for the overarching experience. It made clear that the aim of the organization was to be warm, open, approachable, and international. Five different approaches were presented. During the Listening Committee meeting, one of the comments on a particular musical concept was "I feel as if I'm in a boutique hotel in Brussels; guests are not wearing business suits. A variety of young people are coming and going, the conversation is flowing, the coffee smells terrific." That multisensory impression proved convincing, and among the five different approaches, the one that evoked that comment was the one chosen as the core brand identity. While the brand music was being developed, the brief for the brand voice was also being produced. Sixième Son was convinced that the brand archetype would reveal aspects of the archetype of a Sage but would also be warm, open, approachable, and international. After several ideas, the team landed on the persona of an emissary or ambassador who travels widely and speaks several languages. The language would have to be English, but the accent would preferably not be from an English-speaking country, to convey the idea that the speaker speaks more than one language. In the end, the group chose the voice of a Frenchman who had spent some of his childhood in California and some of his adult life in Toronto. You can compare the experience of listening to the Alexa voice, then hearing the same content spoken by the "ambassador," and finally, the ambassador's voice paired with the music from the sonic brand. You'll see for yourself how each modification increases your engagement with the Open Voice Network brand. Visit https://www.voicemarketingbook .ai/sonicbrandingexample.

The Mighty Sonic Style Guide

Marketing staff tends to turn over frequently, both in companies and in their agencies. Protecting the brand against people's desire to make their own marks requires a firm hand and some spelled-out rules. The Sonic or Audio Style Guide is your brand's best friend in these cases. It explains the inspiration for the brand sounds and gives clear, detailed guidance around the usage of each element. Some companies prefer the style guide be a fully interactive experience in which each example is playable and downloadable on the spot. A typical Sonic Style Guide will comprise several condensed sections usually arranged in the order shown below in the box.

BRAND SECTION	Podcast Package
The Sonic Identity	Voice App Package
The Sonic DNA	Modular Set of Audio Beds for Videos
The Sonic Logo and Micro Sonic Logo	On-Hold/Customer Service Music
ADAPTATIONS SECTION	GENERAL INFORMATION
Endframe	Frequently Asked Questions
Meetings and Events Package	Legal Information
Micro-Melodies for Product Signals	
and Alerts	

Here's an example of the way a piece of tailor-made music might be described to help people understand and articulate its relationship with the brand.

> The audio identity is an original composition that establishes a distinct audio vocabulary to strengthen the impact of the brand's communications by providing a consistent set of impressions across all touchpoints.
>
> For [brand] it is a unique distillation of the brand values. It conveys an optimistic personality, one that has an enduring commitment to working together to pioneer solutions that will make a difference in the audience's lives.

Depending on the company's appetite for detail, you might go on to describe the more specific design elements of the sound, for example:

> The composition is built around a piano arpeggio that has a distinct, clear melody in a major key, which sets the overall optimistic and bright tone.
>
> The countermelody with the piano and echo effect creates a light, slower contrast to the arpeggios as a way to convey passion and caring.
>
> The addition of the pulse of strings creates a feeling of the aspect of pioneering and forward motion.

Podcasts Keep Proliferating

The rise of podcasts and their many uses has already been discussed in chapter 1. As a fully auditory medium, their sound deserves some special sonic branding attention. The good news is that podcast producers do seem to be cognizant of the need for music to welcome, underscore content, make transitions, and close out a piece. Maybe this consciousness exists because podcasts resemble radio shows and radio show creators are experts in the use of music as a branding tool. These role models may make podcasters more apt to realize that music would enhance the content.

To create the sonic vocabulary for a podcast, you usually start with the core sonic identity and then adapt it to the needs of the podcast program. Sometimes the brand doesn't have a sonic identity, so in those cases, the creator must start from scratch using the process used to design a brand's sound. The audio team usually produces a "Podcast Kit," a collection of pieces that include a sonic logo, an intro, an outro, a bed or two of music to use as a background, and two or three transitions to change the tone between different guests or sections of the show.

Different podcasters use different approaches. A popular podcaster, Bret Kinsella, creator of *The Voicebot Podcast*, a well-known podcast in the world of voice, used music like *2001: A Space Odyssey* for his first 100 or so episodes and then decided it was time to create his own sonic brand. The podcast's current clean, tech-inspired sound was custom designed for his program by his sonic branding agency, Audio Brain. The VoiceBot.ai intro is a short piece that builds to a crescendo followed by music that plays during the introduction of the speaker's bio. Kinsella's preference is to cut the music after the interviewee begins to speak, as he wants the guests to come through clearly. To that end, he also removes crackles and hesitations because he wants his guests to sound the best they can. His podcast ends with a sonic logo that's cut from the same cloth as the music that leads into the episode.

How Do You Measure Up to
Kotler's Five Principles of Brand Success?

Philip Kotler, the ultimate expert on branding, posits that five principles create brand strength. They are the following ones, familiar to brand marketers:

1. Consistency
2. Clarity
3. Continuity
4. Visibility
5. Authenticity

Marketers apply many of these in the visual realm, but in truth, all of these can be brought to bear on brands via the auditory realm.[17]

All your sonic strategy, creation, and deployment blossom into brand strength when they're put into practice thoughtfully and methodically. When your customers, immersed in their own environments, feel the brand fit and the sonic consistency among your voice apps, vehicles, devices, or appliances and your communication touchpoints, they'll experience a sense of recognition. When your advertising and social media creations send customers to voice-enabled experiences that answer them in the same voice they had just heard, the seamless experience will provide a reassuring sense of comfort, completeness, and trust.

 GUEST PERSPECTIVE 1

The Science of Voice Branding

Charles Spence

The power of audio branding is not just based on intuition that you need to account for more than just the visual aspects of a brand; it's based on science. To give you a bit of the science behind it, we asked Professor Charles Spence, the world's leading expert in multisensory perception and experience design, having spent over twenty years researching how people perceive the world around them, to share some of his findings from his Crossmodal Research Laboratory at the Department of Experimental Psychology, Oxford University. In addition, as a world-famous cognitive neuroscientist, Professor Spence is a consultant for brands across the world and the author of Sensehacking: How to Use the Power of Your Senses for Happier, Healthier Living *and* Gastrophysics: The New Science of Eating *as well as the coauthor of* Crossmodal Attention Applied: Lessons for and from Driving (Elements in Perception) *and* The Perfect Meal: The Multisensory Science of Food and Dining. *Professor Spence's studies span the mapping of the musical notes most people associate with different scents, the measurement of the remarkable effect that different musical tones have on perceptions of the same flavor, the speed with which someone can see an object with a coherent sound versus a nonrelated sound. Here's what he had to say:*

The human voice is, or at least can be, an essential element of audio branding. While many brands were once associated in the minds of the consumer with the distinctive celebrity voices of the day in the era of radio, sonic logos and jingles have become much more popular in recent years, as audio branding reasserts its position alongside the traditionally dominant medium of vision. Hinting at the growing popularity of audio branding, the latest YouGov survey conducted here in the United Kingdom suggests that a growing number of younger consumers (defined as those under thirty-five years of age) now prefer those brands that have an audio signature to those that do not. At the same time, however, it is interesting to note how the top choices in terms of the currently most famous sonic logos tend to be instrumental rather than vocal. In particular, according to the results of the YouGov survey of 2,000 people across Britain, the McDonald's "I'm Lovin' It" whistle topped the list of brands having a distinctive sonic identity, followed by Coca-Cola's bottle opening and fizz, and Netflix's "Ta-dum."[a]

Things are, however, once again starting to change with the ubiquitous rise of audio assistants, such as Alexa and Siri. Indeed, it is the rapid advance of these voice-activated devices and audio assistants into the marketplace, more than anything else, that is forcing brands to address the question of what they should sound like. The most obvious solution here is perhaps to go for the sound of celebrity. For example, the sound of George Clooney's voice is likely to be just as effective as the sight of his visage in helping to sell more Nespresso. Clooney's public image—sophisticated, cosmopolitan, expensive—was considered a perfect match for the brand when he first appeared in an ad for Nespresso that aired back in 2006. It is, though, worth noting that the long-standing association actually did as much to raise the actor's profile as that of the brand. According to former Nespresso CEO, Paul Gaillard, Clooney ultimately "vampirized" the brand, becoming better known in Europe as a result.[b]

However, beyond co-opting a famous, and thus hopefully instantaneously recognizable celebrity voice, what alternatives are there to maximize the effectiveness of voice in advertising, and what counts as "right" anyway? It turns out that the human voice provides a rich source of information, providing more-or-less accurate clues as to the speaker's sex, their age, attractiveness, and dominance.[c] Social class, or status, where the speaker is from (in terms of region or culture/country), and race can also often be inferred too. In the era of Black Lives Matter, of course, many brands are understandably now having to think much more carefully about the race of the voices that are used to represent them auditorily.

Over the years, there has been plenty of research assessing the influence of voice characteristics on the effectiveness of driving assistants. Do drivers prefer to hear a male or female voice to provide any verbal warnings and/or instructions, or is the optimal solution to match the gender of the speaker to the assistant? Should the instruction to "Turn left in 100 meters" be barked out as if you are standing in front of the drill sergeant in *Full Metal Jacket*, or should the voice be seductive and sultry, like Siri, instead?[d] In this case of driving assistants, it may be as much a matter of personal preference, or personality, that determines whom we like to hear telling us exactly what to do. And looking to the future, personalizing/customizing the characteristics of brand voice to the customer may not be too far away in the era of big data and machine learning.

Intriguingly, matching the gender and narrative style of the audio guide to the portraits being described in the setting of the art gallery has been shown to enhance people's memory for the sensory and linguistic content.[e]

However, beyond the use of recognizable celebrity voice and deciding on the semantic attributes/properties of the speaker (e.g., gender, age, regionality, race) that are conveyed, is there anything else that a brand can do to help increase the likelihood that the voice they use fits with the brand identity? One potentially fruitful way in which to think about this question is in terms of crossmodal correspondences. This is the name given by scientists to the surprising connections between the senses that can sound almost synesthetic when you first hear about them. For example, we tend to want to associate a sweet-tasting product (think confectionary or cola) with a higher-pitched sound (or jingle) while feeling that bitter-tasting products (think coffee) goes better (or corresponds) with a lower-pitched sound (or jingle) instead. Similarly, we all associate sweet with round shapes (and typeface), whereas sour-tasting products are both angular and asymmetrical.

Perhaps the single most intensively studied perceptual dimension in all of crossmodal correspondences research is auditory pitch. As such, an extensive body of empirical research now shows, for example, that relatively high-pitched tones tend to be associated with stimuli that are lighter, brighter, faster, smaller, higher in elevation, and more angular than are low-pitched tones.[f] Especially relevant to the themes of the present volume, marketing researchers have recently been able to demonstrate that the consumer's perception of product size, for example, can be biased simply by presenting them with a lower-pitched (rather than higher-pitched) sound.[g] The British politician Margaret Thatcher would apparently deliberately lower her voice to try to make herself sound more authoritative.[h]

While the majority of the crossmodal correspondences research published to date has involved instrumental sounds and pure tones, the evidence suggests that the same theoretical framework can also be extended to voice. For example, Simner and her colleagues were able to demonstrate a number of consistent crossmodal correspondences between the phonetic qualities of speech and the four basic tastes (sweet, sour, bitter, and salty).[i] Perhaps more interestingly, however, my colleague and collaborator Kosuke Motoki recently conducted an intriguing series of experiments showing that people expressed a greater intention to buy sweet (or sour) food products when the pitch of a voice-over advertisement was raised rather than when it was lowered.[j]

The semiotics of vocal qualities is, I believe, an area that is ripe for further study and exploitation in the area of distinctive brand sound but also in the area of audio instruction/assistance. Just as when one tries to figure out which scent to pair with a brand, my suspicion is that the long-standing semantic differential technique[k]—this popular technique involves assessing the connotative meaning of stimuli by having people rate on scales anchored by polar opposites such as good–bad, active–passive, dominant–submissive—may provide the most effective way into matching the brand attributes with the qualities that happen to be evoked by a speaker's voice.[l]

"In a sense, then, one can consider the growing interest amongst the more scientifically minded marketers/advertisers in matching the physical properties of a speaker's voice with the most relevant brand attributes as the future of voice branding. One can perhaps think of the growing interest in the connotative meaning of voice in branding as analogous to the growing interest in the physical characteristics of typeface (e.g., its angularity, balance, and weight) in connoting, and thus priming, the properties of whatever happens to be described in written for."[m]

[a] DLMDD, "The Results Are In: Sonic Branding Is Making Consumers Spend," published May 25, 2021, https://dlmdd.com/sound-equals-spend.

[b] E. Cumming, "How Nespresso's Coffee Revolution Got Ground Down," *The Guardian*, July 14, 2020, https://www.theguardian.com/food/2020/jul/14/nespresso-coffee-capsule-pods-branding-clooney-nestle-recycling-environment.

[c] David R. Feinberg, Lisa M. DeBruine, Benedict C. Jones, and Anthony C. Little, "Correlated Preferences for Men's Facial and Vocal Masculinity," *Evolution and Human Behavior* 29, no. 4 (2008): 233–41; J. D. Leongómez, Viktoria

R. Mileva, Anthony C. Little, and S. Craig Roberts, "Perceived Differences in Social Status between Speaker and Listener Affect the Speaker's Vocal Characteristics," *PLoS ONE* 12, no. 6 (2017): e0179407, https://doi.org/10.1371/journal.pone.0179407.

[d] C. Ho and C. Spence, "Affective Multisensory Driver Interface Design," International *Journal of Vehicle Noise and Vibration* 9, no. 1/2 (2013): 61–74. doi:10.1504/IJVNV.2013.053817; C. Nass, et al., "Improving Automotive Safety by Pairing Driver Emotion and Car Voice Emotion," Extended Abstracts on Human Factors in Computing Systems, Chicago, 2005, 1973–76. See also S. Borau, et al., "The Most Human Bot: Female Gendering Increases Humanness Perceptions of Bots and Acceptance of AI," *Psychology & Marketing* (in press).

[e] M. T. Fairhurst, et al., "Voice Over: Audio-Visual Congruency and Content Recall in the Gallery Setting," *PLoS ONE* 12, no. 6 (2017): e0177622.

[f] C. Spence, "Crossmodal Correspondences: A Tutorial Review," *Attention, Perception, & Psychophysics* 73 (2011): 971–95.

[g] M. L. Lowe and K. L. Haws, "Sounds Big: The Effects of Acoustic Pitch on Product Perceptions," *Journal of Marketing Research* 54 (2017): 331–46.

[h] E. Saner, "How Power Changes the Way We Speak," *The Guardian*, November 26, 2014.

[i] J. Simner, et al., "What Sound Does That Taste? Cross-Modal Mapping Across Gustation and Audition," *Perception* 39 (2010): 553–69.

[j] K. Motoki, et al., "A Sweet Voice: The Influence of Crossmodal Correspondences between Taste and Vocal Pitch on Advertising Effectiveness," *Multisensory Research* 32, no. 4-5 (2019): 401–27. https://doi.org/10.1163/22134808-20191365; cf. M. Lowe, et al., "An Overture to Overeating: The Cross-Modal Effects of Acoustic Pitch on Food Preferences and Serving Behaviour," *Appetite* 123 (2018): 128–34, who showed similar results on actual consumer behavior while varying both the pitch of voice and the pitch of background music in an audio advertisement.

[k] P. Dalton, et al., "The Use of Semantic Differential Scaling to Define the Multi-Dimensional Representation of Odors," *Journal of Sensory Studies* 23 (2008): 485–97.

[l] M. Igras-Cybulska, "Analysis of Non-Linguistic Content of Speech Signal" (PhD thesis). AGH University of Science and Technology, Kraków, Małopolska, Poland, 2017.

[m] C. Velasco and C. Spence, "The Role of Typeface in Packaging Design," in *Multisensory Packaging: Designing New Product Experiences,* ed. C. Velasco and C. Spence (Cham, Switzerland: Palgrave Macmillan, 2019), 79–101.

GUEST PERSPECTIVE 2

Black Voices Matter: The Quest for Sonic Diversity

Steve Keller

We talked a few pages back about how to cast a branded human voice for your product or service to be used across all available platforms. But once you start defining the qualities you want in the voice for your brand, you need to think beyond the default selection of a white male (or what has typically been the default for voice assistants, the white female). But before you approach it in your organization, we wanted to arm you with a small bit of history, which is why we asked Steve Keller to provide his thoughts. Steve is the sonic strategy director, Studio Resonate, an in-house audio-first creative consultancy, offering support to brands that advertise on SXM Media's platforms: Pandora, SiriusXM, Stitcher, and Soundcloud. In his work, he engages in collaborative research projects that explore the power of sound to shape our perceptions and influence our behavior. In collaboration with Oxford's Crossmodal Research Laboratory, he examined the relationship between sound and taste, with Oxford's Charles Spence, how music, soundscapes, and noise in health-care environments affect patience outcomes and satisfaction. He has also explored the existence of audio archetypes (conducted with Goldsmiths University London) and demonstrated the effects of source bias on evaluations of music aesthetics and worth (conducted with Technische Universität Berlin). His current research has been focusing on racialized listening, the existence of a "sonic color line," and its impact on marketing and industry practices, particularly in the context of voice casting. Here are Steve's thoughts on the topic:

There is perhaps no more intimate a sonic expression of an individual than their voice. In the opening to her book, *The Race of Sound*, Nina Eidsheim asserts that "the foundational question asked in the act of listening to a human voice is Who is this? Who is speaking? Regardless of whether the vocalizer is visible or invisible to the listener, we are called into positing this most basic question."[a] For Eidsheim, the question of "Who is this?" wasn't simply a reference to knowing the identity of the person speaking. It was also a reference to knowing things about the person speaking, the idea that in the sound of a voice is the embodiment of mood, emotion, authenticity, gender, race, and more.

What are the implications of Eidsheim's question in the context of designing voice user interfaces (VUI) and by extension, voice user experiences (VUX)? While the interaction is between a human and a voice interface, it is an interaction, nevertheless. On the one hand, there is an interface that "hears" the human voice of the user. How has the "listening ear" of the machine been trained to hear the voice speaking? On the other hand, there is often a voice that users hear in response to a prompt or an inquiry. What does that voice say about the designers who programed it or the brand that's chosen to use it? And (pause for effect) why does it sound white?

We're not accustomed to thinking of sound as a racial construct. While political structures and visual symbols can, and do, perpetuate racism, research has shown that there are sonic markers that are just as powerful in defining how we hear (and represent) the world around us. Binghamton University professor, Jennifer Lynn Stoever, in her book, *The Sonic Color Line*,[b] coined the phrase to describe the existence of a hierarchical division between the perceived "whiteness" and "blackness" of sounds, derived from listening practices exerted by a dominant culture. These listening practices perpetuate sonic stereotypes so effectively that, over time, we have been socialized to associate white voices as representative of the general market and in the United States, with the voice of America.

It might help if we put these demarcations of "white voice" and "Black voice" into historical context. Descriptions of ads in local papers seeking to find runaway slaves[c] often used sonic markers of voice (e.g., course, hoarse, loud, manly, strong, whiney), coupled with other sensory markers (e.g., large mouth, think lips, black complexion). These sonic markers appeared in popular forms of entertainment, where the imitation of racial tropes through blackface minstrelsy served to extend the sonic color line from the antebellum South to the postbellum North and beyond. "Minstrel caricatures of slaves served not only to define African-Americans in the minds of the dominant culture, but their performances also contributed to the growing sense of 'whiteness' among an ethnically diverse population in the urban North and, in the decades after the American Revolution, to a sense of a unique, albeit problematic, American national identity. In short, the minstrel tradition not only demeaned Blacks; it helped define what was white and, consequently, what was American."[d] In the late 1920s, as the stage phenomenon of white performers in blackface was beginning to wane, shows like *Amos 'n' Andy* and *Two Black Crows* allowed for a type of racial ventriloquism where white entertainers starred in exaggerated, racially charged audio sketches. Implicit in these performances were sonically telegraphed images of Black males as buffoons, who were uneducated and incapable of speaking proper English. Ultimately, Black voice actors seeking radio work would be required to play to these stereotypes. A few were ultimately able to play against type, though this required the adoption of the dialect, diction, and announcing style that mimicked their white colleagues.[e]

The sonic color line is so indelible that we continue to hear it today. Two recent films, *Sorry to Bother You*[f] and *BlacKkKlansman*,[g] feature the stories of Black men who discover the key to success in their careers lies in their ability to adopt a "white voice." These stories address the tensions that exist when we begin to contemplate crossing the sonic color line, and what it means to understand not only one's authentic voice, but the history that may have shaped it. We can see (and hear) the impact of these sonic stereotypes on the continuing evolution of America's lingua franca, addressed by John McWhorter in his discourse on Black English,[h] where he explores how the myriad issues around being Black in America have undermined the recognition of Black English as a major cultural force in the world.

This short (but by no means exhaustive) foray into the history of sonic racism should serve as a cautionary tale as we consider the growing adoption and evolution of voice UI/UX. Given the pervasiveness of the sonic color line in popular culture, it should come as no surprise that designers and brands that are developing VUI and VUX aren't immune to its effects. When white voice is accepted as the "default voice" of the general market, we find the sonic color line perpetuated not only in market communications and professional practice[i] but even in the development of new technologies. Consider the fact that voice recognition systems have been shown to engage in sonic discrimination, with platforms developed by Amazon, Apple, Google, IBM, and Microsoft all demonstrating racial disparity by more accurately "hearing" white voices than Black voices. One cross-platform study[j] found an average word error rate of 0.35 for Black speakers, as compared to only 0.19 for white speakers. Ironically, even with advancements in voice recognition, Black individuals still need to "sound white" to be heard.

More evidence-based, quantitative research needs to be devoted to understanding the impact of both the sonic color line and racialized listening on the design and experience of voice technology specifically, and how it's marketed more broadly. When it comes to audio-only or audio-first communications, this kind of research is practically nonexistent,[k] and rarer still are studies that explore the subject in the context of VUI/VUX. Are we favoring voices that conform to a particular bias? How does this bias affect the effectiveness, adoption, and appeal of voice technology and experience? Are we being rewarded for maintaining practices that may be, at their core, systemically racist? These are all important areas of inquiry. Consider the implications for targeting, adapting voice experiences, and/or marketing to the listening ears of the end user. We're still left with questions about what it means to "sound Black," not to mention the potential for targeting to become a further segregation of sonic spaces. While the research to date may speak to the potential effectiveness of racially targeting specific consumer demographics (or ineffectiveness, as mono-ethnic targeting may have an adverse effect),[l] it does little to help us gauge the impact of our sonic choices on general market communications, where the concept of "general market" itself can be racially charged.

As we begin to think about crossing the sonic color line and advocating for more sonic diversity in the design and marketing of voice interfaces and voice experiences, it may be difficult to know where to start. Here are three suggestions, offered less as a prescription, and more as a point to begin the conversation.

1. Retrain our listening ears. Even as we work to cross the sonic color line as marketers, brand managers, and/or designers, part of this journey is personal. It begins with active listening, tuning into how we hear the world, and acknowledging the sonic color lines we draw and play within every day. It's a journey of identifying what has shaped our personal listening ear, and how that ear shapes the ways in which we hear (and use) our own voices. This is a journey

with implications for all of us, regardless of our personal racial identity. It is a task that requires discipline, humility, and gut-wrenching honesty. It is through these kinds of intentional listening practices that we can learn to hear, and address, issues of sonic diversity in our VUI/VUX work.

2. Encourage sonic DEI. From a corporate perspective, having diversity, equity, and inclusion in hiring practices is key to creating a diverse workplace and ensuring that diverse perspectives are considered in the development and marketing of voice products. Yet crossing the sonic color line isn't a given just because diversity is visible in the headshots of company leadership and employees. It's one thing to see diversity. It's another thing to hear it. We need to experience sonically diverse and inclusive environments. When considering the implications of the sonic diversity in the context of VUI/VUX, it's important to remember the sonic color line isn't limited to the interaction between voice tech and the user alone. Voice experiences often occur in spaces that have sonic markers of their own. Diversifying our understanding of the sonic spaces voice tech inhabits can be tricky to navigate. It's important to listen, hear, discuss, and create dialogue around our multisensory experience of the world around us, and how our voice technology and voice experiences connect with those diverse worlds.

3. Take a stand. Finally, as we identify ways in which our industry culture and practice might be perpetuating a type of systemic sonic racism, we need to be bold enough to act. We won't always get it right but putting our fingers in our ears and ignoring the problem won't make it go away. The issues are complex. Only by working together, sharing experiences, and holding each other accountable will we be able to learn, grow, and cross the sonic color line.

Though I've focused this essay on issues surrounding Black voices, it's important to note that true sonic diversity includes all BIOPC voices. A much deeper dialogue is needed, but hopefully this will serve to start the conversation. The journey of a thousand sonic miles begins with a single step—and a pair of listening ears. Moving forward, may we all be aware of how we're hearing the world, aware of how our listening ear shapes our interactions, aware of the sonic color lines we (or others) have drawn, aware of changes that need to be made, and determined to use our voice to address them.

[a] N. S. Eidsheim, *The Race of Sound: Listening, Timbre, and Vocality in African American Music* (Duke University Press Books, 2019).
[b] J. L. Stoever, *The Sonic Color Line: Race and the Cultural Politics of Listening* (reprint ed.). (Postmillennial Pop, 2016).
[c] See Stoever, *The Sonic Color Line*, 29–30.
[d] R. L. Hughes, "Minstrel Music: The Sounds and Images of Race in Antebellum America," *The History Teacher* 40, no. 1 (2006): 27, https://doi.org/10.2307/30036937.
[e] W. Barlow, *Voice Over: The Making of Black Radio* (illustrated ed.) (Temple University Press, 1999).
[f] B. Riley, dir., *Sorry to Bother You*, United States: Annapurna Pictures, 2018.
[g] S. Lee, dir., *BlacKkKlansman*, United States: Focus Features, 2018.
[h] J. McWhorter, *Talking Back, Talking Black: Truths About America's Lingua Franca* (reprint ed.) (Bellevue Literary Press, 2018).
[i] C. Kumanyika, "Vocal Color in Public Radio," *The Transom Review* 15, no. 2 (2015), accessed August 25, 2020, https://transom.org/2015/chenjerai-kumanyika/.
[j] A. Koenecke, et al., "Racial Disparities in Automated Speech Recognition," *Proceedings of the National Academy of Sciences* 117, no. 14 (2020): 7684–89, https://doi.org/10.1073/pnas.1915768117.
[k] See C. L. Corsbie-Massay, "Manipulating Race and Gender in Media Effects Research: A Methodological Review Using the Media FIT Taxonomy," in *Race and Gender in Electronic Media: Content, Context, Culture*, ed. Rebecca Ann Lind (Taylor and Francis, 2016), 125–43, https://doi.org/10.4324/9781315636801.
[l] T. C. Licsandru and C. C. Cui, "Ethnic Marketing to the Global Millennial Consumers: Challenges and Opportunities," *Journal of Business Research* 103 (2019): 261–74, https://doi.org/10.1016/j.jbusres.2019.01.052.

EXTENDED CASE STUDY

McDonald's UK Mobile Voice Ordering

McDonald's has always embraced the concepts of speed and convenience, although occasional issues might have interfered with continually achieving these goals. Research indicated that two in five consumers said that they had used voice search to ask for directions, an address, or business hours of a nearby location. Research also indicated that a sizable majority were also interested in quality reassurance and safety, dietary information, offers, and most importantly, the ability to order by voice, especially if it were easy, making this new form of customer interaction the next big opportunity within the restaurant industry.

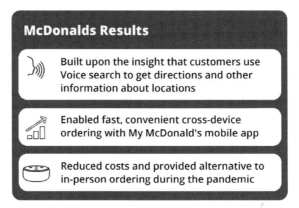

Figure 3.2. Here are the results McDonalds UK achieved with their voice-based ordering.

However, despite the high customer expectations and research confirming that voice was about to emerge with a force in the UK market, voice adoption in the quick-service restaurant industry had been slow. Ever the leader, McDonald's then seized on this opportunity, because they knew it could increase value for their customers. And McDonald's saw voice as an opportunity to advance their brand mission: to be their customers' favorite place and their go-to way to eat and drink.

To develop the experience, they partnered with Vixen Labs and together, they created a new way for customers to enjoy their McDonald's experience, safely and swiftly.[a] Launched during the pandemic, this voice skill was the first official McDonald's one in the United Kingdom.

Working with the My McDonald's app and enhancing some of its top features, this official voice skill allows fast food lovers to check the latest McDonald's offers, find information on their closest restaurants, ask a question, and even start an order via voice. Intuitive, touchless, and customer first, this is a great addition to the McDonald's customer experience arsenal.

The skill also introduced the restaurant finder—a feature that satisfied customers' top priorities: to check their nearest location and its hours of operation—and provided answers to the most common questions regarding McDonald's through a guided conversation, and since the target audience was budget conscious, updates on promotions right from the moment they opened the skill. They also implemented a send-to-phone feature, enabling a fast-ordering experience across devices. As a result, users can check offers and initiate orders in the skill by asking Alexa to send a link straight to their phone. For those who have the My McDonald's app already installed on their phones, the skill directly opens the app.

Following the launch on Amazon, McDonald's wanted to provide value across multiple voice platforms. As a result, they developed the McDonald's Action available through Google Assistant, which offers similar features to the Amazon Alexa Skill but with Google-specific functionalities.

Connecting even more families to McDonald's on Google Assistant, the Action added to McDonald's customer excellence arsenal by making joyful moments easier for everyone. As a result, McDonald's was able to enhance the perception of their value and to reward customers' loyalty—all while reducing their costs across other channels as well as relieving the demand to provide face-to-face customer service during a pandemic.

Support for the voice skill and action also increased the awareness of the My McDonald's app, with a subsequent boost in downloads and app usage. Imagine a safe, easy, frictionless ordering process via voice—it is now a reality! Because of the ease of creating voice apps, we see other fast food and fast casual chains—even fine dining restaurants that offer take out—getting into the voice arena!

[a] Vixen Labs, "Ordering Made Easy with Send to Phone Feature—McDonald's Skill UK," published October 29, 2021, accessed January 13, 2022, https://vixenlabs.co/amazon-send-to-phone-mcdonalds-skill-uk.

CHAPTER

4

Understanding the Audience for Voice

One of the most basic tenets of marketing is that the marketer must fully understand the brand's audience, so, thankfully, we don't need to spend any time convincing you of the importance of understanding the users of voice technologies. Although some people in marketing ignore this discipline and base their judgments on a "gut feeling," there are few who don't value customer knowledge.

For that reason, we are going to move right into the differences between the three main segments, defined by use of the technology: one segment is people who already use a voice assistant, one segment is people who are regular internet users but do not use a voice assistant, and one segment is people who are not regular users of the internet. The third segment may seem irrelevant, but some believe that many nonusers of the internet will become regular users because of voice assistants. That's because, as we mentioned in chapter 1, it's easier for people with lower literacy levels to access the internet through voice application. In this chapter, we'll explore how to provide added value to these three segments through the development of voice applications. Finally, we'll look at audience attributes that you'll need to understand for a successful voice marketing initiative.

But to start, we are going to look at a new model product adoption that we drew from the research Scot and Susan Westwater conducted on voice assistants. In a broad way, it will help you get the most out of your voice-based marketing activities (as well as out of other major innovations). Combined, these sections can help you identify the segments that you want to reach and to formulate how to approach your strategy for using voice technology in your marketing efforts.

Before we look at the new model, let's look at the diffusion of innovations model, which is the classic way of segmenting users of new products. Developed by Everett Rogers in 1962,[1] the diffusion of innovations model focuses on how soon a person adopts the new technology, relative to others, dividing the adopters of an innovation into five categories: (1) innovators, (2) early adopters, (3) early majority, (4) late majority, and (5) laggards.[2]

The Path to Adoption

Rogers also describes what he believed was the process for learning about and adopting an innovation. The steps that he identified in his model are Knowledge > Persuasion > Decision > Implementation > Confirmation.

While this theory can be helpful in benchmarking adoption stages and understanding the general maturity of an innovation, it does not provide strategic guidance on how to drive product adoption—to help speed up the process—and it could even limit your view of the new product's early-stage potential. Rogers's theory merely looks at adoption volume in each stage and then offers generalized segment descriptions, but it doesn't offer insight to what truly matters to each group. What's more, these descriptions can bias the marketers in their efforts, because innovators and early adopters are framed in a more positive light than late adopters and the laggards who make up the final phase.

A new model for learning about and adopting an innovation comes from a platform of original research, the 2022 Voice Consumer Index,[3] conducted by two of the authors of this book, Scot and Susan Westwater, with Vixen Labs and Delineate. The research revealed a consistent pattern in how innovations have been either resisted or adopted into the fabric of the adopters' lives. We believe this new model can help you get the most out of your voice-based marketing activities (as well as out of other major innovations).

Like most of the other basic models, it is based on users' levels of familiarity. As the prospects become more familiar and comfortable with the innovation, they go through a major shift in mindset. The pattern of the mindset change—"the path to adoption"—is consistent across adopters in all of Rogers's categories, from innovators to laggards. The phases map the users' progression to full adoption—when the innovation becomes viewed as an essential resource or tool for daily life. To ignite the desired mindset change, you aim to anticipate and influence this consistent pattern. The phases identified by our research are identified as the Skeptic, the Experimenter, the Explorer, and the Adopter. Following is a description of each.

Resistant: In the first phase, prospective adopters, even those described as innovators, might not readily see the value of a particular innovation. "Why would I need that? Why would I want it?" Some will be willing to find an answer on their own—some may be hostile to the new idea. At this stage, the marketer's objective is trial, and the message is reasons to try, or what a benefit of trial might be. For instance, in the introduction of the first-generation Apple iPod, the tagline "1000 songs in your pocket" was a powerful reason to try. It's also important to include the "how" in messaging so the audience finds an innovation easy to try.

And keep in mind, it is not just the technology provider who needs to help people understand the value of the innovation. It's also the app builders and content providers and supporting product marketers who create a community around an innovation. They all depend on marketing that will help the new idea get trial.

01

Resistant

Why would I need this?

Perception: Gadget/Fad

Mindset: Unwilling to try

Example: Why would I want a smartphone?

02

Experimental

What is this?

Perception: Novelty/Toy

Mindset: Skeptical but willing to try

Example: I just downloaded a beer "drinking" app that my friend showed me.

03

Explore

What else can I do with it?

Perception: Utility/Task Focused

Mindset: Finding more ways it can help with daily life

Example: I track all my meals and workouts on my smartphone.

04

Essential

How did I live without this?

Perception: Essential Resource

Mindset: An essential part of daily life

Example: My smartphone is the center of my digital universe.

Figure 4.1. An overview of the four phases of a user's progression to full adoption.

Experimental: When a prospect becomes willing to try the innovation, the mindset shifts from resistance or skepticism to curiosity. The prospect wants to understand what one might be able to do with an innovation. Innovations at this stage might be seen as novelties or toys. Prospects are not necessarily willing to commit. And if at this stage, you present a complex use case, your prospect might be overwhelmed.

But finding ways to let the user lightly sample an innovation can speed the adoption process. Here's an example: users playing with Snapchat filters, with all their frames, visual effects, and decorations, get comfortable with augmented reality. Uploading and manipulating images to create virtual versions of themselves ceases to be a big mental leap. Comcast

Xfinity Remote got customers comfortable with voice commands by empowering them to change channels through a spoken request. If trial uses are as reliable as they are simple, then trust can be built on a foundation of successful experiences.

Explore: As prospects experiment successfully with an innovation, they develop a comfort level that moves them to find out what more they can do with it. They want to know where else they can apply it—how else it can be of help to them. Now, the applications can become a bit more complex. Marketers can build on the trust gained by the success of previous experiences and begin to address deeper usage occasions.

Essential: When the user has integrated an innovation into daily life, there is another mindset shift. "How did I get along without this?" "Why did I do things the other way?" At that point, the adoption process is complete, and the marketer can focus on brand differentiation and on looking for the next innovation, which might replace this one.

Consider the FAX machine. Early adopters wondered how much they'd ever use them. Then everyone used them. Today the only users are governmental offices and perhaps a few businesses, replaced by scanning and sending via email.

A similar thing may be happening with voice adopters. Once they become familiar with the basic uses of a voice assistant—quickly checking the weather, a more controlled way of selecting music to listen to, and finding other news—they want to know what else a voice assistant can do. To support this curiosity, marketers can use channels like social media, newsletters, and websites, to show what you can do with the voice application. That's what marketers did back when the internet was still taking hold to show newcomers how to access sites and what content they'd find when they got there. Now, when the new technology is conversational AI and voice, marketers need to tell their audiences the benefits of the branded voice experience and learn how to access them.

You can see a similar transition from simple usage to richer interactions in other categories, too, including food products. Look at the adoption of plant-based milks—and new condiments like sriracha. These began as simple replacement products—almond milk for cow's milk, sriracha for ketchup. Later, they become key ingredients in multilayered recipes.

We see a similar shift in technologies. The emergence of voice is the fourth major technological shift in the past thirty years. First was the shift to computers and the web in the 1990s. The advent of smartphones in 2001 fundamentally changed how we create and consume content. It opened a new marketing channel that hugely altered consumer purchase behavior. (The IBM Simon Personal Communicator was launched in 1994 and a prototype of it was premiered in 1992, but it was not connected to the internet.[4]) Social media followed with the launch of Facebook and Twitter in 2007 and 2008. (Yes, Myspace existed before Facebook, but the impact was not as pervasive.)

Now there is voice, which is quickly becoming a main brand contact point for consumers. Instead of competing for eyeballs, marketers and advertisers are now competing for "ear prints," and yet again, we have to teach our audiences how to interact with us. But this user-centric approach can facilitate faster and smoother adoption of your branded voice experiences. By understanding prospect mindsets, marketers can focus on the features and usage occasions that meet the audience's comfort level and offer a basis for bringing people to the next stage. Studying that mindset can teach you which features are most important in early stages and which ones will help move users from simple trial to complete adoption. Both needs and objections need to be understood. A common mistake is to prioritize a complex, sophisticated task when the audience is still deciding whether the innovation is worth bothering with.

Who's Currently Using Voice?

In the aggregate, voice adoption is huge. Voicebot.ai's Smart Speaker Adoption Report says that 35% of US adults now own a smart speaker, up from less than 20% in 2018,[5] while the frequency of use has also increased by 23% between 2018 and 2020.[6] And according to the 2022 Voice Consumer Index, cited earlier, 63% of Americans, 65% of Britons, and 54% of Germans currently use some form of voice assistance.[7] Amazon Alexa and Google Assistant are the most-used voice assistant platforms. Usage is up 6% and 7% year over year, while reported Siri usage is down slightly.[8]

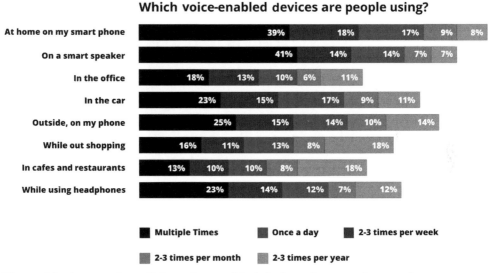

Which voice-enabled devices are people using?

	Multiple Times	Once a day	2-3 times per week	2-3 times per month	2-3 times per year
At home on my smart phone	39%	18%	17%	9%	8%
On a smart speaker	41%	14%	14%	7%	7%
In the office	18%	13%	10%	6%	11%
In the car	23%	15%	17%	9%	11%
Outside, on my phone	25%	15%	14%	10%	14%
While out shopping	16%	11%	13%	8%	18%
In cafes and restaurants	13%	10%	10%	8%	18%
While using headphones	23%	14%	12%	7%	12%

Figure 4.2. An overview of the voice-enabled devices that people are using.

Source: Voice Consumer Index 2022

Among those who have adopted a voice assistant, 38% use it daily and 28%, more than once per day. A full 95% of voice users in the United States, United Kingdom, and Germany connect with their voice assistants over mobile devices, and 66% use smart speakers. (Obviously, the segments overlap.) Most adopters access voice assistants across multiple devices, laptops, desktops, mobile devices, and smart speakers. Brands, then, must have a vision for how their voice content will be available through all the devices their audience will use to access it. This will deliver voice experiences where users want them today and possibly, emerging channels in the future such as the metaverse.

Usage of voice assistance is spread across all age groups

	18-24	25-34	35-44	45-54	55-64	65+
Alexa (Amazon)	22%	31%	30%	32%	38%	52%
Google Assistant	17%	29%	42%	46%	34%	24%
Siri (Apple)	56%	34%	23%	19%	25%	24%

Figure 4.3. An overview of the age segments using voice by assistant.

When we think about early adopters of a new technology, we might focus on the young and the digitally adept. *Not so with voice.* Most frequent users by age are the twenty-five to thirty-four group, followed in order by the thirty-five to forty-four, forty-five to fifty-four, fifty-five to sixty-four, and sixty-five plus age groups. The eighteen- to twenty-four-year-olds, in fact, are last in line.[9] This means that there's an opportunity for all brands, not just those targeting Gen Zers. Users are about evenly split, male/female. Many are parents with children still living at home. Usage is distributed among income levels, with the low-medium, medium-, and high-income brackets using the technology the most frequently.[10]

Platform choice depends on company and age group. In the United States, eighteen to twenty-four and twenty-five to forty-four-year-old users prefer Apple's Siri. Other age groups use Amazon Alexa more often. In the United Kingdom and Germany, Amazon Alexa and Google Assistant are used most often. Despite being available on mobile devices, Amazon Alexa is used most on smart speakers, while Apple's Siri is used most on smartphones. Google Assistant is in a unique position, with high usage on both smart speakers and smartphones.

How Customers Are Currently Using Voice

For new purchases within the home, according to Mintel's US Smart Homes Market Report 2021,[11] 32% of consumers say built-in voice assistants such as Siri and Alexa are important to them when selecting smart home devices. In the US Home Entertainment Technology: Hardware and Services Market Report 2021,[12] 43% of consumers are interested in controlling home entertainment systems with their voices. A whopping 70% of all consumers say smart home technology makes life more convenient, and 71% believe that voice assistants are fun to use (which is more than current usage of voice assistants).

Most use their voice assistants for searching, shopping, and consuming content—both at home and on the go. About 92% of voice consumers ask their voice assistants top-of-funnel awareness questions. And 86% search for service and product information. Another 79% search for information about local businesses, and 78% search for information about brands. Perhaps most important, 59% of voice consumers indicate that they use voice assistant to make a purchase—which is up 18% from 2021.

Yet more interesting for marketers, 82% of those who start researching a brand through voice search will eventually visit the brand's website. So search activities on voice assistants align with the steps consumers take in a traditional marketing funnel, from awareness to consideration to purchase and retention. That means you can organize voice

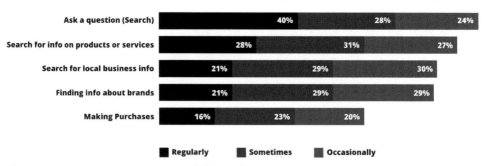

Voice activities align with the marketing funnel

	Regularly	Sometimes	Occasionally
Ask a question (Search)	40%	28%	24%
Search for info on products or services	28%	31%	27%
Search for local business info	21%	29%	30%
Finding info about brands	21%	29%	29%
Making Purchases	16%	23%	20%

Figure 4.4. How various voice activities align with the marketing funnel. Source: Voice Consumer Index 2022,

Source: Voice Consumer Index 2022

content for the stages of the conventional customer journey. Note also that adopters of voice assistants are highly engaged with the platform. Many say they're following the development of its technology.

People who adopt voice assistants generally begin with music, news, and weather—natural entry points for smart speakers. The interactions are similar to interactions with "broadcasting" devices. When they start asking questions, they're starting to use the interactive qualities of voice. They begin to ask about directions, food delivery, health and wellness, and restaurant brands. Susan and Scot Westwater's research also revealed that 45% of US users and 39% of German users would be interested in searching fashion-related topics via voice applications—interesting because some would see this as a highly visual topic.

Currently, trial and error is the way most users learn about the capabilities of their voice assistants and find their favorite applications. Next most common is asking friends and family. This points to an opportunity for marketers to promote their voice experiences in other low-cost channels, such as product packaging, websites, and social posts.

Once users have conducted an initial search, they're likely to seek more information on the brand's website as well as its mobile app and YouTube channel. Many users would like to be able to continue with voice down the path to purchase. So marketers should voice enable their websites, by providing content that's read by a voice assistant—creating a specific Amazon Alexa Skill—or even integrating an owned voice assistant on their website and within their mobile app.

Note this about the marketer's website: The frequently asked questions need to be more robust than usual. Marketers should make sure they are drawn from the actual questions that prospects are asking. They'll be easy to find in a voice search, and they will satisfy the prospect's need for quick, accurate answers. The goal: your brand's website should outrank Wikipedia.

The trick is to optimize SEO for long-tail phrases, instead of just keywords. When people use voice search, they tend to speak in descriptive phrases, sentences, or questions. Also, be sure to monitor error logs to see what people are asking for that's not getting a satisfactory answer.

Consumer use of voice search by industry

Weather	75%
Music	71%
News	64%
Entertainment	62%
Retail	54%
Food Delivery And Restaurants	52%
Healthcare And Wellness	51%
Consumer Packaged Goods	49%
Local Services	49%
Making A Reservation	47%
Fitness	46%
Fashion	45%
Travel	43%
Finance	42%
Other	42%

Figure 4.5. A summary of how customers are currently using voice search by industry.

Source: Voice Consumer Index 2022

Because of the explosive adoption of consumer smart speakers, we see a tendency to think that smart speakers are the only way that brands can use voice to engage. But voice goes well beyond smart speakers. With over 500 million monthly active users on Google Assistant on mobile, plus Siri's enormous consumer mindshare, many brands should consider voice enabling their mobile applications. The April 2020 NPR Smart Audio report says the primary method for interacting with a voice assistant is via a smartphone.[13]

There is a growing group using voice to automate homes and control appliances—even holiday lights. Turn them on and turn them off without getting out of bed. Entertainment controls led the way, but Mintel's 2021 Smart Homes Market Report identified lights, security systems, thermostats, vacuums, garage doors, smoke detectors, carbon monoxide detectors, refrigerators, microwaves, and ovens as targets for smart home automation via voice. For all of these categories, voice automation is a marketing opportunity that enhances the experience of the brand.

Trust and Privacy Concerns—in More Ways than One

The 2022 Voice Consumer Index Research identifies "trust" and "privacy" as two major barriers to adoption of voice assistants by nonusers. In addition, Mintel found that 71% of consumers are concerned about companies listening in to their conversations, and 69% of consumers are concerned about smart home products getting hacked.[14]

Platform providers such as Siri, Alexa, Bixby, and Google need to show how each one is protecting the data. One way is using verbal "cues" attached to each product, to remind users that security standards are in place. Another is to make sure that information about platform security is easy to access. People need to believe that their data, including search histories, is protected. And that requires "trust."

Cognitive psychologist and philosopher Paul Thagard, in an article for *Psychology Today*, outlines five definitions of "trust": "1) trust is a set of behaviors, such as acting in ways that depend on another; 2) trust is a belief in a probability that a person will behave in certain ways; 3) trust is an abstract mental attitude toward a proposition that someone is dependable; 4) trust is a feeling of confidence and security that a partner cares; and 5) trust is a complex neural process that binds diverse representations into a semantic pointer that includes emotions."[15]

While Thagard ultimately argues that the feeling of trust is a neural process, all the definitions have a bit of truth—and they demonstrate the fact that there are many different dimensions to trust.

Another way to look at dimensions of trust builds on the work of Lewicki and Tomlinson. Their article "Trust and Trust Building" offers a framework that might fit the tasks of marketing. They say that "trust in another individual can be grounded in our evaluation of his/her ability, integrity and benevolence."[16] Replace "another individual" with "a brand," and the marketer can begin to see what needs to be done. For "ability," substitute the belief that the brand will perform as promised. "Integrity," when translated to marketing, is "how much the brand adheres to principles that are acceptable to the trustor"—the prospect or customer. Contributing to the perception of integrity is the brand's "past actions, credibility of communication, commitment to standards of fairness, and the congruence of the other's word and deed."[17] Sounds familiar to those who work to build a brand.

Finally, "benevolence" to the marketer means that the brand is seen as advancing the welfare and goals of its prospects and customers. Think of brands' role as badges—and of brand activism as two ways brands can build the benevolence dimension.

What does all this mean? For starters, how your brand performs—and how your brand speaks and acts in other channels—will inform your prospects' expectations that your voice application will deliver on its promise—and deliver the desired content. It also means that if they feel they are being treated fairly in other encounters, they will expect that they will be treated fairly in the voice experience. That's important considering the privacy concerns we have mentioned. Each time a brand fulfills one or more of its dimensions, the bonds of trust grow deeper and stronger. They become better at withstanding doubt.

Beyond the wish for data privacy and the trust needed to overcome the fear of data breaches is another key consideration for brands that develop voice applications. It's spatial privacy. People have concerns about being overheard by people around them whom they do not know. For some, the spatial privacy issue might be more of a hindrance than data privacy issues. Fewer than 27% of current adopters in the United States report feeling comfortable using voice applications in public. This comfortable population drops to about 20% in the United Kingdom and Germany.

Because of concerns with spatial or environmental privacy, brand marketers need to understand the environment where their application will be used. The Butterball example we mentioned earlier (and have a case study about it at the end of this chapter) would be accessed in the kitchen. So spatial privacy would be less of a concern. But a search for the address of a punny named retail outlet that takes place in public might be very different.

It's important to note that while privacy is a concern—both data privacy and spatial or environmental privacy—the quickening pace of adoption for voice assistance suggests that these concerns are not an absolute barrier to adoption. It appears that the overall value that users receive from voice assistance exceeds the cost of the privacy they are giving up (or slightly reducing). So for brands, if you offer value to your prospects in your voice experience, people will access it—especially those who are already using a voice assistant. The only caveat is that the application you create must reassure your prospects through each of the three trust dimensions we described above. Of course, if people trust your brand in other realms, they will be likely to trust you here too.

Some predict that the adoption of voice technology by nonusers will be hindered by self-consciousness. We believe that most self-conscious feelings will dissolve over time as people become more comfortable using their voice assistants out of the home. But it needs to be seen as a real issue. Nonusers of smart speakers in the United States report the lowest percentage of self-consciousness of the countries measured (12%). It is also the country with the highest percentage of smart speaker adoptions by previous nonusers. Germany, which has the lowest percentage of smart speaker adoption, has the highest number of people reporting that they feel self-conscious. (There might also be other cultural factors, but none are widely hypothesized.)

While it is good to understand users of voice assistants in general, what marketers need most is to understand how the segments your brand is currently targeting overlap with the whole broad group of voice users. First, look at your current audience, and see who among them are most likely to be accessing voice. Some key questions to ask:

How do they typically speak? What are their word choices. Understand the words and phrases they're using—the natural language—and adjust accordingly. Find out if there's a mismatch between the name of your product or service and how people refer to it. Within your target audience, note that different generations speak differently and have different language expectations. Older people, for instance, tend to use "please" and "thank you" when talking to their devices, while younger audiences are more informal and prefer slower speech patterns than Millennials and Gen Zers.[18] Understanding how your audience speaks can help direct how your application or skill will speak.

How do people refer to your products and services? Do they use the complete name, a slang term, an acronym, an abbreviation, or something else? McDonald's, for instance, would want people to go to their app if they asked for a Mickey D's Steakhouse—or if in Australia, they want to find a Maccas. In other words, you need to understand all the ways people talk about you—and how they talk about you in everyday language—rather than how you are required to talk about it for legal reasons to remain compliant. Even if you can't use this common language in your response due to the legal reasons, you need to identify it to help them find you and give them right responses.

How do people get to *your* brand? Do they ask for your product or service? Or do they talk about the problem it solves—or the unsolved condition? With medical conditions, for instance, do they use the clinical name or refer to it in some other way—perhaps by shortening the term? In some parts of the United States, people request a soda. In other parts, they want pop—not everyone is going to ask for a Coke or Pepsi. In other words, you need to understand all the ways people talk about you—and how they talk about you in everyday language, rather than the way you are required to talk to avoid legal issues. Even if you cannot use this common language in your response due to legal reasons, you need to identify it to help them find you and to give them the right response.

How do people actually pronounce your brand name and attributes? It's not just how they call it, but precisely how they say it. Do they get the accent right for your brand if it requires one, and do you know all the regional variations of how prospects and customers pronounce your product or service? Even if you geolocate your device, the person asking could be from a different part of the country—or the world. Language, particularly pronunciation, travels with the individual. It is a combination of where they grew up and where they live now. (By the way, you can learn more about algorithmic bias driven by language differences in the Guest Perspective below.)

What is the intent of the request? What do your prospects want from your app or skill? Where do they fall in the path to purchase, and what are they hoping to achieve? You need to know the answer to these questions. If you truly know the audience that your experience will be serving, you can better narrow down the request. If someone asks for Target, are they asking for a retail store, the website, or the corporate headquarters? If the app is for employment, then the request is narrowed down. Otherwise, you may need a question or two.

If someone is searching for a medical condition, do they use the name of it or refer to it in slang? In some low-income neighborhoods, for example, diabetes is referred to as "the sugar"—using the phrase "I got the sugar." Remember that voice is not about what *you* want the app to do, not about what's new and cool. It is about, and only about, what your prospect wants.

What do prospects expect from the application? The theory of mind[19] indicates that people adjust their speech patterns—from simple to complex sentences—and the words that they use—to the imagined cognitive abilities (in the prospect's mind) of the recipient. Think of the words you would choose and the complexity of your sentence structure speaking to a young child versus the ones you'd select speaking to an educated, middle-aged adult. Clearly, they would be different. When you have spoken and have some idea of the hearer's response, you'd adjust again. Did the recipient understand and respond as expected? If not, the speaker will adjust the next utterance—and will continue adjusting until accurate communication is achieved. Understanding what your prospect expects from your application or skill can speed up and shorten these adjustments.

The more you know about your audience, the better off you'll be. Clearly, it's not just the words that matter. Rather, it's the tonality, pronunciation, and context as well. When you understand your audience and its environment, you'll truly be able to fulfill their needs.

 GUEST PERSPECTIVE

Algorithmic Bias in Audio AI

Kalinda Ukanwa

There's bias in everything. Part of your job is to understand it so you can account for it. When you do, you can overcome it so you can reach and serve your intended audiences. To help us understand it, we reached out to Kalinda Ukanwa, who is assistant professor of marketing at the University of Southern California. A quantitative modeler, Professor Ukanwa's research focuses on how algorithmic bias, algorithmic decision-making, and consumer reputations impact firms. She is the winner of the 2018 Eli Jones Promising Young Scholar Awards and a finalist for the 2018 INFORMS Services Science Best Student Paper Award, 2019 Howard/AMA Doctoral Dissertation, and the 2020 AMS Mary Kay Doctoral Dissertation Award. In prior life, Professor Ukanwa was an industrial engineer, financial analyst, and finance executive at Walt Disney, Citigroup, Viacom, and Kaplan. Here's Kalinda's answer:

Louise Kennedy, a well-educated Irish veterinarian with two university degrees, was about to lose her home because of an automatic speech recognition (ASR) algorithm. A native English speaker, Kennedy aced the reading and writing portions of an English test to obtain an Australian visa. However, the ASR algorithm failed Louise on the oral portion because it did not recognize her Irish-accented speech as spoken English. Failing the test prevented her from obtaining a permanent visa to stay in the country with her Australian husband and child.[a]

In recent years, multiple sectors of society have exponentially increased the use of ASR, a type of audio artificial intelligence. Organizations use audio AI services for multiple tasks such as screening immigrants or job candidates and recording and transcribing documents.[b] Indeed, the prospect for widespread adoption of this technology inevitably means that it will have widespread impact on our everyday lives.

However, stories like Louise Kennedy's highlight the rising concerns of algorithmic bias in audio AI. Algorithmic bias is systematically unfair algorithmic outcomes that arbitrarily give one group of constituents an advantage over another.[c] Bias introduced in algorithms generally comes from any or all of three sources: the training data, the algorithm's design, and improper use of the algorithm. There is a common belief that artificial intelligence produces fairer decisions. After all, a machine cannot have emotions, right? In reality, there are now numerous documented cases of algorithmic discrimination in sectors such as financial lending, health care, law enforcement, education, and various online digital spaces.

Audio AI is vulnerable to the same potential for algorithmic bias as other forms of AI. This is far more troubling when audio-based algorithms impact highly consequential decisions such as immigration. In the case of Kennedy, the ASR algorithm failed her in the English test because of its high error rate in recognizing English spoken by those who are not White American or English speakers.

Research published in 2020 demonstrates that the ASR systems of Apple, Amazon, Google, IBM, and Microsoft, which are the engines behind speech-to-text transcription and AI assistants such as Siri, Alexa, and Cortana, have average word error rates of 35% for African American voices versus 19% for White American voices.[d] Another study found evidence of gender and regional bias in YouTube's ASR system used to generate automatic captions for its videos. The system's error rates were markedly worse for women (over 50%) than men (approx. 35%) and for Scottish (over 50%) versus speakers from the United States (approx. 37%).[e] A third study found evidence of not only gender and nonnative speaker bias, but also age bias in ASR algorithms.[f] Furthermore, research has shown that biased algorithms can be harmful not only to consumers but also to the organizations that employ them. For example, a study by Ukanwa and Rust[g] demonstrates that organizations that use biased algorithms are more profitable in the short run but less profitable in the long run than organizations using unbiased algorithms.

In an effort to prevent problems like these from occurring, US and European lawmakers have recently proposed expanding regulation of AI algorithms. Their efforts are in response to growing concerns that algorithmic decision-making can easily reproduce, accelerate, and amplify discrimination. For example, in April 2021, the European Union proposed new, stricter regulations that oversee algorithms used for a broad class of decisions, including hiring, law enforcement, health care, and lending—all of which are vulnerable to bias in audio AI. These new regulations have the potential to be as widely adopted as its regulatory cousin, the EU's General Data Protection Regulation (GDPR). At the time of the writing of this article, there is no comparable and comprehensive US regulation of algorithms. However, the trajectory of legislative activity on AI regulation has increased in recent years: in 2015, only two bills were introduced in the US Congress that contained the term "artificial intelligence." By 2019, that number had increased to 51.[h]

There are five primary areas where audio AI is vulnerable to algorithmic bias:

1. Automatic speech recognition can produce algorithmic bias in the lack of recognition of non-native speakers or minority (race, gender, age) speakers of the focal language. The case of Louise Kennedy is an example. This is often due to the ASR algorithm being insufficiently trained on representative or diverse voice data.

2. Audio-initiated web search and audio search engines can produce algorithmic bias in terms of the search results generated from the search query. Search algorithms learn from the search behavior of users. Search algorithmic bias is typically due to word associations that are embedded with historical or societal biases from the collective search queries of other users. For example, an audio search for pictures of "nurses" and "doctors" may return a preponderance

of pictures showing women and men for each respective term, which reflects gendered stereotypes of these professions.

3. Natural language processing (NLP) of audio sources can produce algorithmic bias because NLP algorithms are known to pick up language patterns and word associations that reflect societal biases. Word embeddings, the core of NLP algorithms, identify words that co-occur with each other in the training language data. Biased word embeddings can reinforce and propagate these biases in tasks such as voice to text, text generation, translation, or web search. They can also influence decision-making in tasks such as resume screening, test grading, and law enforcement document screening. For example, Amazon had to shelve a resume screening algorithm using NLP after the company found it was biased against female candidates.[i]

4. Audio classification can produce algorithmic bias because the classification process often starts with manual classification by human classifiers. This process is susceptible to human biases because humans will interpret and classify data based on their world view, which can be biased. As a result, the classified data used to train the algorithm will transfer the inherent biases of the human classifiers to the learning of the algorithm. For example, a manual classification process whose goal is to label a sound file according to the emotion of the voice could be vulnerable to biases if the human classifier perceives the voices of some racial or ethnic groups as angrier than other groups.

5. Gendered voice use in AI assistants can produce bias in that the systems are often given female voices. These gendered voice-role associations serve to amplify and reinforce stereotypes that can be negative in some arenas. For example, the female default voice for well-known AI assistants (a role historically associated with women) such as Siri, Alexa, Google Assistant, and Cortana helps to reinforce stereotypes of women in submissive and subordinate roles. AI assistant responses to commands can themselves be subject to gender bias. As of 2019, Samsung's AI assistant, Bixby, had different, gender-stereotyped responses to commands depending on whether the female or male voice was activated. In response to the command "Let's talk dirty," the female Bixby would respond "I don't want to end up on Santa's naughty list." In contrast, the male Bixby's response was "I've read that soil erosion is a real dirt problem."[j] These gender-stereotyped roles and interactions with AI assistants cause social harms by reinforcing stereotypes of women in submissive, subordinate, and sexualized roles. As professor Safiya Noble asserted, AI assistants are also "powerful socialization tools, and teach people, in particular children, about the role of women [and] girls . . . to respond on demand."[k]

The enormity, influence, and widespread impact of audio AI calls for an increase in research into the causes, consequences, and remedies for algorithmic bias in audio AI. Furthermore, stakeholders such as consumers, organizations, and policymakers have shown that they are eager for solutions to mitigate harms from bias due to audio algorithms. Five remedies that institutions can consider to address the issues with audio algorithmic bias include the following:

1. Invest in an algorithmic bias team that is dedicated to detecting and rooting out algorithmic bias. A team with the expertise to do so can partner with the machine learning/AI teams in the design of the algorithms and in the collection and use of the training data. Such a team should be diverse so that it can benefit from multiple perspectives in identifying potential causes of bias.

2. Institutions should find ways to collect demographic characteristics in their data so they can audit their algorithms and determine whether they inadvertently discriminate. There are a

number of tools freely available to evaluate whether bias may be an issue. For example, IBM's AI Fairness 360 and tools from Microsoft's FATE research group aim at reducing bias and increasing transparency and accountability in AI.

3. Institutions could immediately put systematic practices in place to ensure a collection of representative data for training the algorithm. For example, if audio samples of Irish speakers were used to train the ASR algorithm used by the Australian immigration authority, the case of Louise Kennedy could have potentially been averted.

4. Algorithms should be designed to make decisions using context-specific data about individuals rather than groups. An individual's audio command for search, for example, could be more informative of what the individual will do with the next audio search query than using the audio searches of the collective.

With careful design and management, audio AI algorithms have the potential to produce fairer outcomes. As algorithms increasingly make consequential decisions about our lives, from immigration and hiring decisions to educational and medical decisions, we must be vigilant about the potential for discrimination from algorithms. There are strong ethical and moral reasons to do so—it is just the right thing to do. However, there is also a case to be made that algorithmic bias can hurt organizations in the pursuit of their goals too.

[a] A. A. Press, "Computer Says No: Irish Vet Fails Oral English Test Needed to Stay in Australia," *The Guardian*, published August 8, 2017, accessed June 26, 2021, https://www.theguardian.com/australia-news/2017/aug/08/computer-says-no-irish-vet-fails-oral-english-test-needed-to-stay-in-australia.

[b] Juniper Research, "Digital Voice Assistants in Use to Triple to 8 Billion by 2023, Driven by Smart Home Devices," published February 12, 2018, accessed June 26, 2021, https://www.juniperresearch.com/press/digital-voice-assistants-in-use-to-8-million-2023.

[c] Batya Friedman and Helen Nissenbaum, "Bias in Computer Systems," *ACM Transactions on Information Systems* (TOIS) 14, no. 3 (1996): 330–47; Solon Barocas and Andrew D. Selbst, "Big Data's Disparate Impact," *California Law Review* 104 (2016): 671; and Cathy O'Neil, *Weapons of Math Destruction: How Big Data Increases Inequality and Threatens Democracy* (Crown, 2016).

[d] Allison Koenecke, Andrew Nam, Emily Lake, Joe Nudell, Minnie Quartey, Zion Mengesha, Connor Toups, John R. Rickford, Dan Jurafsky, and Sharad Goel. "Racial Disparities in Automated Speech Recognition," *Proceedings of the National Academy of Sciences* 117, no. 14 (2020): 7684–89.

[e] Rachael Tatman, "Gender and Dialect Bias in YouTube's Automatic Captions," in Proceedings of the First ACL Workshop on Ethics in Natural Language Processing, pp. 53–59, 2017.

[f] Siyuan Feng, Olya Kudina, Bence Mark Halpern, and Odette Scharenborg, "Quantifying Bias in Automatic Speech Recognition," arxiv.org, published March 28, 2021, https://arxiv.org/abs/2103.15122.

[g] Kalinda Ukanwa and Roland T. Rust, "Algorithmic Discrimination in Service," SSRN, published August 20, 2020, https://papers.ssrn.com/sol3/papers.cfm?abstract_id=3654943.

[h] Yoon Chae, "US AI Regulation Guide: Legislative Overview and Practical Considerations," *The Journal of Robotics, Artificial Intelligence & Law* 3, no. 1 (2020): 17–40.

[i] J. Dastin, "Amazon Scraps Secret AI Recruiting Tool That Showed Bias Against Women," Reuters, published October 10, 2018, https://www.reuters.com/article/us-amazon-com-jobs-automation-insight/amazon-scraps-secret-ai-recruiting-tool-that-showed-bias-against-women-idUSKCN1MK08G.

[j] Rachel Adams, "Artificial Intelligence Has a Gender Bias Problem—Just Ask Siri," The Conversation, accessed June 30, 2021, https://theconversation.com/artificial-intelligence-has-a-gender-bias-problem-just-ask-siri-123937.

[k] Emily Lever, "I Was a Human Siri," *New York Intelligencer*, published April 26, 2018, accessed June 26, 2021, https://nymag.com/intelligencer/smarthome/i-was-a-human-siri-french-virtual-assistant.html.

EXTENDED CASE STUDY

Butterball Turkey Voice Hotline

For over forty years—since 1981 to be exact—Butterball Turkey has maintained a "turkey hotline" during the Thanksgiving holiday in the United States, which is typically one of the first big holidays that either a new couple or homeowner hosts. It's a big meal, and often a big gathering of friends and family, so hours of planning and effort go into it. The Thanksgiving dinner also has many feelings and memories tied to it, making it exceptionally emotionally charged. So even if you think of yourself as an experienced home cook, it's often an incredibly stressful event.

Since the traditional main course of Thanksgiving dinner is a whole turkey, Butterball recognized an opportunity to reinforce its brand as the leader in the category and make sure its product was optimally presented. To do this, the company offered a Butterball Turkey Talk-Line to help relieve some of the stress of preparing the dish. Originally available via an 800 number, the chat line gives advice and tips on how to plan and cook the perfect turkey dinner (or at least how to avoid a culinary disaster). After adding text, online chat, and social media support to answer the nearly 100,000 questions they receive throughout the holiday season, Butterball wanted to make their experts available 24/7 and to support home cooks when they need it most—without having to make a phone call or send a text message.[a] Since Alexa-enabled devices are often located in the kitchen, they found that an Amazon Alexa Skill was the ideal way to bring their sage advice and reassuring expertise of the Butterball Turkey Talk-Line experts right into the homes of home cooks.

A voice-first experience also meant that Butterball could preserve one of the most appealing aspects of the talk line: the kind, helpful voice of an expert there to answer every pressing turkey question. To prepare the Alexa Skill, Butterball had three of their actual experts (Beth, Christopher, and Marge) record responses to the most common questions covering how to prep, cook, and carve a turkey. The skill even included calculators to help determine the size to buy, how long to thaw, and how long to roast. It also had step-by-step instructions and how-to videos for viewing over Alexa-enabled devices with screens such as the Amazon Echo Show. To further add a personal connection, the voice experience also included the talk line experts' bios, memorable stories, and recipes. You might have Marge tell you the ideal cooking temperature for a turkey or Christopher help you figure out how large a turkey you need for twenty people. All of this and more is just a question away. Best yet, there's no need to call and wait on hold; simply ask your turkey question to your Alexa device and you can just go on with your day.

"Every year it's evolved a little bit to help people as the times change. This will be my sixth year with the Turkey Talk-Line and I'm one of three voices on the Butterball skill," Butterball expert Beth Somers explained as she demonstrated the new service. "The app is filled with our most frequently asked questions and those are based on 37 years of call data. Some of those questions include thawing, how to prep your turkey for roasting, how much turkey you're going to need to buy, things like that. It's pretty comprehensive, especially for a first-time cook."[b]

When the Butterball Alexa Skill launched, Butterball made sure its audience knew about this new way to engage the turkey experts. Working with their agencies (Edelman and Mobiquity), Butterball ran a campaign during the Thanksgiving holiday periods in 2018 and 2019. Their website and social media accounts featured a video about the skill, and Amazon featured the skill in several prime placements including the Alexa Skills Store Billboard, Echo screens, and its emails. The 2018 campaign resulted in 1 billion impressions and was featured on the *Today Show*, *Food & Wine* magazine, *WIRED* magazine, and many other media outlets. In 2019, the skill saw its year-over-year sessions increase by three times, answering over 43,805 questions.

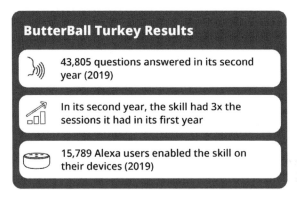

Figure 4.6. The results Butterball Turkey achieved with the turkey hotline.

With the content for the voice experience coming from all the previous call scripts and the Talk-Line experts lending their voices, there was consistency with the phone, chat, and text messaging experiences. The chef or cook's questions didn't change, so there wasn't a need to change the information. But the mode of interaction did change, so the marketers' work focused on making the conversations flow well. Butterball didn't reinvent the wheel; they simply made it run more smoothly and showed their customers they were willing to be wherever their customers wanted to engage with the brand, making the venerable Talk-Line more relevant in today's world.

[a] Amazon, "Butterball Case Study," published April 2020, accessed December 19, 2021, https://build.amazonalexadev.com/rs/365-EFI-026/images/Mobiquity_Butterball_Final05082020.pdf.
[b] Adam Campbell-Schmitt, "Butterball's Turkey Talk-Line Hits Amazon's Alexa This Thanksgiving," *Food and Wine*, published November 1, 2018.

Data Privacy and Ethical Considerations

When you begin to explore the possibilities and potential of voice marketing, expect a wave of optimism. Voice is exciting. It lets us connect with audiences in an incredibly personal way. And it's poised to reset the whole marketing landscape. But you will need to understand and consider a range of ethical and privacy concerns so you can create a voice experience to meet your marketing goals without unintended consequences.

To prevent privacy problems, you need to ensure, just as you do with other digital platforms, that your audience is aware of the kinds and amounts of data you collect, that your data is stored securely, and that it will not be used for nefarious purposes.

To address some ethical concerns, first, be alert to negative and damaging stereotypes. Be certain that they are not expressed in the experiences you create. Second, it's important that you design brand experiences that are inclusive rather than exclusive. More detail to come.

In chapter 4, we reviewed some of the concerns about privacy and trust that people reached by voice technology will experience. In this chapter, we'll expand that discussion to examine in detail the three key issues: (1) privacy and security, (2) inclusivity, and (3) social responsibility.

Data Privacy and Security

The structure of voice technology creates some new and urgent concerns about data privacy. The core feature of a smart speaker is that it listens and responds to what the user says.

This ability makes the interaction more humanlike and natural. But it also sparks an immediate concern about what information is being captured by the device that responds to a human voice. It raises a concern about who can access that information. In response, Google, Amazon, and Apple have rolled out feature updates addressing user history and security, to help the users of a voice assistant take more control of their data.

That's a start. But customers still have a heightened sense of awareness of what it means to have smart speakers and other voice-activated devices in their homes. That sensitivity is magnified because the two lead manufacturers of the most popular smart speakers happen to be Google and Amazon—two organizations famous for harvesting customer data for business purposes.

But smart speakers aren't the only devices that can hear a conversation. Smartphones can listen in. Home devices like smart thermostats and Ring cameras can listen in (we should note that Google owns Nest and Amazon owns Ring). Smart appliances, such as many from Samsung, and remotes from Comcast can also listen in. In-car assistants can hear and remember what you say. But most users don't seem to be as wary of all these when it comes to data privacy, data security, and personal privacy.

In the 2022 Voice Consumer Index Study, in which two of our coauthors were closely involved, both users and nonusers of voice assistants indicated that one of their most important concerns about voice technology is the protection of privacy.[1] But it turned out the respondents in the study had a different interpretation of privacy than the research team had originally imagined.

Initially, researchers thought that "privacy" referred to the respondents' data and their personally identifiable information. That's a natural assumption because this technology captures what a user says verbatim so that it can provide an appropriate response. But in fact, users are also concerned with their privacy at the moment of speaking to the device. They worry about what might be heard, and who might hear it, and whether what someone overhears might trigger a school or business or family response.

It's also important to remember that, while the voice device may be registered to an adult, it might actually be used by someone under thirteen, an age group that falls under a different set of rules for marketing, data collection, and permissions. The range of Amazon Alexa Skills, Google Actions, and other voice applications that already exist show that compliance for younger users can be managed. For an example, see The Story of Lucky Charms, in chapter 2 of this book. But noncompliance—even accidental noncompliance—can have serious consequences. Due diligence is necessary and usually not difficult.

If you are considering a voice app for kids (under thirteen in the United States and under sixteen in most of Europe and several other countries), here is a useful set of regulatory boundaries. It's a list, from a site called Alexa Skills Kit for Developers, of all the reasons Amazon would use to *reject or suspend* a skill designed for those age groups.

1. "It is a custom skill and you are not an Amazon-approved developer."
2. "It promotes any products, content, or services, or directs end users to engage with content outside of Alexa."
3. "It sells any physical products or services."
4. "It sells any digital products or services without using Amazon In-Skill Purchasing."

5. "It collects any personal information from end users."
6. "It includes content not suitable for all ages."[2]

Another concern that was uncovered through the 2022 Voice Consumer Index research was the widespread confusion that surrounds the topic of security. Privacy and security are related, but they are not the same thing. "Privacy" refers to the rights you have (or don't have) to control your personal information and how it's used.[3] (This is often addressed in the privacy policies shared on websites and mobile apps.) Data privacy is a concern of people who design or use voice assistance because the devices operate by listening to what the user says, processing that data to find the most appropriate response, and then delivering the response to the user. "Security," on the other hand, refers to the specific means by which that information is protected. To get people to trust your voice application, you will need to address both.

Most of the privacy and security issues are not new to digital marketers. "In fact, one of the keys to creating a successful online business in 2016 was to show people your site was secure and trustworthy." You see, "customized experience comes at a price for the consumer—the need to provide personal information. So marketers must seek a balance regarding how they can meet both needs and build their brand along the way."[4]

The General Data Protection Regulation (GDPR) in Europe and the California Consumer Privacy Act (CCPA) were created to address privacy concerns and to define who owns data and how it may be used. GDPR, for example, says, "One of the main provisions of this governance is that an EU citizen must provide their consent for the use of any personally identifiable information (PII) before it can be captured or used."[5] That is, the digital "provider," the brand that placed the digital message, controls the data generated by clicks in America. But individual Europeans, even those living in the United States, own and control their own data. That makes it harder for marketers to capture and sell that data. CCPA provides similar protection for residents of California. (One consequence of this is a tactical shift. Because those regulations make it harder for marketers to capture and transfer visitor data, in-bound marketing becomes more important than outbound, because in-bound marketing doesn't require the use of data.)[6]

A New Set of Data

A challenge for voice marketers is that they now have a new set of data. Words chosen and language used uncover intent. Capturing this data will inform the language models being developed. It will "teach" the voice app to better understand the users. And that will improve performance of existing voice platforms. Most people probably are fine with this limited type of data capture.

But with voice, there is another type of data that can be captured—and that is the physical characteristics of the individual voice, as well as the "behavioral choices" of the person speaking. These biometric aspects of a voice can indicate far more than what a speaker is consciously and deliberately sharing. For instance, analyzing these aspects of a user's voice can "indicate underlying medical conditions or gauge disease risk."[7] Vocal factors like pitch, rate, rhythm, tone, volume, and word choice of an individual can potentially reveal psychological issues like depression, PTSD, and suicide risk—conditions that a person might want to keep private—in addition to physical conditions like Alzheimer's, concussion, heart disease, migraines, and Parkinson's.[8] It's also possible to use one's voice to authenticate identity. The use of two-factor voice biometrics identification can be more accurate than facial recognition.[9]

Alternative Ethical Systems

There is no short and simple answer to the many ethical issues—no universally agreed procedure for applying the user data captured across the many digital locations a person might visit. The answer for your brand might depend on the model you choose for ethical reasoning. In addition to the major non-Western ethical systems, Islamic, Hindu, Buddhist, Taoist, and Confucian—ethicist and business school professor Robert Zafft, in his book, *The Right Way to Win: Making Business Ethics Work in the Real World*, identifies four main Western-based systems for ethical decision-making. They are (1) cost/benefit, (2) golden rule, (3) blind bargaining, and (4) virtue.[10]

Each one has its benefits and drawbacks, but we, like Zafft, endorse the fourth system, because it's based on values—the very values that, if lived by your organization, will come to be important and visible assets of your brand. If you know and consistently embrace those values, they will give you clear direction on what data to collect, and how to use that data ethically to help your customers. Meanwhile, some of the ethical answers are already clear.

If you are collecting data, you need permission to do so. And if you collect it, then you must protect it. And the first question you must answer is "Do we really need this data?"

Voice as an Engine of Inclusivity

One of the most exciting aspects of voice technology is the potential for enabling greater inclusivity for populations who have been underserved or lumped in with larger groups. It can enable people with varying levels of literary access to the web, including people with cognitive challenges and other disabilities. Some voice experiences are not yet accessible to everyone—those with hearing loss, for example—and we envision they will be soon. In the meantime, the gains immeasurably outweigh the losses.

There is enormous potential for language and dialect inclusivity. Imagine being able to address French Canadians not just in standard French but in their own homegrown Quebecois. Or to address Brazilians from Cachoeira and Brazilians from São Paulo in their quite different dialects. As language models become more robust, it becomes feasible to provide information in a greater variety of languages. It becomes possible for the user to request information in a variety of ways, even capturing the request through sign language if the user has a camera connected to the device. We can picture the day when an avatar will be able to respond in sign language to an individual requesting it.

What's more, for people living with vision impairment, voice assistance can provide a faster interaction and an additional level of support. Users can simply speak their request or ask a question, rather than reading a screen. Vision impaired users might otherwise be two to four times slower to interact than the visually unimpaired.

While we have these possibilities, the voice marketer needs to worry about *unintended exclusions*. These might range from functionality problems to language problems to the personality of the assistant. Many of them can be eliminated by the crafting of the voice app. Here, the most important issues are *who* the potential audience will be and *what specific problem* the voice experience will solve for them. When you think about the problem you are hoping to solve, it is tempting to cut out the "edge cases." But you need to remember that, if you do not account for the needs of these segments of your audience, you may create the perception that your brand is comfortable ignoring groups of people.

We believe that all the potential unintended exclusions can be avoided if the brand is careful as it develops the voice application.

Right from the start, the brand needs to identify who can and who cannot use the application. The key is to make certain that you aren't inadvertently locking someone out. There will be times when you should exclude a segment. An alcohol brand might prevent children from using their experience. But you don't want to exclude anyone who is part of the most broadly defined target audience, even if the segment is small. These accommodations are easy if you recognize them early. Down the road, there will always be the challenge of developing a more elegant solution that eliminates or reduces inappropriate audiences.

Step one in crafting a solution: Are there any audience limitations that might affect your solution? Not just differing levels of ability—you might, for example, require adjustments if children are a potential audience. They have different privacy rules, but more important, they have different styles of internet behavior. They will interact with a voice application differently than, for example, someone sixty-five-plus.

Different segments may need different conversational styles, different levels of formality or complexity. Younger audiences may prefer less formality and require understanding of contemporary slang. Older audiences might want more "please and thank you." You need to think through the conversation and see if it fits with all of the key audiences, if it incorporates the words and phrases your audience would choose, or if you need to craft conversations that are segment specific.

You need to determine the languages your voice experience will support. Typically, these types of decisions are driven by the languages of the regions and audiences who will be using it. But you will need more than just translations. Statements should be localized—they should accommodate the idioms of each customer region and correspond with local cultural norms and mores.

It is critical and not simple to create a voice assistant whose persona clearly reflects the culture of the user. This requires a team with at least one member who is intimately familiar with that culture or ethnicity of each segment you want to reach. We have often seen marketers make assumptions about cultures and ethnic groups, which result in semi-offensive stereotypes or even caricatures. Any misstep could alienate your customers and prospects or even create a PR nightmare for your brand.

Social Responsibility

Voice experiences usually require the creation of a system persona with whom users will engage verbally. This step has social implications. From the very outset of planning and design, when building out requirements for your features, you must look beyond the good outcomes that are possible and try to imagine what harm could come if someone were to use those features with a negative intent.

It is also important to question whether your chosen persona might invoke a problematic stereotype or suggest a potential harmful trait in your user group. It's been pointed out that both Amazon Alexa and Google Assistant (among others) have female voices as the default, potentially perpetuating a gender bias.[11] That doesn't mean that they were a bad choice. But the stewards of a brand have to examine even faint and far-flung possible negatives and risks. Any potential issue or risk will be vastly easier to address during the design phase than any step following it. No one wants reactive fixes or mitigation moves.

Perceive and discuss the tough questions in the early phases of your voice project—all of them—however hypothetical they may be. It could be time consuming and controversy creating. And it's not nearly as straightforward as "due diligence" makes it sound. But it is a vital step in the development process—and perhaps the only way your team can put its best foot forward from the very start.

Questions to Ask before Creating a Voice Experience

Based on your situation, you might want to create a list of key questions to ask during the initial phase. In the meantime, here are three starter questions:

- **How does this voice experience truly solve my audience's problems?** It should solve the spirit of the problem, finally and unequivocally. It should not be just a short-term fix.
- **Can everyone in my audience use this solution?** Are there any "edge cases" missing? It's important to keep asking if the problem is being solved for every audience member. It can be helpful to think about solutions in terms of who can and who can't use them. That creates an implied challenge to develop a more elegant solution (not just an accommodation) to make the "can't" population smaller.
- **Is there any way this solution can be used to cause harm?** What possible unintended consequences might come from using this solution? We must challenge ourselves to break with the optimism of a solution and make certain that we are aware of the vulnerabilities or trade-offs that come with using our solution. We must think about the risks at least as much as the rewards.

It's important to have these conversations during the planning and design phases versus having to devise a workaround during development or after launch. It's amazing and fun to think through all the ways that a voice experience can solve problems or change the world, but it's at least as important not to create new problems as we move toward a more inclusive and helpful world.

GUEST PERSPECTIVE

Trust: The Essential Element in the Growth of Voice Assistance

Jon Stein

Increasing trust goes together with the willingness of prospects to adopt a new platform. The more one uses a new platform, the more that person's trust in it grows. But what are the other ingredients in building trust? That was the question that led us to approach Jon Stine for his thoughts. Jon is the executive director of the Open Voice Network, which is a "non-profit industry association dedicated to the development of the standards and ethical use guidelines that will make voice worthy of user trust" (https://openvoicenetwork.org/). Building trust is the responsibility of those who are providing content for it, namely, marketers. After all, if web and mobile marketing are the historical guide, you'll be providing the largest amount of content for it. So let's hear what Jon has to say.

Highway 6 in Oregon runs roughly fifty-one miles (eighty-two kilometers) from the western suburbs of Portland to the dairy and tourist town of Tillamook, which nestles against the Pacific Ocean. For most of its length, Highway 6 is but two lanes wide. Its asphalt is often cracked by winter freezing and thawing and by the shifting of rain-drenched soil beneath. It climbs up and over the summit of the Oregon Coast range and runs at length beside the swerving, curving, white-water Wilson River.

Highway 6 is an economic lifeline, not only to the town of Tillamook, but to the surrounding county. On most days, roughly 5,000 vehicles run the length of Highway 6. It hosts eighteen-wheelers, milk tankers, and log trucks as well as cars, campers, recreational vehicles, and working pickup trucks. Speeds average fifty-five to seventy miles per hour—less uphill and more on the downhill side. On summer weekends, motorists heading toward the ocean beaches whiz past (separated at times by inches), convoys of bicyclists for whom the Portland-to-Coast ride is a there-and-back two-day challenge. For all the danger of the road—let alone the visual distractions of waterfalls, endless Douglas fir forests, and an untamed river—traffic generally moves quite safely, which is a good thing. Because when Highway 6 is closed, all kinds of economic opportunity evaporates. When it is open, opportunities multiply.

Which provides a number of lessons for the community of voice assistance, especially on the subject of trust. The fact that thousands of individuals drive Highway 6 each day in a safe and efficient manner is due largely to the formation and maintenance of societal trust. Societal trust is the web, the glue that holds communities together.[a] It provides a shield of protection for individuals, a safe haven for human interaction, and a stable, accessible ground for economic development. Our common goal is to devise the trust-building standards for this new communication highway and to educate the audience of developers, linguists, users, content creators, and marketers on the rules of the road.

Voice assistance is now at a critical stage in its societal development and economic maturation. What was once technological magic is now a mainstream feature; what was (and often still is) a toy for amusement is poised to become a tool for revenue growth and operational efficiency. In other words, voice assistance is poised to become big. Big in functionality that will grow from today's command-and-respond experience to one that is conversational and ever more predictive. Big as an interface on every digital device in a world where every device (and every automobile, every appliance, and perhaps every environment) is digital. Big as the interface to a tomorrow's world of ambient computing, to the connected constellation of artificial intelligence-driven content destinations. Big as a remarkably deep well of personal and actionable data.

As it becomes big, voice assistance will—much as the internet and mobility did in prior decades—reshape personal and communal behavior in the home, on the job, and (even now) in the car. In our work and in our leisure. Voice assistance will also reshape organizational and corporate behavior. It will become a strategic consideration for every marketer and operations chief. A line item on every enterprise and organizational technology budget.

Yes, voice assistance is poised to be big. But it's not big yet. For many, it's still very much a toy and not a tool. For even more, it is a capability that is rarely if ever used. If we compare the availability of conversational agents (now measured in the billions of devices) with the adoption of voice usage, as measured by regular monthly use of those agents, we'll find a significant gap between the two. (Note that we're talking about monthly use, not daily use.) If we compare adoption and the complexity of use—that is, voice assistance used to provide a weather update or tunes from Spotify, as opposed to using voice for search, scheduling, or commerce—there's another significant gap. In short, there's a lot of available voice assistance not being used. And when it's being used, it's for relatively simple things.

Historians would tell us that these gaps between availability, adoption, and complex use are not unusual for a new technology, especially a consumer-facing technology. Technological innovation is often in front of consumer interest. Geoffrey Moore's seminal technology text, *Crossing the Chasm*, pointed out more than thirty years ago the challenge that technologists face in reaching past the early adopters to the majority of a market.[b]

The question for the voice assistance community is one of gap closure. How and how quickly will voice assistance become the next normative, game-shaping technology, the next internet or mobility? How and how soon—in the Moore model—will voice cross the chasm? Or—gasp—will voice assistance never close the gaps, much as assisted and virtual reality struggle to find a market? Will it be a toy for some, a tool for a few, and out of mind for the vast majority? The answer lies partially in time. It simply takes time for users to try, experiment, stumble across the mobile phone app.

The answer also lies partially in technological advancement. Highway 6 became viable for thousands of motorists with improvements in road construction and vehicle performance. Voice assistance will become more viable as technology improves, as models are developed for more languages and dialects, as dialogue context is remembered and used to shape conversations, and as the data scientists push the boundaries. However, the voice industry must recognize that the answer does not lie fully in the technology, nor in the patience of time. As with Highway 6, there are important and multiple elements of trust that must be in place—and widely shared—for the journey of voice to be pursued.[c]

The gaps between availability and adoption, between adoption and ever-complex usage, are gaps of both technology and trust, which must be closed in a timely manner. The success of voice—the realization of the game-shaping potential of voice—depends upon the closing of tech and trust gaps. Let's look at these gaps of trust for voice assistance. Our Highway 6 analogy is instructive. Few, if any, would drive the highway (or any highway) if they did not trust that they would arrive safely at their destination, if they did not trust that other motorists would know and observe the rules of the road, if they did not trust that other vehicles would be of standard size or trust that the road would be paved and painted.

Trust is a foundational issue for the future of voice assistance. And let us be clear: Trust is far beyond the issue of user and data privacy.[d] Voice distrust is found in issues both small (Will it understand me?) and large (Will this make my life better?). The distrust is at individual levels

(What is this doing with my data?) and at organizational and enterprise levels (Will this create tangible, sustainable value?). The economic future of voice assistance—at both consumer and organizational levels, for developers and designers—is dependent on our ability to make voice assistance worthy of user trust.

How can the voice assistance ecosystem form the necessary bonds of societal trust? One seminal academic paper that points to two essential elements.[e]

The first is termed institution-based trust. It's a widely held belief and confidence that complete strangers will observe laws, regulations, or industry standards and do so with behaviors that benefit the community as a whole. Institution-based trust is made up of two parts.

1. **Structural assurance**, where participants are secure in their belief that protective structures are in place. In our example of Oregon Highway 6, this includes laws for driving on the right side of the road, standards for lane and vehicle width, and the painting of yellow reflective lines on the asphalt. In voice assistance, this might be developed through the broad adoption of standards for the interoperability of conversational agents or for the protection of data.
2. **Situation normality**, where participants are secure in their belief that structural processes and rules are widely accepted—and will be accepted tomorrow and in the days ahead. These are expectations that are regularly met. For Highway 6, this might begin with the expectation that everyone will drive on the right side of the road. In voice assistance, this belief will take root through the practices of leading organizational users—businesses, nonprofits, and government agencies.

The second major element evolves from the first and operates at the individual level. Again, two parts:

1. **Trusting intentions** is about the willingness to depend upon another party—another driver, for instance, or in voice, a natural-language-processing software or system provider—even though negative consequences are possible. Trust can't be created through deterrence or fear; it's confidence within a position of vulnerability.[f]
2. **Trusting behaviors** translate intentions into actions.[g] Here, it's a voluntary dependence (with the feeling of security) upon another person—even though negative consequences are possible. It's the expectation that the dependence will not be abused.

This institutional-individual framework is very applicable to voice assistance. At the institutional level, there's a need for protective structures—structures that take the form of communally-accepted technical and usage standards—in areas such as privacy, consent, authentication, platform interoperability, destination management, and access. Structures that will allow us to connect as we wish with conversational agents anywhere in the coming constellation—and do so accurately, safely, and quickly.[h]

There's also a need for protective structures at the individual level, which for voice assistance, is about the human-to-assistant relationship. Yes, there are privacy issues at stake. But there are also accuracy and inclusivity issues[i] and value-creation issues that have much less to do with technology and time and everything to do with the smooth, seamless integration of voice into business processes at the right time, for the right reasons, providing the easy experience.

However, the institutional-individual framework is a top-down view, instructive from a strategic level, but not so much for the tactical. What we need is a ground-up, user-centric view, something like the user-centric trust map shown here as figure 5.1.

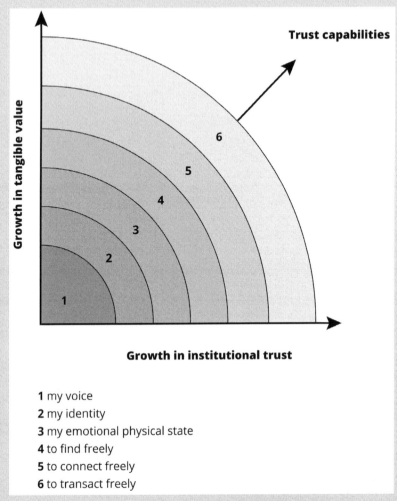

1 my voice
2 my identity
3 my emotional physical state
4 to find freely
5 to connect freely
6 to transact freely

Figure 5.1. The user-centric trust map from the Open Voice Network.

Source: Open Voice Network

Our user-centric model begins with the question that every individual and enterprise user will ask: Will this bring value to me? Do I trust that voice assistance will bring an incrementally positive, sustainable benefit—or just momentary amusement (or frustration)? Do I trust that, within the systems and ecosystem of voice assistance, I have the same opportunity as everyone else to gain from this, or is the game rigged for someone else's benefit? From this basis, we can envision the growth of "trust capabilities" that are delivered through the communally developed standards and guidelines. As trust capabilities grow, so will overall institutional trust (as shown on the X axis) and the opportunity for tangible economic value (shown on the Y axis).

Level 1: Begins at the most basic level of voice assistance: the user's voice.[j] Here, the trust issues are not only of accuracy, but of recognition. Will the conversational agent recognize my voice, even if it reflects a regional dialect or a language that is in minority? Will I receive the same recognition and respect as that of the developing engineers? If I'm able to work my way through to a third-party conversational agent, will it understand me? Needed: commonly accepted standards, guidelines, and systems to enable and deliver multilanguage, multidialect recognition and accuracy.

Level 2: Here it's the user's identity, and the trust issues are not limited to biometric identification.[k] Using current data sets, voice data can be used to infer—with a high degree of accuracy—such things as gender, ethnicity, relative height and weight, age, educational level, and geographic region. This is a Pandora's box of trust issues. How will identity and identity-inference data be used? Who has access? For reasons of convenience, users may wish to pay with their voice or use their voice to authenticate identity (your voice as a password). For reasons of surveillance, those in authority might gather voiceprints. Usage context will make a big difference. Needed: commonly accepted standards, guidelines, and systems to guide voice assistance providers and organizational enterprise users in their use of voice-based identity data.

Level 3: The user's emotional and physical state. An analysis of voice recordings can not only tell us who said it, and what was said, but how it was said.[l] We can determine the emotional state of the user—for instance, sad, confused, angry, joyous—and identify characteristics that will imply the credibility of the user. Is he telling the truth? (Keep in mind that a lie detection test is simply a form of voice analysis.) The analysis of voice recordings can also identify intoxication and leading indicators of physical ailments such as Parkinson's disease, respiratory diseases (COVID-19, as shown in recent tests), and mental illness. Envision, for a second, a retail conversational agent that adjusts its responses to the words and emotions of the human shopper. Is the shopper hesitant? Confused? Drunk? How might a sales-oriented conversational agent respond? Needed: commonly accepted standards, guidelines, and systems to guide voice-assistance providers and organizational-enterprise users in their use of voice-based emotional and physical state data.

Level 4: Moves us into trust capabilities that enable unfettered, free actions by the user. Here, it is the ability to find—quickly, clearly, accurately, openly—any global digital destination. Without being bound by platform restrictions or competitive issues. Needed: commonly accepted standards, guidelines, and systems for a global registry of uniquely identified, voice-found destinations. Such a registry—akin to the internet's Domain Name System—would connect users to the constellation mentioned above.

Level 5: Takes it a step further where not only is the user able to locate any destination anywhere, but the originating conversational agent is able to share dialogs (and corresponding context, controls, and data) with any conversational agent, regardless of platform parentage. Levels 4 and 5 will move voice assistance from its current mobile OS model—apps contained within a platform—to the interoperability and value model of the internet. This will be a huge step for organizational users of voice; a single conversational agent would be able to reach all constituents or customers, and monies could be spent less on maintaining agents on multiple platforms (each with their own update cycles) and much more on content and experience innovation. Needed: commonly accepted standards, guidelines, and systems that will allow conversational agents—regardless of platform—to share dialogs, including context, controls, and data.

Level 6: Addresses an important issue for both individual and organizational users of voice assistance: the ability to transact freely. For an organization, there are three parts to this: a unique identifier and the ability to be found (level 4), the ability to connect regardless of platform, and the ability to protect commercial/proprietary data. This is the ability (and the freedom) to share competitively sensitive information with a prospect or a customer—and to do so without a host platform listening in. Needed: commonly accepted standards, guidelines, and systems that will allow conversational agents to share dialogs with privacy.

When we activate a voice assistant, we begin a journey of exploration and discovery. It may be a simple journey—a simple question, with a simple answer. In years ahead, it will most likely be a complex one, involving dozens of conversational agents, all working together to resolve a multivariate query. We'll begin that journey only if we have trust that we will reach our destination and that we'll be recognized and respected; that when privacy is desired, it will be granted without hesitation; that ongoing technology innovation will enable all in the voice ecosystem to have an equitable opportunity at the creation and capturing of value through a level field, and that the rules are known and observed.

We in the voice community have the opportunity now to build the structure that will allow institutional and individual trust to germinate, grow, and flourish. Voice is poised to be big. Whether it will be is up to us.

[a] Edelman, "Edelman Trust Barometer 2021," January 2021, https://www.edelman.com/sites/g/files/aatuss191/files/2021-03/2021%20Edelman%20Trust%20Barometer.pdf.

[b] Geoffrey A. Moore, *Crossing the Chasm: Marketing and Selling Technology Products to Mainstream Customers* (New York, NY: HarperBusiness, 1991).

[c] B. Briscoe and B. Tilly, "Metcalfe's Law Is Wrong," IEEE Spectrum, published July 1, 2006, accessed February 20, 2023, https://spectrum.ieee.org/metcalfes-law-is-wrong.

[d] Microsoft Corporation, "Trust: Lack of Trust Is a Significant Factor Hindering Usage of Smart Speakers and Digital Assistants," 2019. https://about.ads.microsoft.com/en-us/insights/2019-voice-report

[e] D. H. McKnight and N. L. Chervany, "Trust and Distrust Definitions: One Bite at a Time," in Lecture Notes in Computer Science (including subseries Lecture Notes in Artificial Intelligence and Lecture Notes in Bioinformatics), vol. 2246, Springer Verlag, 27–54, Workshop on Deception, Fraud and Trust in Agent Societies, held as part of the Autonomous Agents Conference, Barcelona, Spain, June 4, 2000.

[f] J. Emborg, S. E. Daniels, and G. B. Walker, "A Framework for Exploring Trust and Distrust in Natural Resource Management," *Frontiers in Communication*, April 17, 2020, https://doi.org/10.3389/fcomm.2020.00013.

[g] Gary Burnison, "As Good as the Last Promise Kept," Korn Ferry, March 28, 2021, https://www.kornferry.com/insights/special-edition/as-good-as-the-last-promise-kept.

[h] L. M. PytlikZillig and C. D. Kimbrough, "Consensus on Conceptualizations and Definitions of Trust: Are We There Yet?" in *Interdisciplinary Perspectives on Trust: Towards Theoretical and Methodological Integration*, ed. E. Shockley, T. M. S. Neal, L. M. PytlikZillig, and B. H. Bornstein (Springer International Publishing), 17–47.

[i] Kimberly Nevala, "Ethical AI Isn't the Same as Trustworthy AI, and That Matters," VentureBeat, published November 28, 2020, https://venturebeat.com/ai/ethical-ai-isnt-the-same-as-trustworthy-ai-and-that-matters/.

[j] Mark Webster, "Voice Technology's Role in Our Rapidly Changing World," Adobe, published October 27, 2020, https://xd.adobe.com/ideas/principles/emerging-technology/voice-technologys-role-in-rapidly-changing-world/.

[k] K. K. Christi Olson, "Voice Report: From Answers to Action: Customer Adoption of Voice Technology and Digital Assistants," ReadkonG, accessed May 7, 2023, https://www.readkong.com/page/voice-report-from-answers-to-action-customer-adoption-of-9795944.

[l] Shira Ovide, "Should Alexa Read Our Moods?" *The New York Times*, May 19, 2021, https://www.nytimes.com/2021/05/19/technology/alexa.html.

EXTENDED CASE STUDY

Sony Hand Wash Tunes Help Families Fight COVID-19

Since 1929, Sony has been an innovative force in the recording industry, with a huge catalog of recorded music. When COVID-19 came along, highlighting the need for healthier handwashing habits, they saw an opportunity to provide support—with an experience that would help keep people safe, while building their attachment to the brand. That's because, after COVID hit in March 2020, most knew that you needed to wash your hands for twenty seconds. While it may not seem like very long, few people were able to gauge that span of time.

As a basic guide, people had been advised to sing "Happy Birthday" twice, to ensure that they were washing their hands long enough. That's an easy guideline, but not necessarily the most entertaining option.

Now, nearly a third of customers across all age groups use voice assistants daily, and almost half of them use voice assistants weekly. And 40% of people were conducting health and wellness–related searches. Sony saw an opportunity to create something a bit more exciting and fun—while also engaging with music fans and driving their awareness of Sony's artists. The timing presented an interesting challenge. On the one hand, Sony only needed content that would keep people engaged for twenty seconds. On the other hand, they had only twenty seconds to give people an engaging experience. Clearly, variety would be important.

Calling on their epic roster of artists, Sony assembled a collection of twenty-second handwashing tunes. It was a fun and helpful voice experience. To avoid song-licensing issues—costly and legally challenging—they invited artists to record reworked versions of their songs—or else submit a wholly original handwashing tune.

Artists were excited to get involved, and soon a collection of fun and unique songs from a dozen artists had been assembled. "It's great to be able to do something, however little, to help people. So we were delighted to work with Sony Music on a handwashing skill," said Roy Stride of Scouting for Girls. "We hope 'She's So Lovely' can entertain people during these times."[a]

Sony's voice design agency, Vixen Labs, then built an app that provided users with a randomized handwashing tune every forty-eight hours, helping to ensure that the experience would stay fresh and surprising. Users also had the option of choosing their favorite tune multiple times.

The uncertainty and anxiety brought on by COVID-19 made the project urgent. So the team sped from ideation to launch in just six weeks. Given the truncated timeline, Amazon was invited to help with marketing to launch the skill with a splash.[b] They created a promotional card to run on devices with screens such as the Echo Show. For two weeks following the launch, Alexa displayed "Hand Wash Tunes," inviting users to try the skill. Some artists also promoted their involvement by posting videos of themselves using it.

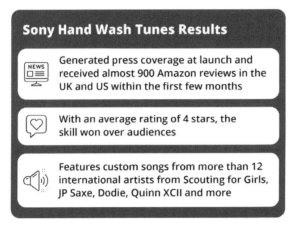

Sony Hand Wash Tunes Results

Generated press coverage at launch and received almost 900 Amazon reviews in the UK and US within the first few months

With an average rating of 4 stars, the skill won over audiences

Features custom songs from more than 12 international artists from Scouting for Girls, JP Saxe, Dodie, Quinn XCII and more

Figure 5.2. A summary of the result Sony Music achieved with their Handwash Tunes Alexa Skill.

Hand Wash Tunes launched with a flurry of coverage. It got almost 900 US and UK Amazon reviews in the first few months, averaging a four-star rating. Users emphasized the mix of fun and helpfulness. Many mentioned how much they enjoyed it as a family. Hand Wash Tunes demonstrates how seamlessly voice can bring together a variety of elements, distilled into a single, intuitive experience. Showing the value of direct voice interaction between artists and fans, it laid the groundwork for future Sony voice skills such as Number One Fan.

[a] Sony Music, "Sony Music Launches 'Hand Wash Tunes' Skill for Amazon Alexa," published May 29, 2020, accessed January 13, 2022, https://www.sonymusic.co.uk/sony-music-launches-hand-wash-tunes-skill-for-amazon-alexa/.
[b] Amazon, "Alexa and Amazon Devices COVID-19 Resources," updated May 31, 2020, accessed January 13, 2022, https://www.aboutamazon.com/news/devices/alexa-and-amazon-devices-covid-19-resources.

Goals and KPIs for Voice Marketing

In chapter 4, we looked at some of the ways that people are using voice assistants, including the platforms they choose, the problems they try to solve, the questions they try to answer, and the experiences they desire. We also explored who is using voice technology. But to achieve your optimal return on investment (ROI) on any platform, including those for voice AI, you need to do more than just place content on it, even the content that your customers want. It's critical to satisfy customer needs where they overlap with your organization's marketing goals—and this starts with actually setting those goals. In this chapter, we're going to explore how to make voice an effective marketing tool for your brand.

To start building your voice marketing strategy, you need to take two basic steps:

1. You need to **define your current situation** so you can then choose the most useful objectives; you might want to start by asking: Does it make sense for your brand to focus on acquisition or would a retention-focused solution result in a bigger impact? Once you have narrowed things down to the phase in the customer journey you want to focus on, you can identify the key performance indicators (KPIs) that will then help you to know whether you are reaching those objectives. To fully describe your situation, think about the typical "paths to purchase" for your brand and the behaviors you want to activate in your prospects at each point along the path. What are the typical steps your prospects go through? Cover everything from first engaging with you to the final behavior you are trying to produce. What hurdles in that path are likely to interrupt, slow down, or break off that process? Additionally,

what can you provide at each point to speed up the process, shortening the prospect's time along the path? Do they need information, entertainment, a short-term
opportunity to increase value through discounting, gift with purchase, larger size, or
something else? What are other decision points and how might they be simplified
or eliminated or somehow improved with the help that a voice app can provide?
In other words, think about your customers' journey and where they encounter
friction. Is your audience using voice search, and is your web content being served
when they do? Or do they need something big to inspire or entertain them during
the awareness phase, or do they need more support during the retention period after
initially trying the product or service? You likely already know many of their pain
points along the path, so this is your opportunity to soften those edges and improve
your customer experience. Once you have your answer, you can build the voice
experience to address a customer problem or a business goal.

2. **Identify your goals or objectives.** Usually, the best way to describe objectives
   involves observable consumer behavior so you can tell how well you are succeed-
   ing. It is almost always possible to choose behaviors that are both observable and
   a clear indicator of your initiative's success or failure. For instance, a consumer
   electronics brand might have trouble with product onboarding, which contributes
   to low usage and retention numbers, so they create a hands-free voice onboarding
   experience to ensure their customer knows how to get the most out of the product,
   which then contributes to generating positive word of mouth. At the same time, an
   entertainment brand might have a discoverability problem and simply want to make
   it easier for their audience to find and watch their programming, so they build a
   voice-enabled discovery engine that works across the devices their audiences use.
   Lastly, a consumer-packaged goods brand might have a goal of increasing product
   reorders, so they create a voice-enabled customer relationship management program
   to remind their customers when it's time to purchase the product again.

But sometimes, it is useful to measure progress or change or activity in behaviors that are
partway to an objective or contribute somehow to success, without being a major goal.
For this, we use an intermediate measure, usually, a consumer behavior called a KPI. In
the digital space, there are lots of behaviors that can be tracked to measure progress or the
absence of progress that will later contribute to meeting a goal or that diagnose a problem
with meeting the goal. Which KPIs are relevant will depend on several factors. What type
of organization is it? Is it a retailer, overwhelmingly focused on driving purchase behavior,
or is it an information provider, focused almost entirely on engagement and time spent with
its audience and the information sharing with others? What kind of product or service is
involved? Is it an impulse buy or a seriously considered purchase?

Good KPIs are behaviors that are easy to measure and have a clear relationship to
success or failure in meeting larger goals. The KPIs you can start with are not that dis-
similar from those found with other digital tactics you're likely familiar with. With search,
for instance, you can look at the formation (and length) of the query. When using voice
to search, people tend to use longer phrases (often referred to as long-tail search), which
contain more nuance and context than you typically see with keyword-based searches.
These long-tail phrases—and more specific and nuanced questions—can indicate that the

prospect is ready to purchase, while more general questions typically indicate that they're just starting down the path. On the other hand, a retailer might look at such KPIs as the number of questions answered as well as the number of questions that were asked but were not matched to an answer (more on how to analyze and enhance your voice experiences in chapter 9). They can also look at usage and repeat usage and whether the customer was able to make a successful purchase or hand off to their mobile app to complete a transaction. Finally, a pharmaceutical brand might have the goal of increasing patient adherence to therapy and will want to keep an eye on the KPIs that demonstrate successful medication tracking or prescription refills. The point is, voice is a tool critical to meeting marketing goals and is not separate from your overall marketing goals, so the KPIs need to be measured as part of a total program.

Now consider some issues specific to voice as a strategic marketing tool. In conversations with brand managers, we are often asked, "How can voice deliver value to my brand?" and "How do you create experiences that drive growth or reduce costs?"

To answer, begin by looking at voice through two different lenses: individual voice applications as a product and voice applications as a component of your bigger customer experience. These two approaches are vastly different from each other, and depending on the industry you work in and the type of organization that employs you, one or both approaches may apply. To help you determine whether your brand's voice application should be a product or an integrated part of your total customer experience, ask yourself, "Will the voice experience be the customer's end destination, or will it be something that works within the existing brand ecosystem?"

Voice as a Product: Stand-Alone Experiences

A stand-alone voice application exists to solve a consumer problem or meet a need. Think, for example, of Clubhouse, the audio-based social media platform. Or think of the many voice-based games you can play through Amazon Alexa or Google Assistant. Question of the Day, Assassin's Creed® Odyssey Spartan, and even classic game shows like Wheel of Fortune, Jeopardy, or The Price is Right are all examples of stand-alone games. There are also plenty of stand-alone voice experiences in the Amazon Alexa ecosystem that are not games, including skills that help a user listen to a radio station or podcast, convert measurements, access educational content, or stream music or provide the weather forecast and more.

As time goes on, we can imagine where businesses create voice experiences that work in concert with other technology and information to help you become more efficient with a recurring task (or even fully automate it). Imagine how useful it would be to be able to dictate your notes after a client meeting, perhaps in the car right after the meeting. Even better, imagine if you could have your meeting and a transcript was automatically generated using an AI-based voice app on your phone. This is possible today and is only the beginning of how voice technologies and AI will improve productivity in the years to come.

This type of voice experience is typically monetized by offering in-skill purchase opportunities of enhancements or access to premium content. In addition to generating revenue, many stand-alone experience creators have a secondary goal of increasing their user traffic and retaining their audience after the initial use.

Voice as a product vs. voice as part of a customer experience

Voice as a product

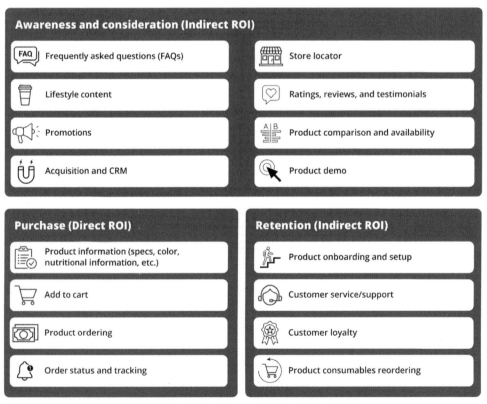

Tend to be stand alone experiences

- Education
- Games
- Utility
- Entertainment

Voice as part of a customer experience

Awareness and consideration (Indirect ROI)

- Frequently asked questions (FAQs)
- Store locator
- Lifestyle content
- Ratings, reviews, and testimonials
- Promotions
- Product comparison and availability
- Acquisition and CRM
- Product demo

Purchase (Direct ROI)

- Product information (specs, color, nutritional information, etc.)
- Add to cart
- Product ordering
- Order status and tracking

Retention (Indirect ROI)

- Product onboarding and setup
- Customer service/support
- Customer loyalty
- Product consumables reordering

Figure 6.1. Opportunities to use voice technology within your brand.

Voice as Part of a Larger Brand Ecosystem

When used as a brand touchpoint, voice can play a key role in building the brand image while driving your prospects down the path to purchase. It will rarely be the user's final destination, though it could be if the business offers a voice-based shopping experience. These applications likely won't replace an existing process but could provide an enhancement or a shortcut for the audience. Consider some of the ways that voice can be used to improve brand and channel experiences. Voice can:

- Make it faster for your audience to search for the product or brand information they're seeking, such as the McDonald's UK Amazon Alexa Skill we described in chapter 3. The increased search capability through voice applications is especially helpful during the awareness and consideration phases of the customer journey.
- Build the brand image and equity so the marketer can increase preference and eventually loyalty for the product and prospects can purchase it down the line. For instance, P&G created Chompers,[1] an Alexa Skill, for their Oral-B and Crest Kids brands. It not only got kids to brush two times a day and longer each time through the use of storytelling, but it also built a relationship with the parents who might then be more inclined to purchase the supporting brands when they needed toothpaste for their child.
- Speed up customer support by handling less complicated questions that don't require an agent's intervention. Think of the Butterball example we provided in chapter 1 or look to the Health-Care Perspective in chapter 10 for examples.
- Support sales by making it easier to find basic information that people need during the awareness and consideration phases of the customer journey.
- Provide an extra revenue stream through sponsored content within the overall customer experience.
- Drive sales through direct purchase or store locator/product lookup functionality. Again, think of the McDonald's UK ordering skill we described in chapter 3.

With that big duopoly in mind, here's a broad list of some ways your brand communication can use voice to make itself sharper and more engaging as well as speed up communications. Make your website voice enabled. The user experience of almost every website and mobile app can be enhanced with voice technology. According to the findings in the latest Voice Consumer Index, consumers are interested in using their voice to search, log in, and interact with various features of websites and mobile apps and even talk to a chatbot simply by speaking.[2] The biggest benefits are in speed of engagement, comprehension, and task completion. That's because you can:

- Optimize your web content to be found via a voice search. People tend to speak in complete phrases when using their voice to search, so you need to make sure that your website is optimized for not just keywords but long-tail phrases as well.
- Communicate promotional extensions to make them more compelling and easier to understand.

- Provide voice tools that interact with your physical product much like how Philips Signify Hue lightbulbs can be controlled from Amazon Alexa, Google Assistant, or Apple's Siri.
- Supply critical information about product use, like that found in the Amazon Alexa Lysol Skill.
- Provide a voice experience that allows you to place a new or repeat order, such as the customer experience applications at Domino's and Starbucks.

As you can see, there is a powerful collection of reasons to provide voice assistance internally as well as externally. Voice enhancements can have a powerful effect on consumer adoption rates. To start, go step-by-step through your customer's path to purchase to find the places where your voice enhancements belong.

Voice and the Marketing Funnel

The goals and KPIs that you establish for voice should be much like the ones you use with other marketing tools. For instance, if your goal is to convert top-of-funnel Amazon Alexa smart speaker searches into website users, you'll need to track how many people use your Alexa Skill and how many people are deep linked into your website—or perhaps how many people request links for more information. The amount of referral traffic from Amazon Alexa experience to your website is the KPI to keep an eye on.

If your product team has integrated voice assistance into your mobile app, you'll want to track how much more frequently your audience uses specific app features and if that increase leads to more engagement, measured by better customer-experience scores, an increase in product sales, or decrease in customer churn.

Finally, if you sell a physical product, provide your audience with a step-by-step, hands-free onboarding process that they can use while they're physically unboxing it. Maybe provide a step by step on how to set it up. It's the most useful kind of help and right when you need it most. And it probably preempts a lot of customer service requests (and can lower call center cost), some of which improve customer relationships, and some of which don't. So track to see if traffic to the help section of your website or the number of calls to your call center decrease.

At the end of the day, consumers are hoping to use your brand to solve a problem. In the 2022 Voice Consumer Index research, Scot and Susan Westwater of our team identified many of the behaviors of the voice consumer that all digital marketers will recognize. In their research, an overwhelming majority of customers (92%) were asking top-of-funnel kinds of questions, and 82% of voice users follow up the search by visiting the product's website or branded app.[3]

Some KPIs You Might Measure and Track

The KPIs you choose to track may also vary based on the characteristics of your segment, your brand goals, and the path to purchase that your prospects tend to take. Many marketers start with broad and obvious KPIs but get more specific and subtle with experience. A few of the common starting points include:

- Number of people who went from an Amazon Alexa–based experience to your website.
- Percentage of people who used your voice assistant on your website or within your mobile app.
- Number of people who used your voice assistant on your website or within your mobile app and made a purchase.
- Frequency of use of your voice experience.
- Repeat usage of your voice experience.
- Requests for more information.
- Increase or reduction of clicks to access a particular feature.
- Conversion rates as measured by CRM software.
- Changes in Customer Experience and Net Promoter scores.

If your goal is to drive more organic searches during the awareness or consideration phases of the path to purchase, then you'll need to optimize your web content for a long-tail search, with a large variety of phrases your audience uses when describing their problem or the task they are trying to complete.

There are specific voice tactics that can help move prospects down the path to purchase through the awareness, consideration, and retention portions of the path to purchase. Frequently asked questions may be a lackluster tactic in print or on a visually focused website but be much more compelling when you hear them spoken. Content, where you get an explicit spoken answer to a user-submitted question, can also be powerful. A step-by-step voice-driven product onboarding or troubleshooting experience can have a huge effect on retention. If you can hear as you are unboxing the product how to set it up or how to get it started, without having to read a manual or go off and view a video, that appears to transform the product-introduction experience. Offering product registration or (if appropriate) reminders to maintain a product can go a long way to providing user value and increase satisfaction of the brand.

Finally, voice can expand your revenue streams. However, it should not be thought of as a new revenue stream but as simply a new way to purchase or experience the brand. If you're a brand marketer, think about how the voice experience can impact the purchase. Voice can make the product information more dramatic, more persuasive, and easier to absorb. It can give product comparisons a visual and verbal impact like a video, but quicker. It can make purchasing and tracking the purchase as simple as verbalizing a request. Where it is possible to make a simple purchase your objective, you obviously have an instant, easily detectable, and highly persuasive KPI. In the cases where you don't have direct sales as your key objective, your KPIs would be determined by a measurable behavior that you want your prospects to exhibit.

Are Your Customers Familiar with Voice?

Understanding your customer's mindset and where they fall within our customer maturity model (we covered the customer maturity model in chapter 4) will give you a solid baseline to work from and help you focus your efforts on the things the prospect needs now and what they are willing to do in the future. How familiar and comfortable are they with voice assistance? How likely are they to do whatever you ask them to do? Voice is a newer kind of interface. There is the danger of overengineering—of trying to create something too complex for the unpracticed user. This approach will give you the best chance for immediate and long-term success.

It's also important to think about the handoff from one tactic or platform to another. How does the voice experience interact with other pieces of your marketing ecosystem? For instance, what is the next step your prospect takes after they find your product or service on their Amazon Alexa device? Does your prospect then go to your website on their smartphone? Do they look up price information on a phone and then request more information by email? What is the path? Where does the handoff happen, and can you help facilitate the handoff in the way that is most likely to lead to purchase (or whatever your desired behavior is)?

Second, how might the path be changed or shortened? As people get more comfortable using a voice interface, can you begin to move the actual purchase into it? You'll know more about this if you track frequency of use and the amount of time spent with your voice experience. You can even do some proactive research with members of your audience to determine which features you should include in a voice-enhanced experience and if they're ready to purchase in this way. Using these techniques is a quick way to understand the impact that voice can have on purchases. Is it because people are more engaged, or is it because they are not quickly finding what they want?

See if your research changes your perception of the path to purchase. It might be even more important to know how many times someone has requested more information and whether it was by email or through SMS. It might be more important to know how many times someone has been able to go to a website through a link that was triggered by a voice experience. A decrease in abandonments might be more important still.

In addition to the many owned opportunities we've identified so far in this book, voice-enhanced ads, while relatively new, can provide brands with a new and exciting way to reach and engage with their audiences. Interactive voice ads have already been used by brands such as Doritos, Ashley HomeStores, Unilever, Wendy's, Turner Broadcasting, Comcast, and Nestlé to engage with their customers in new and different ways. Now brands can place voice-enabled ads and carry out conversations with consumers using the consumer's natural language. With interactive voice adds, brands can connect with their customers and learn more about their needs directly within the ad unit. Once prompted, consumers can "ask the ad questions" to learn more about the product, request more information, and even make a purchase without ever leaving the ad. This can provide a better experience for the customer and yield a level of insight, engagement, and tracking previously unavailable to advertisers.

In summary, voice experiences can provide you with critical information about the awareness and consideration phases of the path to purchase, which might well be where the battle is won or lost. Voice experiences can drive lead generation and help close business deals. As an example, the Sonic Brand Answers Voice app, which Pragmatic Digital created for Sixième Son, does both.

Giving a Sonic Branding Agency a Voice

With the rise of voice-enabled devices like smart speakers, the concepts of audio branding and sonic identities have received increased attention. As brands see the rise of voice marketing, the power of having their sound and voice is gaining traction. However, even though there are iconic examples of powerful sonic brands like McDonald's, Netflix, MasterCard, and Intel, brands don't know enough about sonic branding to know where to start and whom to call.

In other words, the rise of voice assistants like Amazon Alexa and Google Assistant also created a new audience for Sixième Son, the world's leading sonic branding agency, an audience who was not as familiar with the concepts of audio branding and sonic brand systems. To take advantage of this growing interest, Sixième Son needed a bigger presence to help them educate prospective clients about the world of sonic branding. What better way than using a voice experience to deliver the content while showcasing their own audio or sonic branding system?

Sixième Son already had a fully developed content plan that used their website as well as social channels. Where appropriate, the team would provide content and talks to trade publications and relevant associations such as the American Marketing Association. The managing director of North America had even coauthored a book on the topic. However, when talking about sonic brand systems, it wasn't always easy to convey the impact of audio branding.

Knowing that brands were starting to pay attention to their voice experiences and that consumer adoption means a reach of millions, Pragmatic Digital recommended creating a voice application for Amazon Alexa and Google Assistant. Keeping in line with our mantra of starting small and building a foundation, the firm proposed a simple question-and-answer experience that included a lead generation component. Measurement objectives would be divided across three areas: user experience and engagement, search, and lead generation. A voice experience would enable prospective clients to learn about sonic branding while hearing how impactful it could be when applied correctly. It would also allow Sixième Son to begin staking a claim on relevant long-tail search phrases with audio content.

Working with the Sixième Son team, Pragmatic Digital identified the most effective content and the most asked questions by prospects and marketers. The original plan was to develop around fifteen responses, but after the first beta test, they quickly grew the amount to more than twenty responses.

With the conversational content in development, Pragmatic Digital turned their attention to how the experience would sound. With audio being so important to the experience, they collectively agreed that the experience needed its own voice to demonstrate the impact of thoughtful and deliberate sonic branding—and that the expertise was coming from Sixième Son. The team then discussed all aspects of the literal voice and tone so that they could create the right personality who could inform and help users.

After developing the system persona, the Pragmatic development team was fortunate to realize that one of Sixième Son's own team members had the voice they wanted. It helped that she was a trained singer, so she was no stranger to recordings or performing. Despite the pandemic keeping people out of studios, it was possible to get the recordings completed so that the project could keep moving forward.

The development team created a conversation flow that allowed the users to ask questions and request a link be texted to them for further engagement or information. There was a total of three options that were offered at different points throughout the experience. That enabled Sixième Son to include lead generation mechanisms that weren't too aggressive or conflicted with the voice app's helpful and informative persona.

During the early release, Pragmatic Digital found that even though the Sonic Brand Answers Voice app had a distinct voice from Amazon Alexa and Google Assistant, users were still not realizing that they were in a separate experience. To correct this situation, they needed to make it even more obvious that the voice experience was Sixième Son's. Employing "micro-melodies"—composed sounds to indicate that an action has been completed—and sonic signals—short audio pings that can act as prompts for users—that enhanced the user experience and demonstrated how an audio DNA could be applied across a range of channels, resulting in a more polished and richer voice experience. To experience Sonic Brand Answers for yourself, you can simply ask Alexa to "Launch Sonic Brand Answers" or tell Google Assistant to "Talk to Sonic Brand Answers."

 GUEST PERSPECTIVE

Some Notes on Recent Voice Research:
Listen to the Second Voice

Michael Brazeal

To be more strategic with your use of voice, the authorship team asked Michael Brazeal, who had recently retired as associate professor of marketing communications at Roosevelt University, to help summarize the recent academic publications regarding voice. We felt Michael was perfect for this guest perspective, because of his mix of practitioner and academic experience. In fact, before joining academia, Michael spent twenty-eight years in the advertising business, the last eleven as executive creative director at Grey Chicago, where he led a department of thirty art directors, writers, and producers and helped to manage the agency. His work includes national TV campaigns for car waxes and corn herbicides, shampoos and spice blends, fuel additives, fruit juices and food stores, drugstores, deodorants, and dotcoms, as well as internet marketing and sales promotion. His creative awards include the Addies, Tellies, Eagles, Towers, Windies, Louies, Mobius, and NAMA Gold. He is the author of RFID: Improving the Customer Experience. Mickey holds a bachelor's in journalism from the University of Nebraska and a master's in advertising from the University of Illinois. Here's what Michael found:

Voice, driven by artificial intelligence, creates a whole territory of human interaction. People who use voice applications for relationship management or marketing need to understand how to use it wisely. A look at some recent psychological and psycholinguistic research, and especially experiments with voice, can help.

Many psychology, sociology, and psycholinguistic researchers are concentrating today on an issue that challenges the use of AI with voice.[a] This brief summary will identify some new learnings, some concepts, and some obstacles you may not have focused on.

Consider an experiment: a controversial message is received by two groups. One group gets a written page. The other gets identical words in a voice recording. The first group has a pretty clear idea of what the message was. The second group also comprehends the message. But in addition, they know, or believe they know, something about the source. They know his/her age, gender, social class, perhaps nationality or ethnicity, perhaps education. They have a point of view about the source's personality and current emotional state. They probably have an opinion about both his intelligence and his honesty. They know these things with confidence enough that they are prepared to act on that knowledge.[b]

Sounds like an exaggeration, but it's been tested many times.

Think of spoken communications as composed of two channels. There is a lexical or semantic channel that delivers its message through the words it chooses and what they mean to the hearer, rationally and emotionally.

And there is a *vocal behavior channel*, which is entirely separate from the words. The human vocal folds produce changes in pitch, volume, timbre, timing, and tone. This little-studied channel is the primary vehicle for communicating and perceiving expressions of emotion and personality. Not the words, but the flavor of the voice—the sounds around the words, the sounds of an individual speaker. It is described by researchers as "paralinguistics" or "prosody." It is the primary tool people use to perceive remotely a speaker's gender, age, status, power, and culture. It is key to the hearer's perceptions of a person's emotions, mood, attitudes, and feelings.[c]

It is the basic human tool for inferring intelligence, which needs to be known but cannot be observed directly. It is central to how people judge honesty and as will be explained later, "humanity."[d]

Endless experiments have demonstrated that it is not the meanings of the words spoken that communicate the speaker's emotion, personality, and emotional state. If you show the written words to the receiver, they are able to draw only limited conclusions about the speaker's personality or emotional state.[e] Both are more clearly communicated by recorded speech. Interestingly, they are not communicated any better when the talking head is *visible*. It is the prosody that matters.[f]

At present, we don't understand very well at all how we actually express those things or how we decode the cues expressed by others. Most individuals don't have full voluntary control over the vocal personality they present or the precise tenor of the emotions they vocally display. Some of their emotional cues are considered and some are spontaneous. Personality cues are even less well understood. There have been many attempts at modeling the vocal cues. We don't know which cues are most important, and we don't know how they operate. But we absolutely, consistently make critical judgments based mostly or entirely on these paralinguistic expressions.[g]

Paralinguistics is also a big source of social cues. People see it as a revealer of whom you are talking to. Two key sortings happen. One is Us/Them. Are you or are you not a member of some self-defined group that I am a member of? It might be ethnicity or nationality or social class or region. A vocal accent is one of many sorters that almost everyone, including young children, is sensitive to. All of them affect social interaction. The other sorting is High Status/Low Status. "Social behavior is different from talking up than talking down. Different social perceptions, communicated by prosody, invoke different responses. It is important to understand that social differences inferred from speech are seen as real, unchangeable, and predictive. If I know how you talk, then I think I know what you'll do.[h]

Paralinguistic information is hugely persuasive. It is not an argument, so it doesn't produce a counterargument the way lexical messages do. It seems to increase the listener's confidence in their judgments, which enhances credibility. It is nonrational, which may make it difficult to attack. In a series of experiments, for example, persuasiveness of paralinguistic communications was not affected when respondents were told that the persuader was paid to persuade. In many cases, that might weaken a lexical persuasion.[i]

Studies say that perceived sincerity powerfully enhances prosody's persuasive power. Previous researchers had isolated three sources of perceived sincerity: visual cues (facial expression, etc.), lexical content cues, and paralinguistic auditory cues. But in comparative research, the paralinguistic auditory cues are far stronger than the other two.[j]

Psycholinguists study "complaint speech" as a speech behavior so emotionally transparent that it may help illustrate how paralinguistics works. In complaint speech, "tone of voice" and other prosody signals appear to have more impact than content. People who do not believe the lexical content are still persuaded to sympathize with the complainer, which is often the goal of complaint speech. Research on complaint speech is helping to identify, though not to quantify, paralinguistic techniques. And studies of complaint speech have pointed out specific paralinguistic techniques that appear to reduce effectiveness, perhaps because they seem less sincere.[k]

When we consider messages in a human voice, generated by artificial intelligence, we cannot entirely avoid questions about how people listen to and communicate with humans vs. nonhumans.

Anthropomorphism is the behavior of thinking of a machine as a person. It may have powerful effects on how the machine is listened to and responded to. Several researchers have suggested that paralinguistic information is what prevents anthropomorphism. Here is an oft-used example. Computer-generated prose, if read to you by a human, is assumed to be created by a human. The reading by a human apparently supplies the prosody that people use to accord humanity. Siri voices reading computer-generated prose do not produce this effect. They are not assumed to be created by a human. It is suggested that they provide less intonation, and less correctly applied.[l]

Now flip this and consider dehumanization. Psycholinguists say that, when we disagree with another person remotely, it darkens our perception of them. We may infer deficient mental capacity. We may dehumanize them—see them as not in the human family with ourselves. This is a long-standing issue in psycholinguistics; it gets modeled and measured and defined. Online exchanges, which empower quick, short, written-only exchanges of intemperate opinion, create an increase in this dehumanization behavior. But if you hear, rather than read the disagreer, something changes. The disputant's mental capacity seems greater. There is at least a little more acceptance of a differing opinion. There is even some attitude change, and there is measurably less "dehumanization."[m]

Effects of prosody appear to transform the learning environment. It has already been observed that prosody sends a flood of social signals. One cluster of studies suggests that social cues transmitted by vocal behavior produce a change in the learning situation. To simplify: the learner can interpret a classroom episode as an information delivery exercise or as social interaction. If it is seen as social interaction, then social conventions apply. The listener has an obligation to help the message make sense, with whatever extra effort it takes, in selecting, organizing, integrating, and encoding into memory. The alternative is to see the experience as an information delivery scenario, which triggers rote processes and a more mechanical level of involvement. And not as much learning gets done. Some computer interactions appear in some research to be perceived as social events, requiring social performance. But one powerful obstacle is the machine voice, which seems to produce the information delivery sequence of nonsocial behaviors.[n]

Another cluster of experiments proposes that, for a business, hiring a previously unknown person is primarily a paralinguistic task. Intellect is inferred and judged based on vocal cues. The hirer's perception of thoughtfulness, honesty, and human sympathy, the researchers suggest, is based on paralinguistic styles and behaviors.

In one representative experiment, a sample of managers is asked to evaluate a small group of prospects, based on each one's resume and statement of goals and intentions. Part of the sample got the information in its traditional form, in a written resume and a letter. Part of the sample got a voice recording summarizing the transcript and the candidate's goal and intentions. And a third section got the prospect's voice presentation on videotape. Candidates were evaluated on competence, intelligence, "thoughtfulness," and likeliness to be the hirer's choice.

The follow-up questionnaire and interviews found that hirers who got a written statement gave much lower scores on each measure than hirers who got the recorded voice presentation. The researcher suggests that those who got the written sample did not perceive clear differences in mental capacity, for example, among the respondents, which were apparent to those who got the voice sample. (The videotape sample produced scores that were similar to the audio recording, but slightly lower and less differentiated than the voice-only scores.) This is one of a series of experiments, but the results and conclusions were similar throughout.[o]

Another group of researchers is trying to clarify the mechanisms of paralinguistic communication by studying the "voice-selective" regions of the brain. Studies identify three cortical regions that respond strongly to human voice sounds but not to nonvocal sounds. The region's architecture parallels the part of the visual cortex involved with recognizing facial expressions. In early studies, *audio frequencies* in the voice appear to play a major role. Responses to high and low frequencies differ. Filtering or reducing the level of the vocal signal reduces performance on vocal perception tasks.[p] These are early studies, and in part, they show how little we know.

You will already be thinking about how this affects speech generated by AI, especially when it is used for managing brand relationships and interactions. Consider three possible concerns.

People who know they are talking to a machine may not respect the judgments or values the machine expresses. There's research on that.[q] For a small number of identifiable interactions, one could presumably hire an actor and get at least some of the prosody right. But you can't hire an actor to say all the possible things. If you use AI to generate responses to new customer speech, not previously anticipated, it is not clear that you can supply the paralinguistic component.

Generating "dead speech"—speech that has clear semantic meaning but is empty of prosody, creates a bundle of unproductive responses. An interaction with an uninfected human voice or with a mildly inflected "Siri's voice" does not trigger the rules of a social encounter with a human being. It removes the reflex to participate in comprehension and respond, to a person. It creates an "information transfer" situation, where only a limited and lower-level attempt is made at learning.[r]

But "deepfakes" are dangerous. If you know you are talking with a machine, whatever prosody is detected may be seen as dishonest. You can probably produce some artificial foolers. But if your deepfake has partial or temporary success, there is a risk of being seen as a fraudster. And right now, it seems impractical to produce a deepfake that could cover whatever topic a customer might bring up, with a credible paralinguistic message appropriate to all of those messages and to the brand. Humans practice inferring intelligence and intention and honesty and human values from messages in prosody all their lives. They will not be easy to fool.

*In the long run, it is going to be necessary that voice communications to people whose judgments we value contain appropriate messages in both the lexical **and the paralinguistic** channel. To create such messages, we need to know things we do not know now.*

a A. Garcia-Falgueras, "Psychology of the human voice." *Psychology and Behavioral Science International Journal* 11, no. 2 (2019): 1–3.

b J. Schroeder and N. Epley, "Mistaking Minds and Machines: How Speech Affects Dehumanization and Anthropomorphism," *Journal of Experimental Psychology* 145, no. 11 (2016): 1427.

c S. Johar, "Psychology of Voice," in *Emotion, Affect and Personality in Speech* (Springer, Cham, 2016).

d J. Schroeder, "Expressing Dissent: How Communication Medium Shapes Dehumanization and Attitude Change," *Advances in Consumer Research* 46 (2018).

e A. Kumar and N. Epley, "It's Surprisingly Nice to Hear You: Misunderstanding the Value of Talking (vs. Typing)," *Advances in Consumer Research* 46 (2018).

f R. E. Mayer, "Principles Based on Social Cues in Multimedia Learning: Personalization, Voice, Image, and Embodiment Principles," in *The Cambridge Handbook of Multimedia Learning*, ed. Richard E. Mayer (Cambridge University Press, 2014).

g J. Schroeder and N. Epley, "The Sound of Intellect: Speech Reveals a Thoughtful Mind, Increasing a Job Candidate's Appeal," *Psychological Science* 26, no. 6 (2015); and Johar, "Psychology of Voice."

h K. D. Kinzler, "Language as a Social Cue," *Annual Review of Psychology* 72 (2021).

i A. Van Zant and J. Berger, "How the Voice Persuades," in *Advances in Consumer Research*, ed. Andrew Gershoff, Robert Kozinets, and Tiffany White (2018).

j A. Barasch, J. Schroeder, J. Berman, and D. Small, "Sincere Persuasion: Cues in Language Used to Assess and Convey Sincerity," *Advances in Consumer Research*, Volume 46 (2018).

k M. Mauchand and M. D. Pell, "Emotivity in the Voice: Prosodic, Lexical, and Cultural Appraisal of Complaining Speech," *Frontiers in Psychology* 11 (2020).

l Schroeder and Epley, "Mistaking Minds and Machines."

m J. Schroeder, M. Kardas, and N. Epley, "The Humanizing Voice: Speech Reveals, and Text Conceals, a More Thoughtful Mind in the Midst of Disagreement," *Psychological Science* 28, no. 12 (2017): 1745–62; and Schroeder and Epley, "The Sound of Intellect."

n R. E. Mayer, K. Sobko, and P. D. Mautone, "Social Cues in Multimedia Learning: Role of the Speaker's Voice," *Journal of Educational Psychology* 95, no. 2 (2003).

o Schroeder and Epley, "The Sound of Intellect."

p P. Belin, R. J. Zatore, P. Lafaille, P. Ahad, and B. Pike, "Voice-Selective Areas in the Human Auditory Cortex," *Nature* 403, no. 6767 (2000).

q N. J. Fast and J. Schroeder, "Power and Decision-Making: New Directions for Research in the Age of Artificial Intelligence," *Current Opinion in Psychology* 33 (2020).

r Mayer, Sobko, and Mautone, "Social Cues in Multimedia Learning."

EXTENDED CASE STUDY

Allstate and Other Insurers

One of voice technology's strengths is it enables a customer to get the information they need anytime they want it, regardless of the time of day (or night) without having to dial a phone or wait on hold until an agent is available to help. When your company's success depends upon how quickly customers can get information and find a service agent, as it is in insurance, that strength can become a superpower. Based on this insight, Allstate Insurance took hold of the opportunity to capitalize on voice technology when it partnered with Amazon to create its own Amazon Alexa Skill.[a] Designed to help existing customers get basic policy information as well as to help prospective customers find an agent, the skill provides easy, hands-free access to information at any time of day to users.[b]

"Allstate has a history of innovation, and consumers expect that to continue from us," said Roger Tye, vice president of Digital and User Experience, Allstate Insurance. "Amazon's innovation with Alexa provided a great avenue for us to connect with our customers in a delightful way, providing them useful information when, where, and how they want it."[c]

While Amazon did much of the heavy lifting to develop the voice application, Allstate used its own internal data to predict how customers would engage with the voice application and what information the voice skill would be able to provide.[d] Once a customer opens the skill, they can find an agent using a zip code search, find their agent's contact information, or check payment due dates for their policies. Although these features and functionality are similar to what other early voice-adopting competitors have included in their voice experiences, Allstate views its Alexa Skill as a starting point with an eye toward future enhancements and even other voice platforms: "We'll use this initial experience to build out a road map," said Tye. "We will continue to focus on Alexa and other devices like it to be able to leverage technology we already built."[e]

Here are some of the things you can ask Allstate via Amazon Alexa:[f]

Customer with the enabled Skill: "Alexa, ask Allstate when my balance is due."

Allstate: "Your balance is due on Thursday."

Customer with the enabled Skill: "Alexa, ask Allstate to find me an agent in 78703."

Allstate: "The agent closest to the ZIP 78703 is Anita Paulihsee."

Customer with the enabled Skill: "Alexa, ask Allstate what my balance is."

Allstate: "Your balance for your auto policy is $120.95."

Allstate Insurance is not alone in its exploration of voice technology, as several other insurance providers, including Liberty Mutual as well as its subsidiary Safeco Insurance, Progressive, and Nationwide have launched voice experiences. For Liberty Mutual, the smart-home features of voice assistants made the voice technology even more attractive to them since they partner with connected-home companies like Nest. In fact, Brian Piccolo, the e-business manager of U.S. Consumer Markets for Liberty Mutual said, "When we thought of initial use cases, connection to smart devices definitely swayed our decision as we could envision a future where our skills will provide value not just to our customers, but to our connected home partners as well."[g]

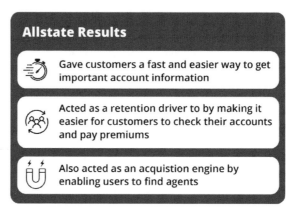

Figure 6.2. Some of the KPIs Allstate used to measure the success of their voice application.

Like Allstate, Liberty Mutual continues to test and use customer feedback to enhance capabilities and optimize the experience itself. Future functionality like quoting and loss prevention services are additional ways that voice assistants can help customers, which in turn, improves their brand experience. "Ultimately we will allow our customers to do business with us when and how they want," said Piccolo.[h]

[a] Speech Technology News, "Allstate Adds Alexa Voice Capability," published February 23, 2017, accessed February 19, 2022, https://www.speechtechmag.com/Articles/ReadArticle.aspx?ArticleID=116524.
[b] Danni Santana, "Customers Can Now Communicate with Allstate through Alexa," Digital Insurance, published February 23, 2017, accessed February 19, 2022, https://www.dig-in.com/news/allstate-gets-on-the-amazon-alexa.
[c] Allstate Newsroom, "Allstate Adds Amazon Alexa Capability," published February 22, 2017, https://www.prnewswire.com/news-releases/allstate-adds-amazon-alexa-capability-300411520.html.
[d] Danni Santana, "How Allstate and Liberty Mutual Got on Amazon Echo," Digital Insurance, published April 3, 2017, accessed February 19, 2022, https://www.dig-in.com/news/how-allstate-and-liberty-mutual-got-on-amazon-echo.
[e] Santana, "How Allstate and Liberty Mutual Got on Amazon Echo."
[f] Allstate, "Allstate Insurance Skill for Alexa," published February 2017, accessed February 19, 2022, https://www.allstate.com/alexa-skills.aspx.
[g] Santana, "How Allstate and Liberty Mutual Got on Amazon Echo."
[h] Ibid.

Developing Marketing Content for Voice

We've talked about how voice-activated technology works and the brand opportunities it holds. We have talked about voice marketing: how to establish your goals and track your KPIs, how to think through what your brand should sound like, and how to differentiate a brand in all the channels where there is no visual to work with. There is one more thing you need in order to drive success with voice.

It's the *content* you use.

In every channel, the marketer's primary goal is to deliver useful and usable information. *Useful* because it meets a need or helps the customer complete a task. *Usable* because it's easily understood and easily navigated.

Content is king. It is the connective tissue that ties together all your channels into a cohesive, consistent, and branded whole. When you integrate voice technology, you add new power, new clarity, new interactivity. But that does not change what a customer wants to know about or to accomplish with your brand's products or services. The first step to ensure that the experience you provide will be consistent across every channel is to make certain that your voice content is integrated with the rest of your marketing ecosystem and clearly expresses the same value proposition. Sounds easy, but it is also the easiest mistake to make. Lack of consistency or a disjointed experience will get in the way of building your brand image and your brand's relationships. It's a roadblock on the path to purchase.

So take a long, hard look. Make certain your voice content matches the messaging from your sales team and on your website and everything delivered through paid and earned

Voice First = Customer First

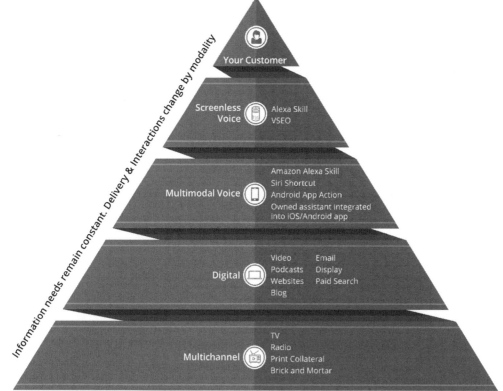

Figure 7.1. Solving for voice-only makes it easier to solve for other marketing modalities.

media channels. There will be executional things that change because of the device your customer is using. Devices without a visual component, for example, may need different expressions of your message to be clear and understandable. But the customer problems solved and the brand expressed must be the same in every channel.

When you're designing a website, you design the mobile version first (mentioned in chapter 2). The mobile environment has more constraints. So first you get your design and content to work in the mobile space, and then you enhance the experience for devices with larger screens and more computing capacity.

Just like mobile, voice-only experiences introduce their own set of constraints. When someone speaks with a smart speaker like Amazon Alexa, there is no screen. Photographs, illustrations, and infographics can't clarify your content. So it must be easily understood when read aloud, with no visual backup. You have to know exactly what information people need, and you have to understand how people process spoken messages.

But if you do a good job in the voice-only channels, you can make it significantly easier for your prospects to get the information they want and need and to give your brand the attention it wants and needs to move down the path to purchase. This is not news to anybody in marketing. But some brands are a lot better at it than others.

How to Write for Audio Only

In any situation where information is offered only in audio, you need to think hard about how people take in information. It has to be simple, direct, and clear because people don't have the luxury of jumping back a few words to see what they missed. They don't have the luxury of a photograph or illustration to complete or clarify the message.

"The most important point to keep in mind when writing for audio is to remain conversational, which means you must talk the way you'd talk with your friends over dinner, to your mom or dad on the phone or even to your kids in the car," says David Berner, a principle morning anchor at the top-rated CBS News Radio Network affiliate WBBM Newsradio in Chicago, during a Zoom conversation (personal interview, April 2022). Berner is also an associate professor at Columbia College. Chicago, where he teaches in the radio program, and he is the author of numerous award-winning memoirs. "Use simple, direct language, because for the most part, people are only going to hear it once."

To make sure your content is conversational, Berner suggests that you read it aloud. "If it sounds odd or clunky and it doesn't sound natural, then it's not going to work," he says. "People don't speak in full sentences. So you can speak in fragments—that's the way we talk. When I write, I say the words out loud because I can catch a word that doesn't fit next to another word, but looks fine in print or on-screen.

"And there are certain sound combinations that the ear doesn't like. It doesn't like 'Peter Piper picked a peck of pickled peppers' unless the use of alliteration is part of your shtick. It doesn't want to hear big words. The ear is not as forgiving as the eye. You could sit on a word for a few ticks when you read it in print. You can't do that with audio."

He says that how you deliver the words could change the meaning. "The fluctuation of how you say it, your tonal quality, and the amount of energy you use make a big difference in how it is perceived. A whisper can be extremely powerful in audio. Silence can be extremely powerful in audio." He suggests that you "read it to someone and if they ask, 'What did you say?' then it is not working. They're not getting the full message."

Berner recognizes that many people might be embarrassed to read their content aloud. If you are one of them, imagine the consequences of skipping this step. "Sometimes the actual act of reading out loud triggers students to talk to me like we are having a beer at a bar, and then it starts to click. But I still find students falling back into what they've written in an essay. They see it in print and use the same line for radio, but it doesn't work the same—it doesn't resonate the same. The minute it sounds forced, clunky, or too long—or the meaning is buried way at the end of the sentence—then it's not working."

Here's some more of Professor Berner's advice:

- **Put the attribution at the start.** "One of the biggest mistakes I see when people work in print or digital, and then move to pure audio, of any kind—is that they still think the attribution can come at the end of the sentence. 'The fire started at six o'clock in the morning, police said,' is fine for print, but it doesn't work for radio. 'Police say the fire started . . . ' is how I'd restructure the sentence to have the attribution come first." You can't put things at the *end* of the sentence that you needed to use to understand the beginning of the sentence.

- **Stop using dependent clauses.** Says Berner, "I don't want to see dependent clauses like 'After the rain fell, I walked the dog.' It is not a sentence we would say in conversation. It sounds clunky when it comes out of your mouth. So if you have more than one clause in a sentence, it probably needs to be rewritten. Not always, but double-check it. There are professional radio reporters who make this mistake over and over again. I see a lot of news stories that have something like: 'After the mayor held her news conference, she visited a church on the West Side. But we don't need to know that the visit was after the news conference. Nobody cares. And it lost the meat of what the sentence was supposed to be about. It pushes the meat to the end."
- **Use sensory language.** According to Berner, this is key. "You can do things you can't do in print or in digital. The spoken word is more powerful than what you read. Remember the songs that you love? You remember the words and the riff because it's powerful. The way it becomes emotive can't be done on a page. That's why you remember a song. That is why you remember the little lines from a famous speech. It's not by the way the words were written on the piece of paper. And descriptions of smell are the strongest," he says. "We remember things by smell more than anything else."
- **Avoid adverbs.** "I would rather see a good verb. I will get a piece of copy that says, 'he ran quickly down the street.' Let's change that to what he actually did. Did he jog? Did he sprint? Did he race? Usually, the verb is far more vivid than any adverb you can put in there. I don't want adverbs. They're usually not necessary, and there's usually a better verb."
- **Turn questions into statements, in your headline or your lead.** "I hate news stories and public service announcements that start with questions. You need to make people interested in a new car—not ask them if they want a new car."

Berner described his process for teaching people to write for radio, which could help anyone who is writing (or judging) audio content. "I have students turn off the computer and just tell me the story—just talk to me and tell me the story. They'll realize it sounds nothing like what they wrote, because that's not how you tell a story. Sometimes I get back short, choppy sentences. There's no flow to it. That copy is probably not good unless you are trying to create a character that has a sort of robotic voice—that's a different thing—but most people don't talk like that if they're having a dialogue with somebody.

"I see lots of dependent clauses, like: 'When it was 5:15 and I lived out in Missouri, when the sun used to shine, I walked my dog.' Since walking the dog is the most important part, it should be somewhere up front, not at the end. I see students who have come from schools where there is a strong English component to the curriculum, and they're writing essays that work fine on a page. But when you start to put it into speech, it's clunky and it's awkward."

Berner reports that he has had reviewers say that there is a rhythm to his writing in his book-length memoirs. "The reason why I have a rhythm to my writing," he says, "is because

I say it out loud. I read all my work out loud even though it's meant for the page. You don't know what that rhythm is, or how it feels, unless you say it aloud. I write for the page when I write. But I am constantly doing what a radio person would do. I'm reading it out loud. I want it to feel musical. Ulysses is a great piece of work, but it's one long sentence in a lot of places." If you want your content to feel comfortable, even online or on a printed page, follow Berner's advice.

The Next Step: Your Content Strategy

Once you have developed your audio-only content, podcasts and radio and the like, you can enhance it with more information for smart speakers with screens. You can enhance it even more for your website, brochures, in-store videos, and streaming or broadcast TV commercials. By identifying the core information needs of your audience, you can structure your approach across all the touchpoints. You'll find this "building up" approach is easier than starting with your most information-intensive elements and then paring back for voice-only applications.

To see the importance of creating content optimized for the voice environment, try this: Ask Amazon Alexa or Google Assistant for information on a major brand like GM or Coca-Cola, or even your own brand. Most likely, the information you get will come from Wikipedia. Currently, voice assistants draw from Wikipedia for product information or information about brands during a voice search.[1] Ask yourself: Do you really want your product or service information—*or your brand information*—to come from Wikipedia? Maybe you'd rather have that information come from your website. But that can only happen when your content is optimized for the voice-only environment.

After you have optimized your landing page content for voice interactions, optimize the FAQs (frequently asked questions) on your website. The trick for the FAQs is to use the actual questions your audience is asking via voice. Build on the foundation you have already established with iOS and Android applications. Identify those key questions, and write the answers to fit them precisely.

Your next step is to develop the content strategy beyond your basic brand messaging. Think of content strategy as a plan for how you will create, deliver, and govern the creation of useful, usable, effective content.

A well-defined content strategy can unify all your offline and online channels, while accommodating the different requirements and advantages of each one. It will help you provide the right message in the right place, at the right time, and—*in the right format.*

There are two ways in which your content strategy can help you better fulfill both the user needs and your brand consistency needs.

1. It defines the methods and style with which we deliver instructions and information important to the user, while reinforcing the personality of the brand.
2. It outlines the rules and guidelines needed to ensure consistency, clarity, and usability for each platform you use.

It's important to keep in mind that the content in a voice environment includes everything from the voice assistant's scripted responses to questions and information requests, and the information that fuels conversations within the brand's voice experience, as well as the visuals that accompany those conversations on every channel with visual capability. It may also include guidance about the conversation flow. Content strategy is the backbone of the whole conversation, because if the input and information is not correct, prioritized, and helpful, it doesn't matter how engaging it is. If it's not reflective of the brand, it can be confusing, ineffective, and even harmful. And if it's not consistent across channels, your message will be confusing.

Think of user interactions as the "front end." At the "back end" is the content structure that makes it possible for someone to ask a question or make a request that is accurately and promptly fulfilled. A successful voice experience must succeed at both ends.

Voice interactions bring a new dimension to brand management. Along with the brand's visual experiences, voice creates a direct expression of tone, personality, and style. It is important for voice and visual to complement each other. Consistency across applications is the rule, and the one exception is interactions in which the standard personality might be inappropriate. As an example, GEICO's Gecko presents a clear, cheeky, upbeat, self-aware style. In recruiting customers, it seems to be right on target. But if, for example, you had a roadside app to help a driver handle an accident, the Gecko might not be appropriate either as visual or as voice.

Tread carefully when you consider adding a *spoken voice* to a long-established brand icon. If this is the first time your icon will make an actual sound, you need to be cautious about casting that voice. Maybe your customers won't think your icon sounds like that. Another approach would be to select a complementary voice that coexists with the long-established icon. Then move toward the new voice as the sound of your visual icon, as prospects and customers get comfortable with it.

Whatever your strategic direction, make certain that your branding doesn't get in the way of the user being able to accomplish the task or obtain the information they need. For the marketer, that's not a new problem, but it's a somewhat different problem in the voice-only channels. Again, you might need to say things differently when they cannot be backed up or clarified with pictures or graphs and must be understood after a single hearing.

If your content makes good use of each different channel's different advantages, it will not be exactly the same across all the channels. Content across channels should feel related like cousins, not identical like twins. Your content strategy will unify the channels, while allowing for executional differences between them. And the way to unify content is with an understanding of the customer's needs, problems, and wishes and how your brand can meet the needs, solve the problems, and fulfill the wishes.

There's definitely discomfort among marketers who begin the process of developing voice AI. It's a newer technology. New skill sets to master. There's concern that it might be hard to do. Maybe there's not much new budget for this new opportunity. And nobody needs a big new task to make time for. You'll remember similar feelings from the early days of internet marketing and again in the early days of mobile marketing. But you're not starting from scratch. It's a controllable group of new channels among a broad spectrum of those you've already solved. If you need to know more about which content resonates, look to your audience for answers—via social listening, questionnaires, focus groups, one-on-one interviews, or a combination of these.

Development Tools for Voice Content Strategy

Voice enables us to address the customer's top tasks and needs and to directly and efficiently answer questions along the customer journey. The best approach, according to William Rosen and Laurence Minsky, in their book *The Activation Imperative*, is first to optimize the point of transaction and then work back to the top of the funnel.[2] That way, you bring more people down the funnel or path to purchase, and you have a better chance to convert them.

Next, inventory all your content. Then evaluate its quality. Content mapping, sorting your content to see how well you serve each segment of your audience or each stage of your path to purchase, might also be useful. Content inventory and content mapping provide a baseline that will help you plan and design your voice experience. A language audit of your customer base and possibly a data ontology study might help you decide how a skill's instructions and commands should be worded.

When multiple content creators are involved, you'll need an explicit set of guidelines for the development and governance of your content system. Its goals: consistent and repeatable messages. Elimination of unintended ambiguity. It also identifies decision-makers, so questions can be resolved quickly and confidently. A comprehensive style guide can help establish the brand personality and identify word-choice preferences. It can set standards that ensure accessible and inclusive language. This is the backbone of the content creation process because it ensures the consistency audiences expect across channels—including voice channels.

Once you understand your audience and how they go about using your brand to solve problems, once you are clear on your business plans and objectives, you can use them to build your voice strategy. Following is a framework for planning and creating useful, useable voice experiences.

Again, the first step is to identify your audience's key wishes, tasks, and information needs for each phase of the consumer journey. Use your findings to determine possible voice-use cases for each phase. Keep in mind the content you already have that does not need to be redone. Then prioritize what you need to create. Be sure your plans are always consistent with the brand's value proposition and its core strategy.

Often the priority phases of the consumer journey are *consideration* and *purchase*. But there are certainly times when the real issue is *retention*, or even *awareness*. You can use the framework with the traditional phases (*awareness, consideration, purchase, retention*), or you can tailor the phases to your own unique journey map.

Think of the opening portion of the framework as value proposition, core strategy, and the phases of the consumer journey that are to be included. Then work through the sections on each phase. Because you are focused on the voice user, start with their needs, tasks, and actions. This will help you to frame your content in terms of audience priorities, and that's the key to creating engaging conversations. Your audience research will help you decide how specific and detailed you need to be. Considerations include:

- **Audience goals** (What are they trying to do?) will inform the list of tasks for each phase.
- **Audience needs** (What do they need to be able to complete their tasks?) will inform the list of questions to be answered for each phase.
- **Audience behavioral goals** (What actions do we want them to take?) will inform the calls to action.

For example, under the awareness phase, the questions might be general inquiries from someone who was just learning about your brand or company, things like:

- Who is this company?
- What products or services do they sell?
- What makes them different?

Meanwhile, the tasks could be:

- Find the location nearest to me.
- Show me the company's product and service story on its website.
- Identify the existing content most relevant to me.

Finally, the call to action could be:

- Find the store, office, or restaurant nearest to me.
- Sign up for our newsletter.
- Read (or listen to) our latest blog post.

Notice that tasks in the awareness phase don't always line up with actions in the drive to purchase. Understanding the progression of phases can help you reframe your calls to action as you move the audience from one phase to the next.

Once the customer information has been mapped out (as above), then turn back to the brand and focus on:

- **Messages:** What brand messages align with the answers to the audience's questions during this phase?
- **Content:** What existing content can be used or leveraged, and what new content do we need to create?

A message "aligns" if it feels like the most relevant answer to the identified need or goal. It might say "Here is how to overcome X; the solution is Y." If you feel that you're force fitting a message that doesn't align directly with user needs, go back and try again. If it feels like a stretch at this stage, it won't feel better during the actual experience.

The result of this exercise should be the identification of the specific actions and tasks for each phase of the journey. It will help you focus your journey phases and identify the content that makes sense in each one.

Your next step is to assess your existing content to determine what might work at each phase. Look closely at effectiveness and consistency. This content will provide a starting point. But keep in mind that you'll need to revise it to work in a voice-only experience, just as you wouldn't copy and paste a brochure section onto a web page.

Here, for example, is a list of some possible existing content that might be adapted to fit in your awareness phase:

- Company brand video
- Commercials for radio and television
- Digital advertising assets
- Sales training materials
- Parts of a call center script
- Press releases or analyst briefings
- Blog posts and articles
- Store list

All of these can help tell the company's story and differentiate its brand. You may find you have a lot more content than you expected. But you may also find that some phases don't have much content at all, or that some important customer needs or questions haven't been answered at all, or that the answers given don't match your current best thinking. Prioritize your content gaps—and fill them.

With the questions, tasks, calls to action, and content needs determined, you can now begin to identify where a voice application might improve an experience or speed the path to purchase. It won't make sense for everything. But what are the possible use cases? You could, for example, solve for someone wanting to talk to an associate to learn more about the product by creating a simple question-and-answer experience that can live on Alexa and Google Assistant. Or maybe there's a relevant "how-to" angle, with a guided activity or tips of the day to fuel a flash briefing. It could even be your podcast content.

Add to your use cases a section on technical requirements and considerations. Here you list the technical needs required to support each of the voice use cases. This will help you understand which content tactics would align with the crawl/walk/run evolution of the voice experience. Something might seem simple as a use case, but when its processes are analyzed, you might find that three different back-end systems have to talk to each other for the solution to work. But once you know the tech requirements, you start to build your road map for development.

By now, you have a lot of information with which to form your strategy. You can see where the content gaps are and the content that needs to be replaced. You have some use cases for voice. At this point, think about why you have so much content in one phase and so little in another. Is your team creating content that answers all the key prospect questions, or are you creating content out of habit. Some marketers find that they're heavying up on content to drive conversion in the purchase phase but maybe aren't doing enough during consideration or retention.

Whether you have focused on one phase of the customer journey or have decided to get a full, holistic view, by now you will have a spreadsheet full of information and possible

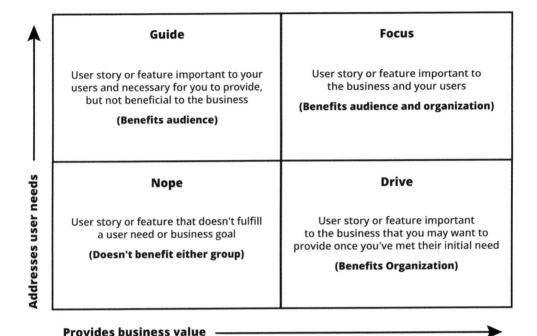

Figure 7.2. Adapted from Meghan Casey's great book *The Content Strategy Toolkit*, this chart can help you prioritize your overall content developed as well as the specific content and features within your voice marketing program.

use cases. The natural, sane response would be that there is no possible way to do all the things that you've uncovered. Now it's time to prioritize your content development. Consider the template developed by Meghan Casey, in her book *The Content Strategy Toolkit*.

The template prioritizes your use cases on two axes: user needs and business value. It divides the space into four quadrants: high and low on each axis. You'll find that it helps you prioritize tactics in terms of what's most valued by the business and the user, rather than falling into the "wouldn't it be cool" category, all too common with new marketing technologies. It also lets you zoom in on what's most critical for your unique situation. And it's great for settling arguments. When you prioritize, you end up with four distinct groups.

1. **Focus:** Rated high in user need and high in business value. Here, you would place tactics that drive purchase or brand conversion, but also anything that will have high impact on both users and the business. These are the content ideas of highest priority.
2. **Drive:** These are tactics that have somewhat lower user need but higher business value. This could be features or content that you can point the user to once you've met the initial need that brought them to you in the first place. It might be an upsell or additional ways to use the product. Something that wouldn't drive initial purchase but will help continue the relationship.
3. **Guide:** High in user need but not so high in business value. This could be something that explains the terminology or provides your audience with information that

helps them move from awareness to consideration. Or it could simply be instructional content

4. **Deprioritize:** Low in business value and low in user need. But this might be something required for legal compliance or corporate policy. Also called *nopes*, you'll want to deprioritize focusing here because you'll want to keep development efforts to a minimum with this kind of content. Try not to say yes to a lot of the nopes.

With the worksheet and the prioritization done, you've got the makings of a robust road map. Together, they paint a picture of what aligns to business goals, what aligns to customer needs, and what's going to improve employee productivity and the customer experience.

GUEST PERSPECTIVE

Content That Keeps Them Coming Back

Sarah Andrew Wilson

It's easy to create a one-time experience, but how do you keep prospects and customers coming back for more in a voice environment? To find out, we asked Sarah Andrew Wilson, who is the chief content officer at Matchbox.io and has been named an Alexa Champion by Amazon, a Top 12 Voice AI Leader by Voicebot.ai, and a Top 40 Voice Influencer by SoundHound. Today Matchbox.io has twenty popular voice applications on Amazon Alexa, Google Assistant, and Samsung Bixby, including award-winning games, utilities, and educational and wellness voice apps. Here's what Sarah had to say.

"Content. Content. Content."
"Content is king."
    These phrases are familiar to anyone in marketing and are especially important when it comes to smart speakers and other voice assistants. Without visual reminders, beautiful graphic design, tools like digital bookmarks, and buttons to select or swipe—components that customers have come to expect when interacting with a brand online—it's easy for a smart speaker owner to use a voice experience once and then forget about it and never return. But if you create an engaging, interactive audio experience with content that's refreshed regularly, you can help your brand stand out and help your customers want to return for more.
    When smart speakers were new, tech-savvy developers jumped on the chance to figure out the new technology and raced to build the first experiences for these platforms. These early voice applications were very simple, one-time experiences. For example, an Alexa Skill named Jurassic Bark offered five different recordings of a dog barking; you would say, "Alexa, open Jurassic Bark," and you would hear a random track of a dog's bark. It was cute and fun and something that perhaps you'd share with your friends during a visit. But it wasn't necessarily something you'd want to return to again, day after day, month after month.
    At Matchbox.io, from our very beginning in 2017, we recognized the opportunity to build voice applications with retention in mind. After all, Amazon, Google, and other companies didn't want their customers to buy a smart speaker only for it to become an expensive paperweight. They wanted their customers to use the smart speaker over and over. So at Matchbox, we asked ourselves, *What can we build that would offer a reason to return, day after day?*

The answer we came up with: Every day, offer brand new, high-quality interactive audio content that doesn't take too much time to consume. The daily content needed to be helpful, or fun, or ideally, a combination of the two.

So we launched a few Alexa Skills that had retention techniques built in, among them, Question of the Day and Daily Poll. These were brief but engaging experiences that lasted between 60 and 120 seconds and allowed users to interact with content we created through their smart speakers. We watched the analytics carefully to learn from our users.

- *How many people were trying the skills? How many returned to use them again?*
- *If a user dropped out before finishing the experience, at what point did they drop out? What was happening at that point? Could we tweak the content or the conversation design to prevent drop-off?*
- *Did certain topics affect retention? Would a question about, say, movies inspire someone to return the next day, more than a question about history?*
- *What was happening month to month? How many people were still using the skill a month after trying it for the first time? Was there another drop-off point with returning users before the thirty-day mark? What could we do to prevent that?*

Of that first batch of Alexa Skills, Question of the Day (QOTD) quickly gained traction. The idea that trivia could be educational seemed to resonate with users, and the question-and-answer format was straightforward. Users were presented with a new trivia question every day—one day's topic might focus on history, while the next day's topic might be science—and regardless of whether the user answered correctly, QOTD provided a two-to-three sentence factoid to help the user learn more about the topic.

We also made sure to gamify the experience, allowing users to earn extra questions, collect points, and compete against others on national and regional leaderboards. We kept it fun, not too easy, not too hard, and with a wide enough range of topics that everyone could find success.

Okay, so we built a successful trivia game. What then?

That's when we looked for additional ways to attract new users as well as to expand on the user experience. *What more could we provide Question of the Day users? What were they seeking? And how could we further use the massive amount of content we had created?*

We launched Facebook and Twitter accounts, once again focusing on content so that we could interact with users directly. We posted FAQs, answered inquiries, and started posting new content to our social media accounts every day—content that was related to the Alexa Skill. (Our QOTD social media pages now have over 20,000 followers.) We learned a lot from our users through social media. For instance, we learned that some wanted longer-form content that they could read to learn more about each day's topic. Others wanted a kid-friendly version, while others wanted a longer experience over their smart speakers.

Using these valuable insights, we built and launched Kids Quiz, an age-appropriate Alexa Skill with different levels, for ages five through twelve. Users could trust that Kids Quiz would have the same high-quality content as Question of the Day, and they knew they could trust us with their kids' attention. For these reasons and more, Kids Quiz soon became one of the most popular Alexa Skills for kids.

Then, expanding our content even further, we launched a Question of the Day–related daily podcast, website, and mobile app. (Yes, we launched all three within six months of each other. Whew!) We hired the best of the best for the podcast: co-hosts Murray Horwitz and Tamika Smith and producer Suraya Mohamed all worked for National Public Radio and had two Peabody Awards and a Tony Award among them. From their years in radio, they knew how to create high-quality engaging audio content. For each four-minute episode, it was decided that Murray and Tamika would discuss each day's question in a fun and entertaining conversation that would be part of the QOTD experience on Amazon Alexa. The podcast would also be available on all major podcast platforms.

Our website AskQOTD.com would provide even more content about each day's topic. If the QOTD was a geography question about the capital of a country, we'd include a few paragraphs about the history, culture, and food of that country, along with a map and photos. If the QOTD was movie related, we'd tell you the backstory of the film, with perhaps an excerpted video or stills that showed a crucial scene from the production.

And our mobile app, Socratix, would further expand the reach of our content from the smart speaker experience, now with eye-catching graphics and touch-and-swipe functionalities. Users would be able to read and hear the question and possible answers, play the game through touch, view who they're competing against, track their game stats, and interact with additional premium content. Plus, they could sync their Amazon Alexa or Google Assistant account, access the AskQOTD.com website, and listen to the podcast, all from within the mobile app.

By focusing on creating high-quality content that users found interesting, using multiple platforms to deliver our content, and listening to and learning from our users, we now have millions of fans around the world.

Users can access our fun and educational content in whatever format they prefer: through their smart speakers, in online articles, on social media, through a podcast, or in a mobile app. And we cross promote to help promote the discovery of our content. For example, podcast listeners are first prompted to check out our Alexa Skill, while folks searching the internet will come across our website, where they're encouraged to check out our mobile app and podcast. And our Facebook followers are directed every day to our website to read more about each day's topic. It's all essentially the same content, just presented differently in each format.

My message to voice tech newbies is this: It's understandable that companies new to the voice-first world don't know where to begin. It can feel strange not to use a screen. But remember to view the technology as just another way to reach your customers. Voice makes it easy for customers to interact with your brand and becomes one of many ways to deliver information customers are seeking. The voice technology infrastructure is here and ready to be used to reach customers. You just have to provide the content.

EXTENDED CASE STUDY
Dominos

When a brand's success is based on the consistent simplicity of its product and the speed of its delivery, one would think its innovation efforts would be focused on just that: product and delivery. Instead, Domino's Pizza has always been a trailblazer, finding ways to innovate all across the delivered fast food category. Starting with the revolutionary pizza tracker, Domino's saw another opportunity for innovation that would make ordering faster and easier, using voice.

"Our online orders regularly exceed 70 percent of network sales, with more than two million pizzas and sides ordered online every week. So, it's important that we continue to innovate in this space. We pride ourselves on introducing new technology that will not only make our customers' lives easier, but make the entire experience more enjoyable," says Michael Gillespie, chief digital officer, Domino's Pizza.[a]

In October 2014 (B.A., or Before Amazon Alexa), Domino's started its foray into the world of voice technology, when they made it possible to order through its virtual pizza assistant, Dom, through a mobile device.[b] Dom was a voice-enabled chatbot that allowed customers to place orders hands free through dictation.[c] Dom quickly became a popular method for ordering pizza, and by the end of 2014, 500,000 orders had been placed through it.[d] When smart speakers started to gain popularity, Domino's expanded Dom's world in February 2016 and introduced an Amazon Alexa Skill that would allow consumers to order a pizza. By the end of 2016, about 20% of all Domino's sales went through Amazon Alexa.[e] Domino's has continued to innovate in ordering methods so that there are now more than ten different ways to order your pizza (including smart TV, Twitter, and from your car),[f] but it all started with Dom and voice.

To achieve this success, Domino's had a clear voice strategy. And it remained true to its reputation for delivering innovation and creative solutions that don't forget about the brand. Since Domino's is known for using technology to give users new abilities that are both useful and fun, there was a need for the assistant to be more than just an automated ordering line with a disembodied voice. The result was a voice assistant that is more than an order taker. It can also recommend additional items and help customers locate deals or coupons—all with a personality that was distinct to the Domino's brand.

Working with their agency CP+B and Nuance, Domino's made Dom into a fun, clever personality, with tons of emotive expressions, thousands of things to say, and answers to a lot of relevant questions. They even gave Dom a visual identity as a happy and hopping microphone with a Domino's cap, seen at touchpoints where visuals were deliverable and appropriate. It was important that Dom's personality reflect the Dominos brand, initially to set it apart from the automated service lines that customers associate with interactive voice response systems. That personality became more important, though, as Dom expanded into other voice platforms like Amazon Alexa, which have personalities of their own.

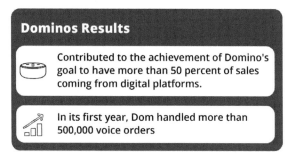

Figure 7.3. The results Domino's achieved through their pioneering voice-enabled ordering assistant.

To ensure that Dom did not go unnoticed, it was featured as the centerpiece of an integrated campaign supporting the launch. The PR buzz was so strong that even before the TV campaign aired, Domino's had already received 200,000 orders through the voice-controlled, pizza-ordering sidekick. In addition to TV, the campaign included online video and social content. There were even talking apology cards, to be sent to those who didn't have a favorable experience during Dom's beta phase, as part of the "Dom is Sorry" consumer outreach component of the campaign. All the components worked together to drive those first customers to use the voice experience.

Multiple iterations and optimizations have been made to Dom. There is a continual improvement in the experience. And the customers' needs remain the driving component of the process. Domino's continues to look for ways to use technology to keep the brand relevant and a part of customers' lifestyles. Their commitment to on-brand fun and useful ways to deliver the customer's pizza needs is what keeps those customers coming back for more.

[a] Amazon Web Services, "Domino's Pizza Enterprises Delivers in Record Time Using AWS for Predictive Ordering," 2020, https://aws.amazon.com/solutions/case-studies/dominos-case-study/.
[b] Alex Samuely, "Domino's Voice-Activated Ordering Assistant Tops Half-Million Orders," *Retail Dive*, published 2017, accessed February 20, 2023, https://www.retaildive.com/ex/mobilecommercedaily/dominos-mobile-virtual-ordering-assistant-dom-tops-half-million-orders/.
[c] Mike Gunderson, "How Domino's Pizza Changed the Way Consumers Order Food," *Respond Fast*, published April 14, 2020, accessed February 20, 2023, https://respondfast.com/2020/04/14/how-dominos-pizza-changed-the-way-consumers-order-food/.
[d] Gunderson, "How Domino's Pizza Changed The Way Consumers Order Food."
[e] Ibid.
[f] Ibid.

The Advantage of Marketing the Voice Experience

As marketers, we all know that if our intended prospects don't know about something, they will never find it. Brands can't rely on customers simply discovering the products and services they provide. Beyond old-school interruption advertising, this also applies to brand communications and related brand experiences—especially when they are built using innovative approaches and technology. Within the voice marketing community, there has been a lot of focus on the concept of discovery and helping audiences discover voice experiences and the features and functionality they offer.

When authors Susan and Scot Westwater first created their process for creating useful and usable voice experiences, they only had three steps mapped out—1) discover, 2) design and develop, and 3) launch and iterate. They quickly came to learn that while consumers are adopting voice-enabled devices, especially smart speakers, they didn't know all the different ways to use them. As with any new technology, discovery and adoption of the applications require a detailed launch plan and support to introduce and train users on why they are valuable and how to use them. So they added an additional step to the process—launch and promote—to account for the planning, promotion, and support needed to generate the awareness required for success.

The concept of discovery has been cited as a core issue when it comes to finding and enabling voice experiences on smart speakers, and there has been much discussion around exactly whose responsibility it is to support it. Some folks feel that Amazon and Google should be leading the charge. It can be argued that they have, though, as in the 2021 Voice Consumer Index, 97% of respondents in all three markets (United States, United Kingdom, and Germany) indicated that they had some familiarity with voice and voice assistants. However, in that same research, respondents were asked how they found voice experiences, and the overwhelming majority, over 70% of respondents in all three markets, said it was through trial and error.[1]

So if most people know about voice, how can there be a discovery problem? Perhaps we should start with the term "discovery" itself. Discovery as a concept evokes the idea of waiting for someone to happen along and find something, which is a passive way to think about something that has been researched, built, tested, and launched with some effort and resources. As we all know, hoping for someone to find you is not an effective strategy (if you want to call it a strategy at all). Instead, if we took the approach of savvy marketers, we'd focus on what we can control, and that is driving awareness and usage. When it comes to voice experiences, that is no different from all the ways that we have had to introduce new technology, such as websites, social media, and mobile apps. All of these have required some form of marketing support. So while there has been a path down to creating the right experience for the right audience and delivering the right content, there is also a need to have a thoughtful marketing plan that focuses on creating awareness and driving traffic to the application.

Traffic and usage are key not just to be able to tell the ROI story but also because they are necessary for any viable iteration and optimization approaches. Quite simply, if you do not have enough people using your experiences that you can learn from how they are behaving, what they are interacting with, or what they're looking for, there won't be a large enough sample size for analysis, optimization, and enhancement. We talk more about the process of analysis and optimization in the next chapter.

Looking back to that research from 2021 asking audiences how they were learning about new voice experiences, there's good news and some not-so-good news. When we look at that trial-and-error number, the good news is audiences are so interested and committed to using voice that they are willingly seeking out those experiences. The not-so-good news is that they are resorting to doing the seeking themselves. Part of this is due to a lack of awareness of voice experiences. Advertising and promotion were mentioned by 51% of respondents from the United States, 44% from the United Kingdom, and 53% from Germany, according to the 2022 Voice Consumer Index.[2] The reality behind these numbers is that many brands aren't providing the guidance and support their audiences need to let them know about the branded voice experiences that exist. Aside from large-scale campaigns that have used Super Bowl TV commercials like the one mentioned in the Coca-Cola case study or the way Roomba's commercials feature its voice-enabled functionality, marketing support for voice experiences is not plentiful.

What this means is that there is a lot of white space to promote your voice experiences with your brand. Audiences want to use voice to find information and help them move on with their tasks. But right now, brands aren't providing a lot of guidance and support to let them know that these voice experiences exist. And that's a huge opportunity for you and your brand to win the hearts of current and new customers.

Leading the way for new technology is a double-edged sword. The upside is that your brand is leading the charge and setting itself apart as innovative and modern. The downside is that you will need to not only promote your brand and experience but also tell audiences how to use that technology.

This is not a new challenge though. The same had to be done for social, mobile, and even the web. One of our authors was working with a major consumer packaged goods company back in the late 1990s when the web was just taking the world by storm and people were learning how to use it to market and not just create simple brochure-ware sites. At the time, she had a senior brand manager for a very large brand who was questioning why a website was necessary and on top of that, why it would be necessary to include the URL of that website on all packaging and the other marketing materials. The brand had a sizable budget, so this was really a question about the viability of the web. Of course, thirty-plus years later when typing in a website is second nature, it seems silly, but at the time, the team had to fight to get a website created and then get that URL put on product packaging because they needed to use every paid, owned, and earned channel to drive traffic. There were messages everywhere: use our website, go to our website, look at our website, here's what you can do on our website, etc. With that effort, it became clear that if we didn't tell our audiences where to go and why, many would not have bothered to find out for themselves by visiting it.

So when it comes to introducing the new technology, there is a need to be intentional and clear to your audiences on how to use it and why. We take it for granted right now that we just say go to our website and users automatically know to get there. When it comes to introducing the voice platform into your marketing ecosystem, it's not enough to simply say we have the experience. That's because the understanding of how to engage and work through voice experiences is not uniform. Therefore, a two-pronged approach is needed. The first part will be explaining why the brand has created this voice experience and how to use it. It's critical to provide the information. But you must also deliver in the brand's marketing messages the benefits and value propositions of using the voice application. Having the two pieces of information in an element means that the content will need to work harder. First, you must figure out the proper hierarchy, because it's carrying the load of two separate messages: one is all about your branded experience and what makes it relevant and great and the other, with the user instructions. It's important to do this because this is what's going to make it possible for someone to go and use your voice experience. This is where a brand is saying, we've created this voice experience, and it's a part of our brand family to make it easier for you to purchase our product and engage with it.

To take advantage of the "news" that comes with launching your new voice experience (as well as launching significant feature releases), you should concurrently create a promotional plan while developing the voice application and any upgrades. Use a launch to reach out to customers and show them you care about their experience and are actively working to improve it every day. There are several approaches that can be taken depending on the audience you're reaching.

Just as there are two key pieces to the marketing messages, there are two phases to the marketing plan itself. One is the launch, which is that great introduction when you'll want to dedicate your efforts to heralding the launch of the voice experience. Since it is an introduction, the plan should be integrated so there are tactics outside the voice channel. Of course, there are strategies for driving awareness among voice assistant users by communicating features and functionality within the description, but it's also important to go outside the voice channel to attract new users and drive them to your voice application such as mentioning the assistant on your packaging.

Launch is important since it announces the availability of the new experience audiences can use. But after launch, it's important to continue to remind folks about the voice experience and to use it. It's going to take some repetition to create the habits that drive usage and engagement. Oracle found in their research that consumers use an average of about six touchpoints when making a purchase decision.[3] While it's helpful to have, it doesn't mean there needs to be a dedicated ad campaign that runs for months and months. It means that after launch, there needs to be a plan for integrating this voice experience, just how you drive to your website, customer support, and even in store. The goal of any marketing support for a voice experience is to make it a part of the larger brand ecosystem and to drive usage. To achieve that will require sustained reinforcement. Launching and leaving it, so to speak, is not an option.

It's also important to remember that the voice experience isn't a silo. It needs to be part of the family and work with all the other marketing efforts in play to have the maximum impact. One aspect of this inclusion is making sure that there are cross-references across the various brand touchpoints that mention voice. Another is shared branding. As mentioned earlier in this book, a brand's sonic identity isn't just for radio and television advertising. Voice experiences can and should use a brand's sonic identity so that there is not just integration with messaging but also the branding itself. The more connective brand tissue there is, the more holistic and consistent the brand expression becomes to their audience.

Voice applications are not meant to replace existing customer experience channels outright. Voice can enhance a customer experience, but it doesn't replace others. That is up to your users and audiences. By offering voice, we are giving users an easy, helpful, and potentially faster way to do things, and although we will help customers find and use voice, we'd never advise forcing them to use it. Think of voice as way to enhance your already robust marketing ecosystem by working in concert with existing touchpoints, not as a replacement for them, especially when you have a loyal user base.

The other part of marketing your experience is ensuring that you're driving not just any traffic but the right traffic. Every marketer knows it's impossible to be everything to everyone. Just as the voice experience itself wasn't created for just any person, you wouldn't want to market it to just any person. Starting with the brand's audience personas or the voice user personas, you can create campaigns that target those intended audiences and drive them to the voice experience. You want to make sure that you're driving your ideal audience members to your experience so that when they find the information needed to make a purchase decision, they will make the transaction you're looking to expedite and facilitate. So that campaign is going to involve working with your existing customer journey, your personas, and a lot of the other things that you've already established as part of your brand's marketing strategy. This will ensure you are driving the proper traffic, getting the right usage, and then using that information to optimize and iterate the experience so that it's even better the next time someone comes back to it.

Ninety percent of customers expect consistent interactions across channels.[4] Therefore, it is important that a voice experience is on brand and consistent with the established ontology and language used elsewhere. If it isn't, customers won't recognize it as part of your brand so it doesn't feel genuine, authentic, or part of what your brand is. So while it's not specifically part of brand marketing, it is important to ask these questions during the development of the voice experience:

- Does this look like it's part of the brand family?
- Does this sound like the brand persona that's been established in other channels?
- Does this feel like a genuine extension of the customer experience?
- Are the behaviors we're driving with voice a natural evolution of how someone would engage with the brand?

If you look at your marketing campaigns and it sticks out or it doesn't seem to match, that's another good moment to check your gut and take a very critical look at what you are launching. While you can make incredible inroads using voice experiences, if they are not done properly, they can damage a customer relationship.

We would be remiss if, in a marketing chapter, we didn't talk about paid, owned, and earned and at least give a high-level discussion about how you can leverage each of these in your marketing efforts. Consider:

- **Paid** is probably the easiest one to get a handle on, and that's when you're paying for access to your audience. That could be digital media, such as banner ads or paid social posts, sponsored content, TV spots, or radio ads.
- **Owned** is any property that you as the brand owner physically have control over. So that's the brand website, product packaging, email, any organic social posts, and even owned podcast content.
- **Earned** media is probably the easiest to think of as public relations. That's where you are physically using other people's properties or voices to get your message out to your audience. Tactics will include any placement and magazine articles, any interviews, and any podcast appearances, which would be considered earned media. Placements from strategic partnerships—website mentions or inclusion on their social content, for example, would also be considered earned media.

If you are creating an Amazon Alexa Skill, make sure that you don't overlook the "store" description. Just as app store descriptions can impact how easily an app is found, the voice application description also plays an important role. Speaking of app store descriptions, if you integrate a voice assistant into your mobile app, make sure to talk about it in the release notes and app store descriptions too. Voice assistant users read the descriptions and pay attention to the reviews. It's worth the extra effort to create a description that provides users with the information they need to know why they will want to use the voice application as well as how to use it. So make sure that you have a description that aligns with keywords or key phrases that would be used in a search of finding something relevant. Go beyond the standard "get answers to commonly asked questions" type of language and go a level deeper. Also, include the various additional invocations to make sure users know how to launch the voice app. And finally, use the example commands and phrases to show what functionality and features are available so that it's clear to the user what they can (and cannot) do.

Website and email content provide opportunities to not just promote a voice application but to also provide a bit of user onboarding. Onboarding should be in the application itself, but with deep linking opportunities and such, it's important to look outside the voice experience to attract those new users. Landing pages are especially good to help your audience learn about voice and how to use it. It's just not enough for a brand to provide the voice experience that helps solve customer problems and meet information needs; it also needs to provide a sustained marketing campaign to make their customers aware that the voice application exists, help onboard them, and ultimately get them to use and then reuse the experience.

An Example: Promoting the Food Network Kitchen Voice App

The Food Network designed its Food Network Kitchen app as a multimodal experience that could work on Amazon Fire TV, Alexa Echo Show, Google Nest Hub, and several other devices. To fully support it, they needed to explain the app and where it was available. As a result, they used a combination of paid, owned, and earned tactics to get the word out to all their audiences. They ran social ads and, in partnership with Amazon, also were featured in the Amazon newsletter and elsewhere like trade and consumer publications.

In their ad creative, the Food Network also integrated the various devices so the breadth and depth of all the ways someone could use the app were clear. So in their TV spot, there was an Amazon Echo show, a Google Nest Hub, and then a mobile tablet that showed how it all worked on their own website for Food Network Kitchen.

To get people to engage, they also offered a complimentary, one-year subscription to the Food Network Kitchen app. The offer was mentioned in blogs, social, and in any press coverage as well as on television. This integrated approach generated excitement so that when the voice application was ready to launch, they had a user base who was ready and willing to use it. The result was adoption and social proof from actual users. With twenty to forty reviews serving as an acceptable amount in the Amazon Skill Store, the Food Network Kitchen app had over 150[5] as well as hundreds of thousands for their Fire TV app. Since, hundreds of thousands of reviews indicate even greater engagement and usage. So that shows the success that comes with taking an integrated marketing approach to support your voice applications.

Another example of a launch campaign to make people aware that a new experience exists is the Headspace: Guided Meditation for Everybody voice application. Headspace took a multitiered approach that also involved using paid, owned, and earned channels to let its audiences know that Headspace's product was now available through voice devices. Using both paid and organic social, there were Instagram, Facebook, and Twitter ads and posts to promote the voice experience, which was available via Amazon Alexa and Google Assistant.

Amazon also featured the new skill in its Amazon Alexa email newsletter. The launch even garnered earned press coverage in trade magazines, such as Adweek.

One notable approach Headspace took was with the landing pages they created to support the voice experiences. Headspace created landing pages specifically for Amazon Alexa and Google Assistant.[6] By doing that, Headspace was able to provide platform-specific context onboarding information to provide users with explanations that were specific to the experience on Google Assistant versus Amazon Alexa devices versus Amazon Fire TV. The landing pages served as helpful destinations for traffic and enabled Headspace to tell a more complete story to drive adoption and usage. The pages were linked so users could navigate between the voice assistant platforms, but it put Headspace in a position where they could intentionally drive to either experience. So, for example, a paid social ad message for Google Assistant users would take a user to a Google Assistant–specific landing page.

Nutella has had an Amazon Alexa Skill for quite some time. What's interesting about their Nutella Creations Skill is that they first began promotion on International Pancake Day and then built on from there. After launch, they started incorporating messaging about the skill into their social organic posts so that there was a callout to use the skill. In some of the visuals of suggested servings demonstrating usage occasions, there would be a smart speaker to provide a subtle reinforcement. There was an intentional message to support the Nutella Creations Skill included on all consumer-facing content talking about Nutella so that it's clear there's a voice application a simple invocation away. On the social platforms, Nutella had videos explaining the experience and giving the invocation phrase to help users get started with using the skill. In addition to that, they did organic posts on Instagram to reach people on their accounts.

When we look at the copy that's in the creative for all these marketing efforts, they make sure to always deliver on the fact that you can be able to get recipes, games, and other information. They always make it a point to share with folks here are the things you can get from it so that they start to manage their expectation. But it also tells prospects why they would want to open it and would want to engage and use it. It was a simple message that didn't overpower the rest of the content, but it served as a constant reminder that helped drive the first time and repeat usage. It's a great example of how you can use your own space to continually remind folks about your properties without having a dedicated campaign.

Ultimately, users will not engage with something if they don't know it exists, regardless of the technology involved. So if you build a voice experience, your audience won't seek it out unless you tell them it exists and how it can help them. There needs to be a concerted effort to drive awareness and traffic to the experiences we have created. It's an important part of the process to develop a promotional plan that will make sure that your target audiences know the voice app exists and how these tools, which is what they are, can help solve their problems. But look at a holistic marketing plan to promote this so you can have a sustained presence.

After launch, there should be continued support of your experience. Weave your voice app into your ecosystem by simply adding invocation prompts or information to marketing pieces and digital properties (it can be as simple as adding it to an email signature). As we said before, if you build it, they're not necessarily going to come. You have to let them know your voice app exists and tell them why they need to start using it.

GUEST PERSPECTIVE 1

Build It and They Won't Come;
Shout It from the Rooftops and They Will

James Poulter

While we presented why you should market your marketing (i.e., your voice app), don't just take our word for it. We asked James Poulter, CEO, Vixen Labs—and previously, the head of Lego Group's Emerging Platforms & Partnerships—to give us his perspective. Here is what he had to say:

"If you build it, he will come." When Kevin Costner flips the breaker switch in what has become an iconic film moment and in an instant, light floods the crunchy soil, making the grass glisten against the dark, we can sense the promise will be fulfilled.

Field of Dreams has long been a favorite film of mine—the promise of one man reviving a place against all odds and giving it new life—and of course, it's that unforgettable phrase uttered by James Earl Jones that has resonated more throughout the voice industry in recent years.

When the Alexa App Stores and Google Action Directories opened up to the developer community, there was much promise of reward, so much so that it felt like this could well be the new gold rush.

However, these stores lacked one thing that Kevin had to his advantage—the floodlights. In this specific case, there was a need for people to "see" or visualize what was available to them in those new audio playing fields.

Okay, I think that may be as far as I can stretch that metaphor.

It's been a well-acknowledged issue for some time now that voice applications are not as intuitive and easy to navigate as they could be—commonly known as "the discovery problem." How is a user supposed to know what that little black or white sphere/cylinder/puck forgotten somewhere in a corner does?

How would people remember all the different phrases or "invocations" pushed out into the ether by brands and studios? And even if, let's say, they could remember them once, how would they find their way back to the same utterances? All these issues required a clear-cut solution.

The URL Is Dead—Long Live the URL

Let's talk about URLs—we all know that start-up that decided to scrap all vowels from its name. Now, imagine what a nightmare the main site URL could be for that! In these new days of the .co, .xyz, and .eth URLs, the situation isn't getting any simpler either.

However, an invocation—a phrase a user utters to the voice-activated device to "invoke" an app or piece of content (e.g., "Alexa, play Justin Bieber")—sounds like a perfect solution to this problem and provides some natural advantages over using the URL or social handle as a call to action.

For one, it replicates natural language—we are used to asking one another things using names, commands, and directions. These frameworks are hardwired into our language patterns from the earliest ages. Parents babble words like *mama* and *daddy* to their babies all the time, we teach children to say *please* and *thank you* as they grow up, and we rely on short memorable phrases in daily life to get things done.

However, since the inception of the web, we've progressively distanced ourselves from natural language and started relying more on visual symbols, hashtags, "hamburger" icons, and strings involving www.enterbrand.com/where_am_i to navigate our online worlds.

Web 3.0 may be quickly becoming littered with even more navigational pathways and acronyms we will have to get used to—worrying already about the gas fees to mint our NFTs on the blockchain. As if it weren't complicated enough already.

The voice ecosystem, however, involves natural language processing and text-to-speech and speech-to-text functionalities, beckoning us to come back to real talk.

We know that users need it. According to the Voice Consumer Index 2021, 86% of voice users primarily discover what they can do with their voice-enabled devices through trial and error. We know consumers are looking to explore their voice devices more, and if you're reading this book, you're probably keen to help them.

Our job is simple—we need to up our game and pick the ace up our sleeve—invocation marketing, which are the words that open your voice application. This can be in conjunction with the platform but is not required. Either way, the words should be consistent. Think of this as your new URL.

Many who started early in the voice marketing game, circa 2017, were either hobbyists trying out use cases and building tools and games for their own pleasure or early voice adopters who recognized the promise of reaping rewards on the voice-enabled web.

Those who came first, in those early formation days of the web, benefited from being organically recommended by the engines of Alexa, Google, Bixby, and the like. That has created an issue for later entrants to the market, as the most generic invocations—such as "Alexa, help me sleep," "Hey, Google, get a banana bread recipe," or "Hey, Siri, play worship music"—were already well served by those early to the party and as such, proved hard to dethrone.

Even today, if you want to ensure success, you need to make certain that the invocation you want a user to say is (a) not already being served by a very popular app or piece of content and (b) that you promote that invocation to your audiences!

I know the latter may seem obvious, but our experience in recent years is that the promotion of these phrases, or what I call "invocation marketing," has been sorely lacking.

The least popular way for voice users to find what they can do with their voice devices was found to be promotion through paid and earned media such as influencers, blogs, and online news.[a]

Brands, in particular, have been slow to invest in many of these earlier projects that have come out of innovation teams, R&D projects, or test and learn programs within marketing departments. This is where the catch-22 of the "discover problem" comes from.

Many who entered the voice market early spent their time and energy on making novel and interesting experiences, but for many, these were new and untested waters, which meant teams were unlikely to invest sufficiently in marketing these experiences to demonstrate the ROI needed to sustain them.

We see now that as Alexa and Google Assistant are growing in popularity, many brands and businesses are reentering the voice market with a more educated approach—but they still face the important dilemma of how-to invocation marketing to their advantage. As with all marketplaces, the more vendors there are, the louder one must shout.

Getting It Right the First Time

Listening first is a good principle for all conversations—whether you're trying to decipher why your wife is complaining that you're always late or listening to the server for the specials, it's better to get all the information you need before piping up yourself.

The same is true in invocation marketing—knowing what your users are already saying about you, how they want to talk to you, and what they may want is the first step to getting this right.

At Vixen Labs, we spend about 50% of our effort in any voice project in "discover and definition"—learning our users' wants, needs, and existing behaviors—how they use language, what they think the brand or business in question does, what more they want from it—before we go near building anything.

It's the art of listening to users that makes truly great voice experiences, whether you're promoting a voice application, trying to discover the latest podcast, or getting the answer to a simple question from the web.

There are a plethora of ways in which this can be done, but I'll suggest a few here to get you started:

1. Focus groups—getting users together virtually or in person to hear direct feedback on what they need from you.
2. Online surveys—have users fill out their own invocation phrases to crowdsource the way your user groups speak.
3. SEO and analytics—look at the long-tail keywords that users are already uttering to their search engines using tools like Semrush.
4. Compare—look at similar apps and content players in your space and review what invocations they are using on the app stores, and content providers like Spotify or Amazon Music to see what other similar apps and products are named.

KISS—Keep It Simple, Stupid

I often say a good conversational experience is like the best dinner guest you've ever had. You want to invite them in, they show up with a gift, they speak politely, and they know when to get out of the way. And, hopefully, above all, they leave a good enough impression to be invited back.

Once you know what your audience wants from you, you need to enable them to ask for it in the simplest and most memorable way possible if you want a chance of being invited into their homes, cars, or workplaces.

The best invocations are unique, simple, and memorable. We know that voice is often the medium we turn to for routine and simple tasks, often when we are doing something else. So phrases need to be formed in short memorable sentences—this isn't the place for fancy marketing copy or clever turns of phrase. Nor is it the place for slang, catchphrases, or improper nouns, as these are the most likely to be misheard by the device your user is speaking to.

But there is another more pressing reason for keeping it simple—beyond the technology of it all—you need to be able to market it.

This means you want to make sure your invocation will work well alongside other marketing calls to action and copy—whether that's in the first three seconds of a TikTok or Instagram Reel, through a Twitter hashtag, or emblazoned on a billboard.

The Field of Dreams

As voice continues to proliferate into all our devices—from our headphones to car head units, from our desktops to drive-throughs, the opportunities to initiate conversations with consumers are multiplying exponentially. We already see clients like McDonald's integrating voice orders in the car, banks enabling voice transactions, and voice-enabled shelving in our retail destinations.

All these sale points, commerce or community, also become new fields for marketers to start conversations with customers—in real language, with real humans, and hopefully some real business value.

It's no longer the stuff of dreams; we just need to turn on the floodlights. If you build it, he will come, but if you voice it, they will all gather around the pitch to make it happen.

[a] Scot Westwater and Susan Westwater, "2021 Voice Consumer Index White Paper," Vixen Labs, published June 30, 2021, accessed June 30, 2021, https://vixenlabs.co/voice-consumer-index.

GUEST PERSPECTIVE 2

Beyond the Smart Speaker

Roger Kibbe

Smart speakers are just the start. Soon voice will be integrated into other consumer touchpoints. To get a perspective on the direction of the voice, we approached Roger Kibbe, a senior developer evangelist at North America Bixby Labs, formerly Viv Labs, which is the home of Bixby in Samsung Research Americas. Before Samsung, Kibbe founded Voice Craft, a voice app development firm that was preceded by twelve years at Gap Inc., where he oversaw customer experience and logistics technology strategy. He also worked at Accenture early in his career. Here's what he has to say:

Smart speakers are truly a phenomenon. They're the fastest adopted new technology in history and have taught the world to interact with computers via voice. We are entertained, served, and illuminated every day by talking with our smart speakers.

But smart speakers signal the beginning, not the end of voice. We interact with technology through our phones, computers, appliances, and TVs. Voice applications can interact with all of the technology we use every day. Regardless of whether we're at home, in our cars, or at work, we should be able to have a conversation with the devices around us. Voice enabling these devices will unlock new and creative ways to enjoy our technology.

So what does it mean to voice enable our appliances? What does voice enabling a TV let us do? What does a conversation with my dishwasher sound like? How do the capabilities of these devices, their locations, and their usage affect how we talk with them? The key considerations for voice-enabling devices include:

- Mobile/stationary: Is the device mobile or stationary?
- Screen and screen size: Does the device have a screen? If so, how big is it? When using the device, are we typically looking at the screen?

- Available modalities: Does the device have a keyboard? Does it accept touch? And does it have buttons?
- General/specialized: Is the device used for general purposes or specific purposes?
- Length and interaction complexity: Do we expect to have a conversation with the device, or does it respond primarily to simple commands?

As we consider enabling new devices with voice capabilities, this matrix becomes useful in helping us design and build appropriate voice experiences for them and helps us unlock the creativity that will enable us to take advantage of unique features and usage occasions. Let's explore some voice-enabled device options:

Phones: We use voice to interact with our phones today, but it is in the simplest way possible. Imagine using voice to interact with your favorite phone apps. Phone screens are great output devices, but swiping and typing, especially if it's anything complex, is suboptimal. Voice unlocks a new way to communicate with our phones.

Phones are inherently mobile. Imagine a voice experience that understands where we are and provides information about what we are looking at, a virtual travel guide if you will. Or imagine a location-based social voice—we would hear tips, tricks, stories, and even digital graffiti from those who have previously visited this location. Location-aware voice experiences will detect if we are traveling a well-trodden path (our commute to work) versus a new location and will adapt. The delivery of information during our commute should be terser and more businesslike than the conversational tone we're open to when we travel.

Earbuds/headphones: These are an extension of our phones but without the rich UI and full swiping/tapping capabilities. Earbuds use the same voice assistant as on the phone but as a voice-only experience. So a rich multimodal phone experience must now adapt to be a voice-only experience. Hence, designing a voice experience for a phone means designing both a multimodal phone-based experience and a voice-only earbuds experience.

Something unique about earbuds is they are stereo. Imagine a voice/audio experience that took advantage of that advantage. What you hear on the left can be different than what you hear on the right. Some innovative gameplay or a location-aware tour guide, as mentioned above, could take advantage of it.

Smartwatch: These, like earbuds, are paired with a phone. A smartwatch has a very small screen, so simple UI elements can be used. But a multimodal experience on the smartwatch would likely be more "voice forward" than a phone would. We at Samsung have extensive data on the usage of different devices, and we know that interactions with smartwatches tend to be short and to the point. Smartwatch voice experiences should be simple, as users are unlikely to engage with multi-turn and complex experiences.

In other words, a more complete voice experience for a phone would require additional thinking. You'll need to have the full phone experience with rich multimodality, a voice-only experience for earbuds, and a reduced functionality/tiny screen multimodal experience with a paired smartwatch.

Smart appliances: The Samsung Smart Hub refrigerator offers unique opportunities for voice experiences. The device has a large screen (essentially a giant tablet), so the experiences are multimodal. Unique opportunities lie in the location and usage of the refrigerator. Being in the kitchen, a chef's assistant, or "GPS for the Chef" as the CEO of SideChef calls it, is low-hanging fruit. Since the refrigerator stores food, how about voice advice for particular diets? Or food information? The kitchen is also a family gathering area and an information hub (think of the fridges full of magnets and notes for the family). How can this be replaced or augmented with voice experiences? How about fridge-based family-friendly multiplayer voice games?

This is just the start. Think of the voice experiences that can be created for other appliances as well. Why should I talk to my clothes washer? What would I say to my microwave? Well, have you ever fumbled over pressing a series of buttons to get these appliances to do something you could describe simply by using your voice? Saying to a microwave "defrost a chicken breast" is much simpler than setting a defrost power level, figuring out how long a chicken breast takes to defrost, setting it, and then finally starting the defrost. What about setting the water temperature, cycle type, and spin time for a clothes washer? It's almost certainly more efficient to do this via voice than using the myriad of buttons on the typical washer.

Television: The TV is one of the most exciting areas to innovate in with voice experiences. Here you have a giant screen with great output modality but poor input since punching buttons on a remote for keyboard input is a horrible experience. What about a rich graphical multiuser game that uses voice for input? Family or friends would gather around the TV to play.

There is a desire, especially among younger generations to have interactive TVs. My teen daughters do not watch TV without a smartphone in their hands. When they have questions about what they are watching, they use their smartphones to answer their questions. Why can't they simply ask the TV? One example of this would be for basketball fans. If I am watching a Warriors game (my favorite NBA team—I'm a Bay Area native), I might want to know how many points per game Stephen Curry is averaging. Or I might see a violation of the rules like "three in the key" and not understand what it is. I should be able to ask my TV using voice, and the TV should bring up an overlaid graphic and voice output to give me the desired information.

The most powerful version of this concept would be if the voice assistant in my TV was context aware and understood what I was watching. There are privacy concerns that need to be addressed, but context awareness would allow a whole new level of interactivity with our TVs.

Automobiles: Autos have been an area of intense interest in the voice world. The nature of driving and the need for safety make voice an obvious interface. Voice control of auto features is a start but what about interactive entertainment? Americans spend 30 billion hours a year commuting; that is a LOT of time. Playing voice games, voice shopping, and audio entertainment are all very attractive for those billions of hours we spend in our autos.

AR/VR devices: Voice is the natural interface for a heads-up AR experience or an immersive VR experience. Games and entertainment are the obvious VR choices. How can voice controls enhance a VR experience? An immersive "other world" voice-controlled experience opens up a new world of possibilities for gaming, as it allows for on-demand information, virtual diagrams/manuals, augmented shopping, or new, yet-to-be-invented experiences. AR and VR devices are still emerging, but as they get smaller, cheaper, and friendlier, they will gain more traction.

All taken together, the future of devices is voice enabled. To effectively get there, we need to consider the where, how, when, and why of our interactions with our devices. Voice technology is the first man–machine interface that forces the machine to learn a human way of communicating rather than the other way around. To enable people to benefit from and enjoy this most human way of communicating, we must consider these characteristics of our devices and our device interactions. When we do so, we will unlock a huge wave of usability, utility, and creativity in voice.

EXTENDED CASE STUDY

Using Your Voice to Share a Coke

Although it's the most valuable soft drink brand in the world,[a] Coca-Cola knows that in a highly competitive category, a brand cannot rest on its laurels and must continually look for ways to maintain that leadership position. Coca-Cola knows that marketing is part of that winning formula and has been behind several iconic campaigns that have spanned decades. However, even iconic campaigns can benefit from adding marketing innovations to keep them relevant and effective at building consumer relationships.

In 2011, Coca-Cola launched the breakthrough "Share a Coke" campaign where Coke changed its packaging and released limited-edition bottles with 150 most popular names in Australia on them.[b] The campaign was so well received (it was launched globally with each country finding a new twist to add).

In 2019, the Coca-Cola Australia team was looking for unique ways to bring that summer season's campaign to life.[c] A creative brainstorm produced the idea to incorporate voice technology, and having worked with Amazon in the past, the team went to Amazon to bring the concept to life on Amazon Alexa.

"Our digital strategy team encouraged us to test and explore how new technologies like voice-assisted platforms could help us create a new and unique experience for people," says Mick Drew, head of e-Commerce, Coca-Cola South Pacific.[d]

The "Share a Coke" voice experience was available via Amazon Alexa as a voice skill and was designed to support the campaign before, during, and after launch. By simply saying "Alexa, let's share a Coke," users were able to open the Alexa Skill. Users who activated the voice experience prior to the campaign launch were presented with a series of messages to keep the experience feeling fresh and to encourage users to come back when the campaign went live. During the campaign, users were asked if they would like to "Share a Coke" and if they did, they went through a simple flow where a text message would send a link to the website where the user could order a personalized Coke to be sent to themselves or a friend. Post-campaign, the voice app shared interesting data from the promotion, such as the most popular names.[e]

"Voice-assisted lifestyles are becoming increasingly popular among consumers so, at Coca-Cola, we are super excited to work with Amazon and build on the success of one of our most iconic campaigns, Share a Coke. This campaign enables customers to Share a Coke in a fun, new, and innovative way via Alexa," says Coca-Cola South Pacific marketing director Lucie Austin.[f]

Initially, the new campaign was intended to run for one week. However, with the attention and interest generated by the integrated campaign that used paid, owned, and earned channels, all available coupons for free products were claimed within a few hours. The Coca-Cola Australia team quickly made double the initial number of coupons available the next day. Later that night, that supply of coupons was also completely claimed. Despite increasing the number of available coupons by 300%, more than 800 unique users still missed out on their free personalized Coke. In addition to exhausting the supply of free products, the voice experience helped increase the number of full-price personalized Cokes that were also being sold.

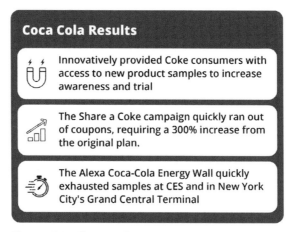

Figure 8.1. The results Coca-Cola achieved with their voice-enabled assistants.

Around the same time that the voice-driven activation was happening in Australia, Coca-Cola was also launching its first-ever energy drink, Coca-Cola Energy, in the United States.[g] Teaming up once again with Amazon, Coca-Cola created another unique pre-release sampling activation at the 2020 Consumer Electronics Show where attendees could request a sample by simply using their voice.[h] When someone standing in front of the Amazon Alexa "Coca-Cola Energy Wall," used the voice command "Alexa, give me Energy," an ice-cold can of Coca-Cola Energy was dispensed through a secret panel in the wall. At launch, consumers were also able to request samples using a voice experience for the Australian version of the Share a Coke campaign.

By challenging themselves to explore the use of voice technology, Coca-Cola was able to build upon an already successful campaign and launch a new product in ways that broke through the noise in a highly competitive category.

[a] Rachel Arthur, "Always Coca-Cola: Coca-Cola Tops Soft Drinks Brand Rankings," Beverage Daily, published August 20, 2021, accessed February 17, 2022, https://www.beveragedaily.com/Article/2021/08/20/Coca-Cola-tops-soft-drinks-brand-rankings#.

[b] Coca-Cola Australia, "What Was the 'Share a Coke' Campaign?" accessed February 17, 2022, https://www.coca-cola company.com/au/faqs/what-was-the-share-a-coke-campaign.

[c] Coca-Cola Australia, "Did You Share a Coke with Alexa?" published August 12, 2022, accessed February 17, 2022, https://www.coca-colacompany.com/au/news/did-you-share-a-coke-with-alexa.

[d] Coca-Cola Australia, "Did You Share a Coke with Alexa?"

[e] Medium, "How VERSA Used One Voice Experience to 'Share a Coke' with Millions," published February 19, 2020, accessed February 18, 2022, https://medium.com/versa-agency/how-versa-used-one-voice-experience-to-share-a-coke-with-millions-887d98f991b2.

[f] Little Black Book Online, "Alexa, Let's Share a Coke," published January 29, 2020, accessed February 18, 2022, https://www.lbbonline.com/news/alexa-lets-share-a-coke.

[g] Coca-Cola Company, "Buzz Builds as Coca-Cola Energy Rolls Out Nationwide," published January 24, 2020, accessed February 19, 2022, https://www.coca-colacompany.com/news/buzz-builds-as-coca-cola-energy-rolls-out-nationwide.

[h] Agen-C, "Voice Activated Coke Energy Launch at CES," accessed February 19, 2022, https://agen-c.com/portfolio/alexa-coca-cola/.

CHAPTER

9

Analyzing, Maintaining, and Refining a Voice Strategy

We have covered a lot of ground in this book from understanding the voice consumer to making your brand stand out in a voice environment through audio branding and even how to identify the kinds of content you should use to create a memorable experience. These individual topics are all important, but they will all have less of an impact if you don't continually optimize and enhance the voice experience, which means you need to analyze how your voice experience is currently being used and based on the findings and your marketing goals, what you can do to improve it.

One of the biggest considerations when it comes to voice experiences (versus many other digital experiences) is that you can't afford to launch it and leave it. Any savvy marketer knows it's critical to have a process to identify how people are currently using your digital asset and to plan for optimizing and refining the experience. Michelle Tucker, adjunct professor at Loyola University and EVP creative director at Edelman Chicago, likes to remind us of the saying that clients are "living in a state of perpetual beta" (personal conversation with Scot Westwater, August 2019). With this approach, it's okay if the experience is not perfect at launch because you'll learn how your audience uses it, the language that they use, and the information they're requesting that you have and haven't accounted for. The more you learn, the easier it becomes to add new and optimize existing features.

With voice, it's even more important due to the nature of the experiences—namely, the natural language inputs that are used to make a request and the AI (artificial intelligence) behind it. Because these experiences rely heavily on the word choices, language, accent, and slang usage of the customer, it's imperative that you monitor not only the KPIs you set during the analysis phase but you also look at the error logs to ensure your experience is handling as many kinds of requests as possible. More on this in a bit.

There is a popular misconception that AI can do anything due to the way it's portrayed in movies and elsewhere in popular culture. Images of Iron Man's computer Jarvis or Samantha the operating system in the movie *Her* often comes to mind. The reality is we're closer to the Robot from *Lost in Space* or Rosie from the *Jetsons*. While AI can do a lot of wonderful things, the reality is we're still in the early days of this technology. As such, there are still some growing pains that can crop up from time to time. By having a plan to monitor performance and enhance the experience as needed, you can minimize the impact these growing pains might have.

Launching your voice experience isn't the end of the journey; it's just the beginning. Once your experience is live, you can then continue to get real-time data about how people are using it. And you can even start to understand sentiment when you start looking at the verbatim utterances, which are what the person said when making their request. While it's also not possible to account for all the different ways that your audience is going to ask for a specific piece of information or even what they will call your product, it's also imperative to look at your transcripts to see what words people are using, especially what words are giving people an error. Are they finding matches with the answers that you already have, or are they not getting answers to their verbal questions? These errors or triggering "no matches" can show you here they want you to go and what you should consider adding to your experience in the future. You'll also quickly find out if your experience is out of sync with the expectations of your audience, or you might find that people are asking for things that are completely out of bounds because they're confusing your brand with another one.

Not only do you want to monitor the words and phrases they are using to make sure that they're matching up with answers you already have, but you also want to use it to train your language model to better understand your audience and get the phraseology and ontology your audience is actually using and apply it in the other channels within your marketing ecosystem. In essence, voice allows you to learn a lot about your audience, and the data that is generated can be used as a proxy for initial customer research since they are using their own words to describe their problem. These insights can be used as the starting point for more in-depth customer research allowing you to uncover opportunities to support your audience faster.

But to do that, there needs to be a measurement plan in place to ensure the desired metrics are captured. Therefore, it's critical to have key performance indicators (KPIs) identified as part of the discovery phase of your process. Examples of voice-specific KPIs are mentioned in chapter 6. Once you have established what success looks like for your brand, you'll need to ensure the KPIs are properly tagged and tracked within the experience so you'll have a clear picture of how people are using the experience and if it is successful or not. You can use these insights to optimize the experience once you have reached a significant amount of traffic to make it better.

KPIs can and should be a combination of hard and soft metrics. Hard metrics are the metrics that directly impact business objectives like conversion, such as email capture rates, lead form completions, or direct purchases. Drop-off or abandonment rates also fall into the hard metric category. If there are other clearly stated objectives like reducing call center time or increasing sales through a specific channel, success would be determined by hard metrics too. Meanwhile, soft metrics don't always point directly to a sale, but they provide additional information that help inform better experiences. Examples of what is captured in soft metrics would be things like tracking the types of questions being asked (are they general or do they relate to a specific product feature?) or how long users are engaging with an experience before they convert or drop off. This type of information can provide guidance for product development by monitoring what functionality or features users are asking about or troubleshooting. Capturing voice intents is an incredible way to understand how your prospects and users talk about your product or service. Similar to how site search information can show where content isn't clear or meeting needs, the "no matches" that are tracked when the experience can't deliver a response or answer are a treasure trove of insights about what users really want to know or don't know about your brand or category. The result is a fair amount of information that can be captured, analyzed, and then used to inform the voice experience and other content your organization creates. All this information also should be collected as anonymous session data to avoid any privacy breaches or regulatory violations.

One of the "big ahas" that you will have once you have your experience out in the wild is in addition to people using different words that you hadn't accounted for, they're also going to ask different types of questions or try to use "features" that you haven't created yet (and that's okay). As a result, your voice experience is also a great testing ground to see the other product features and content areas that still need to be addressed. You can use that intelligence to optimize the experience and then get feedback directly from your users.

While we are talking about what to measure, it should be noted that there are things you think you want to measure but ultimately aren't meaningful or helpful metrics. For example, with website metrics, even though we can track "hits," we have learned that "unique page views" are a better indicator of page traffic (in combination with a few other metrics, of course). Similar to website analytics, metrics like "session length" indicates how long someone is using the voice experience. Without additional information like the number of turns or number of requests in the session, you won't be able to glean any actionable insight from it. Invocations can be helpful in telling you how many people have launched a voice experience, but it won't help inform how to keep someone engaged.

Measuring Your Return on Investment

Because it comes up a lot, we also want to share some words of caution regarding direct return on investment (ROI). While driving purchase is a common objective, it should not be the only reason to create a voice experience. There are other customer experience or marketing goals that voice can help you achieve. For instance, voice can support a user through the shopper journey to drive indirect ROI (attribution can make that a bit difficult to measure as precise as is desired in some instances). It's important, therefore, to make sure that as you are reviewing your road map and your priorities, there is clarity on what your voice experience can accomplish. For example, a coupon or discount offer delivered through a voice experience probably isn't going to move the needle on your brand sentiment but may deliver a short-term uptick in sales (just as any coupon would). A voice experience can help you with onboarding or providing customer support, but it won't fix the customer experience or drive repeat purchase if the product has a lot of issues that require customer support. A voice experience won't be able to completely change the perception of a brand but when developed with the specific objective and purpose in mind—and an on-point experience—it can help improve it. When Comcast rolled out its award-winning Xfinity remote, it had a negative Net Promoter Score (NPS). After the voice-enabled remote was launched, that NPS score improved to become positive. Granted, this voice experience didn't suddenly deliver a massive positive score, but it provided enough of a positive impact to take the score in a positive direction. Voice brings innovation, but there is an onus that needs to be put on the brand to make sure it works so that there truly is an improvement in how it services its customers.

And if you do not take the steps to make sure that it makes things easier, you will put yourself in the same place that got you to where you are in the first place, in a situation that you have a bad experience. It is not a silver bullet. It will not fix all the challenges you have. We do love to talk about the Comcast Xfinity remote, because yes, that is an amazing example of how an intuitive, incredible product feature can raise your NPS. It is possible to increase the score through voice if your challenges are around availability, self-service, and other things that the technology can help address, making voice a very smart place to put some investment even if you can't translate it into direct sales.

While it's not going to fix everything, it can help build up positive consumer sentiment. It can help contribute to a better customer experience. It can improve many of these things. But it is still just one piece of the ecosystem. If you don't address shortcomings that your prospecting is seeing or experiencing in your other channels, voice is not going to be able to be as effective as you expect. It can't single handedly raise all the boats on its own.

With the Comcast Xfinity case study, the initial purpose of the brand adding the microphone button to their remote was to be able to change channels. It was a very simple use case where someone could change the channel by simply saying "channel five" or "NBC." Once people started using the remote and Comcast saw how people were using it, they started adding features so that now you can say "show me the movie where the dinosaur eats the lawyer" and you will get a listing for *Jurassic Park*. That wasn't a functionality for launch but over time, as people got comfortable using it, as they got the usage data, the product team was able to look at other ways they could use voice to enhance that experience. It's improved. That experience has been so positive that it took what was normally a negative NPS for Xfinity or for Comcast and actually made it positive for the first time. In addition to that, the Xfinity voice remote has won multiple Emmys and has been written about in multiple blogs, trade publications, and other mediums.

When some brands were first starting to dabble in voice experiences, we anecdotally noticed that one typical objective was to get good PR to prove that they were an innovative brand, and using technology was their proof. It's an interesting goal but it's selling the impact and purpose of voice experiences short. If we go past the novelty and "shiny object" appeal of voice technology, there's an opportunity to simply make some tasks easier for the customer. Just as we have discussed the different ways that voice can impact your bottom line, there are multiple ways to make things easier. Voice can help with onboarding. It can help with customer support. It can help with someone with product selection. We've seen in research that throughout the entire marketing funnel, there are activities that users are doing that can align with the marketing funnel.[1] As we look at setting our goals, we can look bigger than appearing to be innovative, and we can be innovative by looking and seeing what it is that folks are asking of our experiences. But also looking at how they're talking about our brand as well, social listening, can also help inform us. And by putting metrics together, we're able to start to build a complete picture.

Again, as we mentioned previously, you get a lot more nuance when using your voice, especially in the search context, because people use more words than when they type out their inquiry. So it's not just keywords you need to capture; it's the full phrases that are key. But once you have the full phrases, you can use this knowledge to your advantage by optimizing your web content, blog content, video content, and more to better address the core questions and phrases your audience is seeking. As a result, this is also a great way to inform how content should be rolled out across the entire marketing organization, not just in voice.

As we've talked about taking an iterative approach to developing your voice experiences, it is important to understand that iteration is not a substitute for testing and quality assurance (QA) to make sure that it's properly functioning as your audience starts to use it. Regardless, if there is an intent to optimize after you get user data, you will still need to do QA before you launch. You'll still need to do usability assessments. Launch is just the beginning. You are starting with an informed experience, but over time you will evolve the experience. As your audience gets more comfortable with using their voices, you'll also see that they will get comfortable with using your voice experience to ask you to do different things. This will help inform your road map.

Depending on a voice experience's functionality, tracking can be set up to track direct purchase, add to shopping list, requests for information, email sign-up, etc. To help provide guidance on some of the metrics available with voice experiences, we have put together a summary of some voice-specific metrics that are commonly available:

Metric	What It Tells Us	Why It's Useful
Invocations	How many people have enabled the voice experience and launched it (often can be broken out by device or voice assistant platform)	Invocation metrics can indicate a preference for an assistant or device but also tell us how many people attempted to engage with a voice experience. It also can let us know if our marketing support is reaching the right audience and giving enough information for someone to find the voice app.
Engagements or sessions	How many people opened and used the voice experience (slightly different than those who just launched the experience). This is the total number of sessions, so it won't tell us the number of unique and repeat users.	Number of sessions will indicate how many people are trying the voice experience, which can indicate interest and appetite for it.

Metric	What It Tells Us	Why It's Useful
Session length	How long a user engaged with the voice experience before exiting. This can be expressed as a unit of time (XX seconds or minutes) or by the number of requests or turns.	Session length can indicate if the voice app is not just attracting but keeping users engaged. A very short session could indicate users are having trouble using the app (unless it's designed to be a short exchange).
Unique users	How many unique users have engaged with the voice experience. This isn't always available since use of the voice experience might not require a login or other unique identifier.	Unique users indicates how large a user base is using the voice app.
Errors	What error messages were triggered during the session. These can sometimes be classified as "no match," meaning the system couldn't find a match to the request because it didn't understand the user or there simply wasn't content or functionality available to fulfill the request.	Understanding what error messages are being triggered can help identify if there are issues with the language models (Is the NLU working as it should?), if users are asking for functionality that isn't available, or if users aren't clear on what they can and cannot do using their voice.
Specific content requests	This indicates the number of times a specific response was provided or a functionality was used.	Knowing the nature of what requests are being fulfilled and what questions are being answered will identify what users are interested in and where the experience is getting things right.

The chart above shares some ways to measure how a voice experience is performing, but it is not exhaustive. So there may be other metrics that are in play. Regardless of what metrics are used, the purpose will be to identify where content and functionality can be added or improved. The goal is to understand where and how to optimize the content and the overall features of the experience so that you're creating something truly of value for your audience and your brand. Once you've optimized the foundational experience to a point where you're consistently delivering on your internal goals and audience needs, then and only then should you begin to introduce new features.

GUEST PERSPECTIVE

Voice Analytics: Getting from Learning to Real-World Value

Romina Pankoke

How do you best turn your findings into actions? To find out, we asked Romina Pankoke. She is a certified Conversational Designer and lead VUX designer at Vixen Labs, a full-service voice agency based in London. She works from Berlin as part of the European team developing voice application architecture, dialogue paths, and interaction mapping. Before Vixen, she had had an extensive freelance career working across digital strategy and UX. Romina is also a passionate advocate for the Voice First and Women in Voice communities. She received the Leadership Excellence Award as a Chief Chapters Officer and Board Member of the global Women in Voice organization, and is the cofounder of the Women in Voice Germany Chapter. Here's what she has to say:

As a voice user experience designer, it is my job to develop conversational solutions that meet the users' needs as fast and frictionless as possible, such as helping them get an answer to a question or to complete a task. Voice analytics play a vital role in informing whether this has been done successfully and are the basis of an iterative approach to building voice experiences.

Although voice technology has been around for quite some years now, there are still many firsts in everything that we do. A lot of companies are also just now getting started with conversational AI. Voice works differently from other communication channels in the way users learn about it, interact with it, and the use cases it serves. Therefore, it is important to approach building an Alexa Skill, Google Action, or the like with clear focus on a learning agenda, rather than jumping straight to launch. It may be tempting to rely on knowledge, experience, and data from other channels to guide a voice project, but it's really important to start with the groundwork: who are your users, what are their needs, and how do they even use voice? You will also want to reflect on your own brand's needs, goals, and strengths to find what you have that truly adds value to your customers via voice. Such a discovery process will help identify the most promising opportunities and voice use cases for your business. However, at this stage, many ideas and decisions are based on assumptions. This is where voice analytics come into play, as you will need data to validate the hypotheses you are defining. The first questions to ask are "What do we want to learn?" and "How can we qualify what we are creating as successful?" The next one to ask is sometimes overlooked but is vital to make your insights useful: "How will we measure and validate these criteria?"

Not everything can be answered through analytics data. Therefore, a plan on how to measure your set of criteria will most likely contain additional user testing methodology. Take the time to go through your learning agenda items and success criteria one by one, defining what each item means to the project, what an answer to it should look like, and what will be needed to answer the specific question. This will inform what channels and measurement methods are required and will also reveal dependencies, overlaps, or discrepancies. At the end of this step, you will have a streamlined and prioritized learning agenda, which is a vital aspect to setting up your project for success.

Prioritization is an important keyword here: we want to make sure we are not spending a lot of time and budget only to find out too late that our build is not what users wanted and needed. Unfortunately, words like "agile" and "iterative" are a bit worn out, but they apply here for sure: you will need a phased approach of learning and iteration so that you can base each decision on real insights from the previous step. Define your starting point carefully, considering what needs to be learned first, where the highest user value lies, and what business opportunities are most promising. Set a clear focus, and don't be overly ambitious with the topics and features you are adding. Put the rest on a first-pass future road map, start releasing small chunks, and be prepared to learn as you go.

Once you know what you would like to know, you'll want to discuss how tracking will be implemented to make sure you have the necessary tools and services lined up. When using technology from some of the big platforms such as Amazon or Google, there will be standard analytics reports available in the consoles used to configure your app. The metrics available here are a great starting point, but they will report mainly on technical performance and robustness of the application. When it comes to details on what users are doing and how they interact on a granular level, the metrics available by default are limited. Adding extra tracking tools is extremely helpful here, and there is a range of services available from paid conversational analytics SaaS to classic platforms such as Google Analytics.

When the voice experience is up and has been running for a while, it's finally time to get answers to the questions you have previously defined. Although each learning agenda and set of KPIs are different, let's look at some key areas that are likely to be on your list.

As with other digital channels, making sure a voice experience responds speedily, runs smoothly, and operates without technical hiccups is part of the homework. There is also the interaction model that needs attention, as this is where you'll have defined the prompts the system gives and what utterances can be used to interact with the app. Checking how successful these interactions are is a vital part of monitoring. Enhancing it over time will make sure your users can talk to the experience without hurdles, and your system is able to understand your users properly. For technical stability checks and interaction model investigation, the reports provided by the platforms are usually a good source. It's in their interest that what we offer on their platform works, so in particular the reports available for Amazon Alexa are usually sufficient to find out if there are any problems.

Another area to look into is the user experience and the conversations we are providing: Do users know what they can say and do? Are our prompts clear so that users get their tasks done as fast and frictionless as possible? Where do they drop off, and what could be the reasons for that? Closely linked to this is the content itself: What information, offers, or services are most interesting to the users; where do they go repeatedly; and what choices are they neglecting? For these types of questions, interaction paths, intent funnels, and specific interactions are where to find answers. Some platforms provide interaction path reports, but we usually rely on the implementation of manual tracking and additional tools to dive into this on a more granular level. Of course, investigating every single user interaction would be a bit cumbersome. Therefore, it is best to identify pathways that are specifically insightful for your hypotheses and a set of valuable interactions that will help reveal what decisions users made at important gateways, whether calls to action have been actioned on, and if utility tools responded in a satisfying manner.

The most popular metrics are usually the ones around activation of an experience, total number of users, and new users. Yes, these numbers are important and can be quite exciting. However, one thing to be aware of is that users can have a hard time discovering voice apps on platforms such as Google Assistant or Amazon Alexa, even if they go actively searching in the first place.

Therefore, looking at these metrics in isolation won't give much insight. Instead, they need to be put in relation to the promotional efforts made to draw users to the voice application and should really be used to validate the success of a campaign, rather than the experience itself. To get a feeling for how useful your app is, you will want to check how many users actually return, what services they call repeatedly, and how much time users spend with your app.

Lastly, check your ratings and reviews. Did you find any potential weaknesses in the data you just looked at? Well, maybe you will find more information about it in what users say about your app. You might also discover completely new topics to go and investigate in your data. Public reviews are quite scary, and the negative ones aren't pleasing. But this form of direct feedback is incredibly valuable and will bring a lot of insight.

When looking at the metrics outlined above, it's helpful to remind ourselves that voice works differently from other digital channels. Voice is a lot less linear, and we have a two-way conversation here that often involves on-screen information on top. Therefore, voice applications, and the statistics that come with it, are more complex. Let's take website statistics as an example: A website has menus, buttons, and links for users to navigate within the website. By putting certain navigational elements on a page, you are dictating the pathways users can take through your website, as you simply can't jump to a page that isn't linked. When looking at the statistics of a website, we will have this structure in mind, automatically trying to find patterns and adding up the numbers. Now with voice, user journeys aren't as linear and predictable. People can say whatever they want, so they basically can (and should be able to) move within the voice experience as they wish, independent from the path you may have envisioned for them. Therefore, simply put, numbers may not add up as nicely as they do for other platforms. Also, people can (and will) say silly things and speak out requests you did not plan for. The system will then provide interactions to get the user back on track, which we usually call error messages. This type of data may look scary when seeing it for the first time, but it is a normal part of conversation design and a very valuable source of information.

After going through quite some detail, let's get this summed up. To set your voice project up for success, you will want to start off with your learning agenda and then build your voice experience in iterations based on real findings. This will ensure you make improvements when and where necessary, evolve your content in alignment with what your users really want, and create services that make a difference. Starting small and learning fast will save you time and money, as you are focusing your efforts on what really matters, instead of wasting valuable resources. Improving your voice application that way, you will also be able to generate more leads, earn more money, or reduce customer service costs. The approach outlined here isn't a new invention with voice. It's just time to really take this to heart, as launching and leaving will almost certainly lead to failure of some sort. However, if you really listen to what users tell you through data and are willing to take action based on that, voice will become a valuable addition to your set of communication channels.

By the way, learning from what your users are doing in your voice application can also help improve communication on other channels. You may have never had a two-way conversation with your users before, so this is almost like a free piece of qualitative research.

Feels like a big project ahead? It probably is. But if you are short on time or budget, don't shortcut the process. Instead revise your learning agenda and make iterations smaller.

EXTENDED CASE STUDY

Finish Dishwasher Pro Detergent

Sometimes even the most low-tech activities, like dishwashing, can benefit from the high tech of voice technology. Since 1953, Finish (part of the Reckitt family of brands) has been dedicated to making people's lives cleaner and easier. Finish is a brand on a mission, determined to put an end to water waste and support households with cutting-edge solutions.[a] Knowing their audience often have their hands full (literally and figuratively), Finish wanted to provide an intuitive way to help consumers get the most out of their dishwashers.

Though dishwashers are commonplace appliances, owners know surprisingly little about how to properly use and troubleshoot them. Whether it's choosing the correct cleaning cycle, figuring out which dishes go where, or selecting the right product for the job, it can feel like a frustrating task. But doing it the right way can save water, money, and time. The challenge though is that knowing how to do it the right way meant flipping through a manual or calling customer support.

The Voice Consumer Index 2021 showed that nearly a third of consumers across all age groups used voice assistants daily, with nearly half using them weekly.[b] It also showed that usage was highest in the home, revealing a clear opportunity to connect with Finish users where they needed help the most.

With the rise in voice technology adoption in households, a voice application was a perfect way to support the brand's agenda and provide an easier way to get at the information dishwasher owners needed. Taking into consideration Finish's brand purpose, "Easing the Burden of Dishwashing," voice offered an intuitive and exciting way for Finish to directly support consumers while demonstrating their commitment to pushing technological boundaries.

Starting with a strategic learning phase focused on audience needs, Finish and their partner Vixen Labs set out to create a skill that would cover two primary aims: to reinforce the Finish brand as a modern, technology-savvy brand and to act as a convenient diagnostic and shopping tool for their target audience. Working collaboratively, they settled on a set of features that could bring their dishwasher expertise and brand tone of voice into the home.

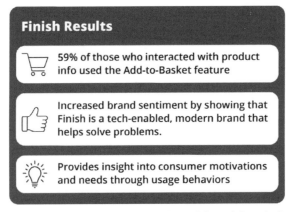

Figure 9.1. The results Reckitt achieved for their Finish Dishwashing Pro Alexa Skill.

Rather than building a platform for users to ask questions, they identified the most common dishwasher issues and created a journey that guided users to the right solution. By simplifying the diagnostic process, the voice skill provided the most streamlined route from problem to resolution. When Amazon invited Vixen Labs to beta test its new Add-to-Basket functionality, Finish jumped at the chance to include the feature to allow users to order directly in the skill. This was a particularly exciting development when considering the learnings from our Voice Consumer Index 2021, in which we found that over 40% of voice users were either already using voice to make purchases or were likely to do so. Add-to-Basket would be a significant leap forward in providing a truly seamless experience for users with a direct path to purchase. Not only was this to propose skill solutions, but it would also actually help consumers implement them.

The resulting voice skill, Dishwasher Pro, is a big help in the kitchen, providing easy tips on how to clean and maintain dishwashers, as well as how to ensure sparkling dishes every time. For users, it provides a seamless diagnostic and shopping experience. Of those who have interacted with the product information section of the skill, 59% have used the Add-to-Basket feature. For Finish, it provides a window into the motivations and needs of consumers through their usage behaviors. Dishwasher Pro is the confluence of customer care, convenience, and contextual marketing that voice unites into an intuitive interface that works for everyone.

Whether you're struggling to get sparkling dishes or you're just interested in seeing what voice might look like for your brand, try out the Finish Dishwasher Pro skill for yourself; just say "Alexa, open Dishwasher Pro," or go to the Alexa Skill Store to search for it.

[a] Claire Metcalf, "Finish Case Study," Vixen Labs, published December 2022.
[b] Westwater and Westwater, "2021 Voice Consumer Index White Paper."

Voice Implementations Across Industries

The way consumers use voice is not limited to just one industry or vertical. Every brand has an opportunity to use voice to improve their customer experience, potentially increase productivity and efficiency, reinforce their differentiation, and build their image. The most basic opportunity presents itself as voice search. The most recent Voice Consumer Index shows significant usage of voice search across multiple industries, which means—as we mentioned in chapter 7—that it is important that your content be optimized, incorporating long-tail phrases instead of just short keywords so that your brand's featured snippets can be found as part of a voice search. Through the 2021 Voice Consumer Index, we also learned that there are some common tasks consumers want to accomplish through voice as well as some industry-specific tasks. You will find within this chapter some of the expected tasks for various industries.

But accomplishing the expected, while a good place to start, is not enough. A marketer's job is to delight their customers. That's why more robust voice experiences matter too. To help you create context around the opportunity that voice offers within various industries, we have asked experts to share their perspectives on how voice will transform their businesses and industries. While we couldn't invite experts from all the major sectors—that would have made this book two or three times bigger than the one you're holding—we believe these perspectives are valuable for readers from all business sectors, as they help indicate the possibilities of using voice in your marketing programs for your brand. Along with the case studies and the other guest perspectives sprinkled throughout the book, we hope they inspire you.

AUTOMOTIVE PERSPECTIVE

Opportunities of Voice Apps in the Car

Shyamala Prayaga

Cars and trucks are at the epicenter of the use of voice technology, which makes sense because it allows a hands-free search. But the use comes with some questions: Is voice safe to use? Does the use of it cause distracted driving that leads to accidents—or are there ways to reduce it? To find out, we asked Shyamala Prayaga. Until recently, she was the product owner for the Autonomous Digital Assistant at the Ford Motor Company—where she oversaw voice and chatbot innovation and worked with cross-functional teams to bring that vision to reality—and today she is senior software product manager, Conversational AI, Deep Learning at NVIDIA, where she continues to work on Ford's voice initiative. Recognized as a self-driven evangelist for UX and voice technology, Shyamala recognizes the societal and cultural benefits of voice tech. She possesses the insight and knowledge that comes with experience and leadership in the design and technical development of voice. Her research into usability, accessibility, speech recognition, and multimodal voice user interfaces has been presented and published throughout the world. And interviews with her have been published in Forbes, Healthy Code, Automotive, *and* TU-Auto *magazines, among others. Finally, she is also a frequent guest on podcasts. Here's what she has to say:*

Voice assistants are very rapidly becoming part of our everyday lives. They are everywhere, from our phones to our homes. We have also seen a surge in voice application usage in appliances and drive-throughs. Voice applications have gained popularity in many industries, such as hotels, health care, banking, and even education, because they enhance the user experience, reduce operational costs, optimize business processes, and help people with disabilities.

The automotive industry is not a stranger to the voice assistant world.

In 2004, Honda, a pioneer, installed voice assistance through IBM ViaVoice. Since then, we have seen constant improvements, innovations, and adoption of voice assistants in the automotive space. As a result, in-car voice assistants have become an almost standard feature in many new vehicles on the market today.

Although many options exist for users to interact with voice assistants in their cars, Voicebot.ai data suggest that 33.2% of people use the in-car voice assistant.[a] The second most common voice option used is the smartphone voice assistant via Bluetooth, followed by Carplay, and at a significantly small fraction, Amazon Alexa. According to Voicebot.ai, 73% of drivers will use an in-car voice assistant by 2022.[b] In addition, over 60% of car buyers who have used voice assistants will consider the availability of a voice assistant in their purchase decision. This research indicates not only the need but the growing user expectations from their voice assistants in the car.

Voice assistants are predicted to be embedded in nearly 90% of new vehicles sold globally by 2028, as per Navigant Research.[c] Amazon, Google, Nuance, IBM, SoundHound, and others are all pushing hard to become the default assistant because being the voice assistant in the automotive world would open a vast market opportunity. Billions of hours are spent in cars monthly in the United States alone, and drivers want to spend those hours being more productive, which leads to distracted driving. In fact, distracted drivers account for around 2.5 million car crashes every year.[d] We hear about these crashes all over the world almost every day.

The three main types of distractions are visual, cognitive, and manual. Some of the top reasons for distractions while driving include:

1. People are lost in their thoughts. It happens more often than we think, especially for people with long commutes. In fact, I once went fifteen miles past my home because I was lost in deep thought and didn't realize that I'd skipped an exit to my house. Imagine being so deep in thinking that you missed seeing the other vehicle getting in your lane. Scary, isn't it? But this is the top reason for distraction.
2. People using cell phones. Using cell phones while driving is something we all have done at some point. Whenever there's a ding on my phone, my mind immediately wants to read the notification. The more I try to resist, the more I feel the urge to see it. It is said that drivers are at a very high risk of crashing when they use their cell phones and that it takes our brain thirteen seconds to refocus after using it.
3. Driver looking at something outside the car. Have you ever seen yourself looking at the cute little dog peeping from another car or the scenic beauty while driving? Drivers get tempted and look around. But taking eyes off the road even for a split second can lead to a disaster.
4. Using a device other than a phone within the car. Any screen-based device, whether the human–machine interface (HMI) or infotainment system in the car or your pager adds an equal amount of distraction as a smartphone. NHSTA sets conscious rules for HMIs to limit screen interaction while driving, but user-owned devices do not have similar regulations.
5. Driver drinking or eating. Again, during long commutes, people are hustling, bustling, and catching up, and they end up taking small bites to control their hunger pangs. But a split-second eye off the road can lead to incidents.
6. Driver adjusting the radio or air-conditioning. Have you ever found yourself shuffling the radio stations or adjusting the climate controls in the car? Maybe the air-conditioning got too cold or hot, and you are trying to readjust. This is me almost every time I am driving. Although climate controls are accessible, they need some attention, which forces us to take our eyes off the road, leading to incidents.

While some of these reasons are beyond our control, the good news is that voice assistants can offer tremendous opportunities to reduce distractions for many of them. Controlling the climate using your smart speaker may be a luxury at home; it will soon become a lifesaver in the car because it reduces distractions and cognitive load. Many other use cases can help reduce distractions and enhance the user experience, including making a phone call, listening to music, sending text messages (or listening to one you just received), asking for directions or information about a point of interest, and other tasks. With the rise in voice commerce, there have been some potential opportunities for ordering food for pickup, using concierge services, and more.

The auto industry is also considering many other uses of voice to help optimize the operations and reduce cost; examples include scheduling your vehicle maintenance, asking questions about the vehicle or its operation (replacing the owner's manual), and providing other customer-care tasks.

As a customer, when you see the fancy red Mustang Mach-E with the fifteen-inch screen on the road, you are amazed by the attention to detail and every aspect of the user experience. But did you know how much effort went into designing every detail? The icing on the cake is when you can talk to the car to ask for help in navigating to a place or calling someone or even drafting an email.

A conversation designer for automotive is faced with many challenges, from regulations to integration, that need to be addressed. Some of the key challenges in designing voice experiences for automotive are architecture, regulations, connectivity, privacy and security, hardware and software, external limitations, and personalization (and that's just the start of the list). Each of these is unique and requires a clear understanding to implement a better voice design strategy for the automotive sector, but they are the basic underpinnings of making voice a part of our everyday automotive experience.

ᵃ Bret Kinsella, "In-Car Voice Assistant Users 127 Million in the U.S. with Strong Adoption in the UK and Germany as Well—New Report," Voicebot.ai, published August 23, 2021, https://Voicebot.ai/2021/08/23/in-car-Voice-as sistant-users-127-million-in-the-u-s-with-strong-adoption-in-the-uk-and-germany-as-well-new-report/.
ᵇ Eric Schwartz, "73% of Drivers Will Use an In-Car Voice Assistant by 2022: Report," Voicebot.ai, published November 17, 2019, https://Voicebot.ai/2019/11/17/73-of-drivers-will-use-an-in-car-Voice-assistant-by-2022-report/.
ᶜ Automotive World, "The Rise of the In-Car Digital Assistant," published October 21, 2019, https://www.auto motiveworld.com/special-reports/special-report-the-rise-of-the-in-car-digital-assistant#:~:text=According%20 to%20Navigant%20Research%2C%20digital,with%20consumer%20expectations%20is%20key.
ᵈ Damjan Milenkovic, "Distracted Driving Statistics and Facts for 2022," Carsurance, published February 18, 2022, https://carsurance.net/insights/distracted-driving-statistics/#:~:text=%E2%80%93%20Every%20year%2C%20 there%20are%202.5,the%20driver%20has%20been%20distracted.

According to the 2022 Voice Consumer Index, the top five tasks within the banking and finance category that US consumers would like to be able to do using their voice are:[1]

1. Checking their balance
2. Finding answers to common questions
3. Getting directions to a physical location
4. Updating account details
5. Finding the nearest ATM

BANKING, FINANCE, AND INSURANCE PERSPECTIVE

Improving the Customer Experience While Improving Operations

Robin Keira

Throughout this book, we explored how voice can help brands enhance the customer experience—while improving operations. To see how voice can help solve common customer experience and operational issues within the insurance and finance sector, we approached Dr. Robin Keira, the founder of Digitalscouting, a platform for thought leaders, entrepreneurs, senior managers, and others in finance and insurance to share best practices, lessons learned, and up-to-date views on tech and business trends around the world. As a global top-ranked influencer and thought leader, Robin speaks on the biggest stages in finance, insurance, and beyond. He also serves as an advisory board member for various start-up organizations as well as an ambassador for the Open Voice Network. Here's what Robin has to say:

Despite all my years working in the insurance and finance industry, I still get surprised with all the innovations we develop each day. We now live in a time where disruption is the new game, where winners are those who bring something new to the table for prospects to talk about. Incumbents who were not able to modernize their legacy systems are out of the game. As a result of the digital transformation that's spreading like wildfire, we're now seeing an endless spurt of growth in the insurance and finance industry.

Telematics now calculates premiums for vehicle insurance, peer-to-peer (P2P) now allows group-friendly insurance, finance now has blockchain for more transparent and efficient process systems, and application programming interfaces (APIs) open a new channel for banking. In other words, insurance and finance are exciting spaces that can never run out of advancements to market to the public. What else is out there that we haven't tried?

The Problem of the Insurance Industry

Insurance is often coined as an underrated industry. Confusing, unnecessary, expensive—these are just among the words typically used to describe insurance. One of the probable reasons for this misconception is that insurance requires a long-term commitment bounded by uncertainty. Unlike many of our purchases, insurance is intangible: You only get what you pay for when something bad happens. We can educate and guide our customers in choosing the insurance policy that best suits them, and we can give the best after-sales service ever, but the dreading moment in between typically leaves the customers wondering if they'd made a wise decision. It is at this point customers slowly lose trust and enthusiasm for insurance. The main problem is we are not part of their daily lives. It is only on the rarest occasions, most often unfavorable, that we reunite with our clients. To keep our relationship with customers healthy and thriving, we must stay close to them in many possible ways.

The Problem of the Finance Industry

Queues, the endless sound of fingers clattering on the keyboard, silent murmurs of complaints from customers waiting in line: This is the scene that will welcome you on a typical banking day. For the longest time, the promise of digital technology to transform financial institutions has not been fully kept. While it solved problems, new ones were also created in the process. The emergence of disruptive technologies and start-ups forces the existing and traditional banks to rethink how they conduct business. It put banks in a never-ending chase to find the right blend of innovative technologies that offer efficiencies for the company, facilitate customer retention, and open doors for more customers. The finance industry is now in a significant cultural shift that offers no room for traditional and conventional process systems. Internal offices are faced with the challenges of handling big data, meeting rising expectations, and complying with an increasing array of regulations, all of which create damaging friction in the business process of many financial institutions.

What Is Voice and How Can It Solve
Insurance and Finance Problems?

A few years ago, having someone to assist you with your simple needs was a luxury. But thanks to artificial intelligence paving the way for language processing algorithms and voice recognition, you can now make specific demands without even lifting a finger with only a digital device and some setting modifications. But the question remains unanswered: "How can voice solve the problems of insurance and finance?"

The emergence of voice was never a problem. We took for granted the gigantic potential voice has in helping insurance and finance be part of our customers' daily lives and reduce the friction inside the offices caused by simultaneous demands. Voice can help us identify nearby locations of establishments, describe policies, and calculate specific amounts. In insurance, it has two critical touchpoints: buying and filing a claim. Voice technology offers the possibility of connecting with customers on a more emotional level.

Government financial initiatives, on the other hand, can be leveraged to make better use of voice. EU and UK governments started the European Union's Second Payment Services Directive (PSD2) and Open Banking to improve the duration of transactions and make payments safer and more secure. These initiatives force banks to release their data securely. They'll allow customers to compare banks and better manage their finances efficiently. There are third-party providers (TPP) involved in PDS2: payment initiation service providers (PISP) and account information service providers (AISP). Enabling the data accessed by these TPPs will make room for insurance and finance in our daily lives. Imagine asking Alexa, "How much money do I have?"

Many companies have already taken extra steps in using voice to step up their game. The results have shown strong customer support and simplified internal processes, among other benefits. For instance, Deutsche Familieversicherung (DFV), which conducted the first InsurTech IPO in the Western world and played a significant role in the German health insurance industry, uses this new approach to meet its clients' demand in real time. The DFV was the first insurer worldwide to conduct a full sales process using Amazon's Alexa.

In addition, LV=General Insurance (LV=GI), one of the UK's largest personal lines insurers, now has car insurance voice skills for its customers with Amazon Alexa and Google Home Assistant. The first of its kind in the insurance industry, a voice skill, launched by LV=GI on February 4, 2020, was able to initially answer over 500 policy-based questions, collated from FAQs on the company's LiveChat and the call center. While it helps LV=GI's customers discover a range of answers about their car insurance policy, it also lessens inquiries received by the company's call center.

According to Statista, more than half of American households incorporate voice-operated personal assistants in their smartphones in the year 2020.[a] While voice assistants gain popularity in homes, cars, and mobile devices, they can also be used as an engine for sales and marketing, bringing a group of insurers such as Nationwide, Liberty Mutual, and Farmers to combine efforts and build Amazon Echo Skills (Alexa). Progressive, on the other hand, joined Google Home way back in March 2017.

The Future of Voice for Insurance and Finance

Voice in insurance and finance is still in its early stages. It will increasingly learn our natural language and the range of services that it can accomplish will expand. People are becoming more and more comfortable talking to machines. Soon, consumers will embrace voice in almost all aspects of their lives as it evolves in ways that fully adapt to consumers' lifestyles. Insurance and finance should take advantage of voice at this developmental stage. Voice promises what all businesses want to achieve: reduced costs and increased efficiency. The opportunities that voice waits for us to grasp are huge but require tremendous investment into IT systems and corporate culture as well as lots of patience. It will take time, but if we start now, we'll do it.

[a] Statista, "U.S.: Voice Assistant Use by Device 2020," https://www.statista.com/statistics/1171363/share-of -Voice-assistant-users-in-the-us-by-device/.

Consumer packaged goods (CPG) seem to be at the forefront of all new marketing technologies, and voice is no different (think back to the Lucky Charms case study in chapter 2 and the Finish Dishwasher Pro Detergent in chapter 9). While brands need those kinds of initiatives to differentiate their brand and add value to the experience, the top tasks consumers say they want to complete with CPG products are a bit more basic. In fact, according to the 2022 Voice Consumer Index, the top five tasks within the CPG category that US consumers would like to be able to do using voice are:[2]

1. Find answers to common questions
2. Track packages/orders
3. Research a product
4. Find where to buy the product
5. Search for product or brand information

Also with new technology, entertainment properties often lead the way in how to use it, as we saw with websites back in the 1990s. And voice is no exception, as we saw with the Sony Music handwashing tunes application in chapter 5. But before entertainment can accomplish the exceptional, they need to master the basic tasks US consumers would like to be able to do using voice. According to the 2022 Voice Consumer Index, these include:[3]

1. Play a song
2. Find answers to common questions
3. Get directions to an event
4. Check show or movie times for TV
5. Browse content

 ENTERTAINMENT PERSPECTIVE

Entertainment, Entertainment Marketing, and Voice Tech

Donald Buckley

A goal of any marketer is to create value for their brand, and one way is through entertainment. So anytime an entertainment executive has ideas how to tie entertainment to marketing, we need to listen. And that is why we approached Donald Buckley, CEO of Treehouse, an entertainment, media, and emerging tech consultancy. He is also media and entertainment advisor at the Open Voice Network and serves on the board of the Experience Center of the IAB. As chief marketing officer of Showtime Networks, Inc., Donald led marketing for such TV series as Homeland, The Chi, Billions, Dexter, *and* City on a Hill *as well as for Showtime Sports and Showtime Documentary Films. In addition, he created and led the marketing organization that launched Showtime's streaming OTT service. Previously, as Warner Bros.' senior vice president, Interactive Marketing, Buckley founded its Digital Marketing Department and was a cofounder of Warner Bros. Online. Among the hundreds of movies released during Buckley's tenure were the* Harry Potter, The Matrix, *and* The Dark Knight *franchises. He is a member of the Academy of Motion Picture Arts and Sciences and currently advisor to media companies and start-ups in voice tech, gaming, streaming TV, content, social, data security, app development, and entertainment market research. Here's what Don had to say:*

When I was about eighteen or nineteen years old, I worked at a drive-in movie theater, which may have been one of the best jobs I have had in my entertainment career. Like others there, I wore white coveralls, carried a long-nosed flashlight, and had a tool belt cinched to my waist. Part of the job was to make sure that all 1,900 speakers worked, that there were no shorts in the underground web of wires that carried the sound from the projectors and ran up through each of the hundreds of hollow steel speaker poles that dotted the field.

In the projection booth in the middle of the field, attended by a lone projectionist, a pair of carbon arc projectors shared the task of throwing images onto the screen some 500 yards forward. The song of the film moving through metal and the flickering light of moving images gave the place an almost supernal, sacred splendor. Beneath the magic, though, were critical interactions between man and machine.

The transparent line running along the edge of the film carried the optical soundtrack, which varied in width according to frequency. It passed through a labyrinth of gears and sprockets, past an exciter lamp and photocell, and was transformed into electrical current, then sent on its way through an amplifier to the buried grid of wires and then finally landed as sound in ears from the speakers hanging on the car windows.

It was a network designed to deliver a customer experience that brought delight to its patrons. They had no idea that my buddies and I in white may have spent the last few hours digging up and repairing the wires that lay beneath them. The way that network ran was an important part of the marketing message too: You will have an enjoyable, trouble-free evening out. You'll have fun. There were 593 drive-in movie theaters in the United States in 1995; only 321 remain today.[a]

During that same period, global users of the internet grew from 16 million to nearly 5 billion today, while streaming video and radio, music, podcasts, and social audio have exploded. Clubhouse, the leading social voice platform that launched in April 2020, has at the time of this writing, over 10 million users and is valued at $4 billion. YouTube users alone account for almost one-third of the entire global internet user base, and the number of OTT video service users in the United States will reach 198 million this year. And it is predicted that there will be more than 100 million podcast listeners in the United States in 2024[b] and that commerce over voice technology is expected to each $80 billion in 2023.[c]

In all forms of entertainment today, the goal is much the same as it was in my drive-in days: deliver a friction-free and emotionally satisfying entertainment experience. Viewers line up to see a movie or choose to watch a show because of how it makes them *feel*, or how they think it will, whatever the genre. The reward for that choice should be a fluid user experience that is easy and even fun, entertaining in and of itself. If businesses do that, the audiences come back for more. If businesses don't, audiences won't.

The choices available to consumers are overwhelming. They now desperately need help choosing what and where to watch, and what and where to hear. The companies that offer the best solutions, some mix of product enhancements and marketing, will emerge atop their competition. The solutions should be elegant, easy, and mostly invisible, like the wires running under the drive-in field. There's a strong argument that at least part of the solution lies in sound, specifically, in voice and voice tech.

We used shovels, wire cutters, and electrical tape in my earlier example. A clean field, crisply focused images on the screen, good sound, and a fair price ensured customers would return week after week, as long as the movies were good and the weather held up. Word of mouth helped sustain the brand identity we created through advertising as well as through the consumer experience.

Now, advances in neural networks, conversational artificial intelligence, conversation design, continuing improvement of natural language processing and natural language understanding, and prioritization of voice and generative AI within media companies will together push development forward and provide an important element in the arsenal of search and discovery, acquisition, and retention. Work is being done every day to make sure there are no shorts in the wires.

It's a pretty good bet that as the science improves, digital natives—whose natural adoptive behavior will favor voice—will rise to power at Netflix, HBO Max, Amazon Prime Video, Hulu, Disney+, Spotify, and others. Even now, there are early, though spotty, beginnings of voice capability for search, discovery, and navigation built into apps, web, smart TVs, and programming platforms, and some users are at the very start of adoption and acceptance of voice as their *primary* choice of TV navigation over the painful process of search and click of on-screen keyboards. It's a good thing too.

On-platform marketing is the clearest, most efficient means of messaging. Viewers have demonstrated their propensity to watch—by watching.

Voice-enabled search and discovery on streaming video, music, gaming, and podcasting platforms isn't just a nice-to-have; it a business imperative. Think about the customer experience. Customer acquisition costs are significantly higher than retention costs, and retention is driven by positive customer journeys. The number one predictor of streaming subscriber retention is consumer satisfaction—that there is fresh and highly valued content. So if you have a *Game of Thrones*, *The Mandalorian*, a library of powerful intellectual property on which to base future productions, and maybe even a collection of major theatrical films, that's a great start. Right after that come variety of selection and ease of navigation.[d] In short, ease of use and lots of quality choices.

Uneven deployment of voice functionality at the networks and services and lack of voice interoperability standards are short-term impediments to a streamlined voice experience, but an urgent issue nonetheless in the battle to attract and retain high lifetime-value subscribers. There is no doubt that it is coming, and consumers will come to demand it. Otto Söderlund, CEO and cofounder of Speechly, which produces a fully streaming spoken language understanding API, predicts, "Consumer expectations will change very rapidly. We remember how quickly swiping was adopted. In the beginning, that was new; a touch screen had never existed before. Adoption was extremely fast. Voice adoption will happen as fast as or faster than touch."[e]

Even as clunky as the experience is at this stage, the use of voice remote function is heading in the right direction. The voice functions on TV remotes now deployed by Roku, Amazon Fire TV, Comcast, and others are just beginning to see slight increases in adoption and frequency of use. A recent study by Los Angeles market-research company Enact Insight showed that among the 1,500 frequent entertainment consumers surveyed, 14% *always* used voice commands to help find and view movies and series on streaming services, up from 11% six months earlier. Those who reported that they *never* used voice commands dropped from 53% to 45%, and those who occasionally use voice commands on remotes number 41%, up from 36% earlier.[f] To move this trend forward, platforms must align with programmers to allow interoperability and a consistent, fluid use experience.

The benefits to the future voice-advertising ecosystem would be priceless, and profitable, as brands discovered the ability to reach, in a comprehensive way, avid, engaged consumers of entertainment even as they are searching and navigating on their screens.

There's more good news. As consumers begin to regard voice, while perhaps not as essential as water and electricity, as a feature, they will sometimes expect to function with as little thought as turning on the tap or flipping the light switch. More than 35% of US adults now own a smart speaker, up from less than 20% in 2018.[g] And even though smart speaker adoption has slowed from its fever growth between 2016 and 2020, daily usage has grown, as has the number of users of voice assistants on mobile devices—11% between 2018 and 2020, while the frequency of use jumped by 23% during that same period.[h]

So it just makes business sense to employ voice because its navigational process is faster and easier, and that leads to a better customer experience. But what about search and discovery? That upward movement tracked by Enact Insight doesn't address the data behind the actions of search, which will be analyzed by networks and services to deliver recommendations that not only consider viewing behavior but might assess mood, sentiment, urgency, and more, all of which will shape the highly personalized, recommended "watch list" of their subscribers.

There is no end to the list of new entrants into the streaming television business as the newcomers and traditional networks and programmers roll out variations of premium and ad-supported networks, like Tubi and Pluto. Competition is tough as awareness is taking a hit. Marketing to differentiate, to dominate, will be essential. And voice marketing will become a critical weapon in the arsenal. Voice marketers will have to think more deeply about how they optimize search for voice, what creative units sound and feel like on established and even custom assistants, and how all of this is integrated into marketing plans, including voice marketing on podcasts and terrestrial and streaming radio and music services.

Another study by Enact Insight, conducted during the run-up to the 2020–2021 Academy Awards, revealed that the majority of 1,500 active entertainment consumers surveyed were not aware of *any* of the eight films nominated for the Oscar for Best Picture. This astounding fact is the result, to some extent, of the consequence of a worldwide pandemic, which forced many theaters to remain fully or partially closed, but the study was not about attendance. It was about awareness.

The velocity of the shift to in-home streaming consumption of movies and series was hastened by the pandemic, but the trending was already there. More people streaming, higher numbers subscribing to streaming subscription services, and growth of cord cutting began well before COVID-19. But in early March 2020, Universal Pictures made an announcement that shocked Hollywood and Wall Street and upended a longtime business model in theatrical exhibition, which sanctified the ninety-day window. With more than thirty international markets already in lockdown, with most theaters about to go dark in the United States, Universal announced that their new film *Trolls World Tour* would be available on demand on streaming platforms at the same time it opened at the few remaining open theaters. Similar declarations from other studios followed. The pull and promise of streaming were simply too strong. There has been some adjustment since then. As Wall Street turns its attention to revenue from subscriber growth, streaming platforms are further challenged, and the theatrical/streaming balance is not so clear cut.

But why haven't even frequent moviegoers and high-volume consumers of entertainment heard of the films nominated for Best Picture? Part of it may be attributed to lower marketing spending and shorter marketing windows, as studios launched theatrical films on streaming services on the same date as their release in a now-limited number of theaters. However, poor means of search and discovery is certainly part of the problem. While vast numbers of the population have subscribed to streaming services, awareness of the Oscar nominees (and hundreds of series, documentaries, and films) still remained low. Those cutbacks in marketing spending typical for theatrical releases and unfamiliarity with streaming platform–marketing strategy certainly contributed to low awareness scores. The issue provides the suggestion of a road map for the future, as consumer expectations and adoption of voice climb, as networks and programmers embrace voice technology in product for navigation, search, and discovery, so must they adopt new marketing strategies and tactics using voice and voice tech.

These Are Early Days in Voice Marketing

Voice marketing is faced with a set of circumstances like those that surrounded the early days of social media, where Facebook, for example, did not accept advertising. There was no model, there were no KPIs, and there were no experts. The result was the proliferation of organic posts by brands on Facebook and other social media channels. Lots of darts were being thrown in an attempt to measure impressions and sentiment. None of it was structured in any meaningful way, but early experiments undertaken by brands later yielded results in platform expertise as the medium matured.

So how does a marketer use this voice platform (which has many different component parts) absent any system of formal paid media? Innovative and creative companies and brands will lead the way with their creativity and innovation, testing and learning and even influencing its future state.

Organic Voice Partnerships

Let's say you're in charge of marketing season three of *The Mandalorian* on Disney+. You have a wealth of *Star Wars* IP from at least twelve movies, a number of animated projects, and including the first two seasons of the show. There is abundant data; there is countless trivia; there are fan facts about characters, locations, story lines, and the canon of the world of *Star Wars* going back more than twenty-five years. There are also dozens, if not hundreds of trivia game skills on Amazon's Alexa alone. If the marketer were to grant a trivia-facts license to the top-performing developers among them in return for a commitment of duration and frequency tied to the return of the show, they would be taking the first steps in developing a voice aspect to their marketing plan. And the trivia creators have the benefit of an association with a premium, globally known brand. For now, it is organic. Later, there will be paid media opportunities, and the innovators will help shape what it looks like and define the KPIs that will become standards. The same early-stage approach can and should be considered by businesses large and small, even if just to get to know the territory, learn the nuances of voice, and come to know the community and influence its evolution.

A Holistic Approach

As more skills are added to the rapidly growing collections, discovery becomes even more challenging. The challenge for businesses will be to differentiate their voice branding programs, integrate them, and create a mosaic of strategically driven tactics that enhance and expand upon each other. This might include branded podcasts, announcer-read podcast ads, sonic branding on web and mobile, and music service ads, some of which will be interactive. After the introduction of voice mode on Pandora in 2019, advertisers including Home Depot, Unilever, Volvo, and Xfinity were beta testing interactive ads, an early program led by SXM Media, the advertising sales arm of SiriusXM, Pandora, and Stitcher. It is clear that integration of voice and audio-enabled advertising across their products is a priority for the company.

Apps on tens of millions of phones represent another nascent opportunity. If you use Waze to navigate or Side Chef to cook, voice is already enabled, and thousands more will be soon. Warner Bros. pictures recently provided a "Batman" voice for Waze among the choices for directions in the navigation experience, and while audio advertising is not currently being offered, it is just a matter of time. Until then, we'll see a number of these "product affiliations" or "voice placements."

Rapid development makes any predictions almost immediately obsolete, but as we look in to the near future, we'll see voice platform routines linked to entertainment experiences, home automation that will help set the tone for the evening, the right music at the right moment under the right light, with new forms of entertainment emerging from multimodal development. What is certain is that attention must be paid, with an almost obsessive level of study, to unearth the vast opportunities that lie ahead in voice.

[a] David Louis, "On Oscar Night, a Look Back at the Past, Present and Uncertain Future of Going to the Movies," Cedar City News, published April 25, 2021, https://www.cedarcityutah.com/news/archive/2021/04/25/dld-on-oscar-night-a-look-back-at-the-past-present-and-uncertain-future-of-going-to-the-movies#:~:text=The%20drive%2Din%20was%20truly,large%20drive%2Din%20theater%20state.
[b] Oberlo, "US Podcast Listener Numbers (2022–2026)" eMarketer, Published November 8, 2022, accessed June 14, 2023. https://www.oberlo.com/statistics/podcast-listener-numbers
[c] Donald Buckley, "Voice Technology Is the Next Big Thing in Media and Entertainment," *Variety*, August 5, 2021, https://variety.com/vip/Voice-technology-is-the-next-big-thing-in-media-and-entertainment-1235031704/.
[d] Enact Insight, "Streaming Platform Intent Study," 2022.
[e] Donald Buckley and Janice K. Mandel, *The Future of Media and Entertainment Informed by Voice*. Open Voice Network, June 2021, https://web.archive.org/web/20211019095002/https://openvoicenetwork.org/papers/The-Future-of-Media-Entertainment-Whitepaper-Final.pdf.
[f] Enact Insight, "Streaming Platform Intent Study."
[g] Bret Kinsella, "Over Half of U.S. Adults Have Smart Home Devices, Nearly 30% Use Voice Assistants with Them—NEW REPORT," Voicebot.ai, published June 20, 2022, https://voicebot.ai/2022/06/20/over-half-of-u-s-adults-have-smart-home-devices-nearly-30-use-voice-assistants-with-them-new-report/.
[h] Bret Kinsella, "Smartphone Voice Assistant Consumer Adoption Report Executive Summary," Voicebot.ai, https://research.voicebot.ai/report-list/smartphone-voice-assistant-consumer-adoption-report-2020/.

Mayo Clinic, Cleveland Clinic, and other health-care brands are expanding to voice to better serve and inform potential patients about illnesses and treatments. And that is not surprising based on the tasks US consumers would like to be able to do using voice within the health-care category. In fact, according to the 2022 Voice Consumer Index, the top health-care search tasks are:[4]

1. Learn about a disease
2. Search symptoms
3. Find answers to common questions
4. Look up treatment options
5. Find a doctor

 HEALTH-CARE PERSPECTIVE

Supporting Post-Op Patients

Sirish Kondabolu

How can we innovate our marketing with voice to enhance the customer experience? Dr. Sirish Kondabolu, orthopedic surgeon and director of Strategic Media and Marketing, Orthobullets, has an answer for health care—an answer (as well as thought process) that could help inspire customer experience improvements in other categories as well. But we'll let Dr. Kondabolu tell the story:

Health care is in the unique business of giving people more quantity and quality of what is truly the only nonrenewable resource—time. Any technology that can help save time for those who work to give us more time is a no-brainer. Voice is one such technology. In fact, voice can optimize patient care, provider care, and therefore overall health care.

It is often talked about in medical circles that health care is at least a decade behind other industries in adopting new technology. For example, health-care organizations were among the last cohort to jump on websites, social media, and podcasting. What is interesting is that long before sharing digital images on Instagram, hospitals have been using PACS (picture archiving and communication system) and DICOM (Digital Imaging and Communications in Medicine) since the 1990s to share medical images and data.

Contrary to popular belief, health care has also been ahead of the times when it comes to voice technology. Long before Alexa and Siri, health-care professionals have been using speech-to-text medical dictation software, a form of voice technology, to document patient encounters. But while health care has long championed new technology for internal uses, it lags in using disruptive technologies to improve customer experience, digital marketing, and business innovation. This lag largely stems from the risk-averse culture of medicine coupled with the regulatory requirements of HIPAA (Health Insurance Portability and Accountability Act).

Although health care has a unique challenge compared to other sectors in this regard, there are many ways voice can be leveraged in this space that does not require HIPAA compliance but can still provide massive value. Delivering the proper information to the proper person at the proper time in a way that the end user can understand is exactly why voice technology is and will continue to be a powerful educational tool for patients and providers alike. This realization is precisely how I stumbled into the voice space in the first place.

My passion for changing both patient and provider education first began in med school. During your first two years of medical school, much like college, you are largely in lecture halls and labs learning material before you start seeing real patients. I found myself falling asleep in most of my lectures and then stopped going altogether when I realized I could learn the material better on my own with other resources on the internet. As we are all now aware on social media, if the content is not engaging enough, then you'll not return. When I was able to find MP3s of more engaging professors, I realized the power audio would have in medical education.

After my frustration with the way medical education was being delivered in lecture halls during my first two years of medical school, my frustration then became channeled on the wards when I saw how many residents and attending physicians talked to their patients about their conditions. If I could barely understand their medical jargon, how could patients possibly understand? I made a conscious effort to experiment with different ways of translating this "medicalese" into plain language and communicating the complex medical information in ways patients could understand through analogies and celebrity case studies.

Unsolicited feedback from patients indicated that my explanation was the first time they could understand what was going on with them, which led me to start my first podcast, *Medicine ReMixed*, a show with an approach of using the things people already paid attention to (e.g., pop culture, sports, music, comedy) as a vehicle for disease education. Think of it as the audio equivalent of parents mixing medicine into something that tastes good so their kids will ingest it. This podcasting experience made me realize that interactive podcasts would be the future of medical education (both for patients and providers) and the technology that would enable that reality was voice.

Without realizing the technology was budding at the time, my fascination with the implications of voice in health care started as a day-dreaming session during the start of my orthopedic surgery residency when I thought about all the time-sucking inefficiencies in a hospital. From looking up medication dosages and management guidelines for orthopedic injuries to who was on call for a particular specialty, my frustration with patient education in medical school had taken a back seat to my rude awakening of how inefficient clinical practice was for doctors in the information age. I fantasized about a future where technology made the lives of health-care professionals easier and more efficient, even if it was just by providing quicker to access information.

Orthopedic interns are not really in the operating room. Rather, you are seeing patients as they come through the emergency room, setting fractures, splinting/casting, reducing dislocated joints, and many other nonsurgical procedures. In addition, you're also responding to issues for patients admitted to the hospital's orthopedic floor before or after surgery. This is arguably the worst job in the hospital because you're on the front lines of one of the busiest departments in all of medicine. You're getting paged all the time, everyone is mad at you all the time, and there is no way for you to hide (believe me, I tried). You are often working over eighty hours a week and then expected to study about the consults you saw in the emergency room before presenting on the daily rounds and for "in-training exams" to test your proficiency in clinical orthopedics.

And if that weren't enough, orthopedic interns and junior residents who are on call oversee the "service line" patients call if they have a question after hours. It's typically used by post-op patients who were discharged home from the hospital or after same-day outpatient surgery. A patient calls the service line just as you're seeing consults in the emergency room while being paged by a nurse to put in a medication order or assess a patient. You're expected to respond within a reasonable amount of time to avoid complaints but are often too overworked and overwhelmed to respond in a timely manner.

Meanwhile, the patients become frustrated because they can't get their questions answered quickly. The questions are often basic: "My incision is bleeding; is that normal?" or "My dressing fell off; what do I do?" or "I have a fever or a rash; should I go to an emergency room?" I remember wondering if the patient got their discharge instructions that address these commonly asked questions or if the surgeon told them what to expect. Even at the most elite hospitals with advanced medical and surgical therapies, post-op and discharge instructions are still just sheets of paper. Even if the instructions make it from the recovery room to the parking lot, they assume (a) the patient can read and (b) if the patient can read, they can understand the content.

The reality is health literacy is a critical issue. The average US resident reads at an eighth-grade level, and the average Medicare beneficiary reads at a fifth-grade level. These statistics have obvious implications for patients, including their ability to understand common medical terms let alone discharge instructions. What's more, doctors only have a few minutes to explain things to patients and are usually rushing to get to their next patient. Meanwhile, the psychology of the patient is often one of "I don't want to seem stupid, and "I'm freaking out about this surgery and only hear every other word my doctor is saying to me." And after surgery, of course, the patient is in a fog from anesthesia. Though nurses often review post-op instructions prior to discharge, patients are typically not in the best mindset post-surgery and post-anesthesia to absorb much of this information. I remember thinking that it would be amazing if I could just record answers to the frequently asked questions (FAQs) and have the service line play them to patients. Now that service line I once thought was science fiction has turned into science nonfiction through voice.

"I bought my first voice assistant in 2017 during my last year of orthopedic surgery residency. I tested it while I was taking a shower and started off with an easy question (for an orthopedist): "Hey Alexa, how many bones are there in the human body?" After it gave me the correct answer of 206 bones, I wanted to see how it would respond to a more complicated question: "How do you treat an odontoid fracture?" Once Alexa fired back with a nuanced answer about how these neck fractures are treated differently in younger patients versus older patients, I was convinced this thing was legit. My third question was one I didn't know the answer to when I asked it: "Hey Alexa, when did Bo Jackson have hip replacement surgery?" It responded with "1992." My mind was officially blown. I had just reviewed two facts and learned a new one while lathering my scalp with my eyes closed! Using a smartphone (not recommended for a shower) would have taken me several minutes to look up and read the answers to each question. I felt the way James Bond must have felt with his voice-enabled gadgets. I realized just how game changing voice technology could be for the way we interact with information—especially in health care.

After graduating from residency, I became that orthopedic surgeon I had hated, by printing discharge instructions for my patients after their surgeries. With how much I was using voice assistants in my daily life and how much my own non-tech–savvy parents were interacting with them, I thought that a simple voice application might help.

I knew nothing about coding or how the technology worked. I just knew that it existed and that it was cool. I wanted to get educated, so I went to some voice technology conferences. Within weeks after visiting one, I had a proof-of-concept Alexa Skill and Google Action for knee arthroscopy post-op instructions. I picked that procedure because it's one of the most common among outpatients (it's done for things like meniscus tears) and the post-surgical instructions are straightforward. I created a skill/action based on the frequently asked questions and made a prototype that is live on both Alexa and Google assistants. My goal now is to add discharge instructions for other common orthopedic procedures and have patients use these voice applications so that we can refine and add to the existing question-and-answer bank.

A potentially powerful option for these post-op voice skills/actions is to have the surgeons record their answers to the FAQs so their patients can hear their own doctor's voice telling them the answers, which will add an extra positive layer to the patient experience. The hypothesis for voice applications like these is that they'll reduce patient anxiety and calls to the sleep-deprived residents or on-call surgeons. Having important discharge instructions on demand improves the patient experience while saving physicians time creating one of the many "win-win" scenarios voice technology can produce.

Accessing health information is one of the most common reasons people use the internet even before COVID-19. It is, therefore, no surprise that one of the top use cases for voice assistants is accessing answers to medically related questions. With this data, health-care organizations and individual providers have a golden opportunity to deliver quality answers to medical questions patients are asking. It's safe to assume that patients' information needs are not going to be different on voice platforms than on other devices but the way the information is delivered and the ways patients interact with it will change, and that is what health-care professionals and marketers will need to figure out. Other common use cases include researching treatment options, finding information about a health-related service provider, and asking about nutrition information. One health-care organization leading the way is Mayo Clinic with several medical information skills, including one for first aid that provides self-care instructions for such common everyday injuries as minor burns and sprained ankles. Voice experiences like this one have the potential to let patients treat or triage themselves if their injury can be safely managed at home.

If the patient realizes they require urgent care, several hospital systems like OhioHealth and Northwell have skills that allow patients to ask their voice-enabled devices about the locations and wait times for the hospital's clinics and urgent care centers. Not only are skills like these providing valuable information while saving them time, but they can also help the institutions manage increased patient loads.

Meanwhile, the Cleveland Clinic has created an Alexa flash briefing that delivers daily health and nutrition tips. This is a great example of a simple voice-based offering that hospital systems, private practices, and individual providers can create as a meaningful way to engage with their patients, providing consistent value regarding health and wellness.

In certain health-care delivery contexts, being hands free is not just a nicety but a necessity. For example, emergency medical service (EMS) clinicians like EMTs and paramedics typically need to focus with both hands and eyes on the patient during emergency situations. However, like all health-care professionals, they'll often have to look up treatment protocols, especially if they are less experienced or responding to an emergency they don't routinely see.

To address this, Brewster Ambulance Service in Weymouth, Massachusetts, recently created an Alexa Skill that allows EMTs and paramedics to reference treatment protocols and procedure steps through voice commands. This type of solution could be useful in other scenarios as well. As a resident, I remember watching one of my young attending physicians pasting the steps of a surgery on the wall. Not only would a voice application help young surgeons easily reference steps during surgery, but it would be useful outside of the hospital in reviewing the steps of a surgery one is about to perform.

There are many other simple tasks where the voice could make the life of a health-care professional a little easier. For one, Mayo Clinic developed a voice app that allows health-care professionals to get an instantaneous answer to the daily task of finding out who is on call, saving them hours every year. Such applications could also be used to directly call or page the provider on call to save the extra step of dialing the number on another device.

One of the biggest pain points for health-care professionals is EHR documentation, given how time consuming it is. Although speech-to-text dictation software is faster than manually typing clinical notes, it still takes considerable time and comes at the cost of either an awkward patient encounter (if providers decide to dictate during patient encounters) or personal time away from family to "get caught up on notes." EHR documentation is often cited as the biggest cause of burnout in health care. Scribe services have exploded over the years to help mitigate this issue; however, there are inherent problems with this solution such as the cost, lack of standardization between scribes, and need for physicians to spend time training scribes and reviewing their work.

One area of voice technology that is addressing the documentation crisis is data extraction applications like Suki, which integrates with EHRs, uses natural language processing software to extract conversational data for clinical note transcription, pulls up data when asked, and even places voice-enabled medication orders. Voice-based apps like Suki, Saykara, and Vocera are helping reduce the burden of documentation so health-care professionals can spend more time on patient care and self-care. While far from perfect, this technology is a huge step in the right direction.

Another promising area is education for medical students and residents/fellows, as well as continuing medical education (CME) for attending physicians. Decades of cognitive psychology evidence suggests that the most effective way to learn new information is through spaced repetition and active recall. Commonly performed with flashcards where newer and more challenging flashcards are reviewed more frequently, while older and easier flashcards are reviewed less frequently to hack the "forgetting curve," spaced repetition enables learners to review information precisely at the time they would naturally forget it. And as the name suggests, active recall stimulates one's memory (through practice test questions and reciting answers to a flashcard question) versus passive learning methods (like reading a textbook or watching a lecture) where information is more likely to be forgotten sooner.

The ideas of spaced repetition and active recall were first described in the late 1800s by German psychologist Herman Ebbinghouse, and learning tools like flashcards have been used for over a century. What is novel however is software algorithms developed over the past several decades to implement spaced repetition models. The reason I give this context is that voice technology has the unique ability to couple spaced-repetition algorithms with an active recall to enable all kinds of students to learn better or in places they could never study before (such as the shower).

For another layer to the voice-based study experiences, applying celebrity voice choices to the flashcards may significantly increase the engagement of students, making studying a little less painful. Imagine a future where Cardi B is testing you on the clotting cascade or Kevin Hart is helping you learn the Krebs cycle?

In my role as the director of Strategic Media and Marketing for a medical education technology company, I have seen the impact of the audio products that I have helped build for orthopedic surgery residents and medical students. Our daily podcasts reviewing high-yield medical topics and multiple-choice questions designed for exam preparation have surpassed our expectations for downloads and accolades, but what is most exciting is how we have translated the passive learning experience into an active recall experience backed with spaced repetition algorithms to train medical students and physicians more effectively.

Another extremely interesting emerging area that could add a layer of value for educational use is vocal biomarkers. Already being used in clinical settings for diagnostic purposes (such as Parkinson's disease, schizophrenia, and depression), vocal biomarkers use human voice features like volume, tone, inflection, and cadence to provide potentially valuable data. Vocal biomarkers could potentially be coupled with voice education applications to gauge the confidence of a student's understanding of the material. This may be especially useful to prepare for several oral exams required in medical training.

These examples are just the tip of the (vo)iceberg exploring how voice technology can create a more sustainable future for health-care delivery. Voice is just one aspect, albeit an important one, in a multimodal strategy to create smart hospitals, clinics, and health-care classrooms. In a way, voice could be the foundational gateway drug to help health-care professionals save more lives while scaling the unscalable—their time.

Let's Get Retail Ready

Finally, according to the 2022 Voice Consumer Index, here are the top expected tasks for voice in retail, food delivery, and travel. To start, the top expected voice tasks for retail outlets are:[5]

1. Check order shipping status
2. Research a product or service
3. Check product reviews
4. Find answers to common questions
5. Compare products

In addition, the top expected voice tasks for retail food delivery are:[6]

1. Find restaurant address/hours
2. Search for nearby restaurants
3. Find answers to common questions
4. Research menu/pricing/availability
5. Find discounts or promotions

Finally, here are the top expected voice tasks for travel purchase:[7]

1. Find answers to common questions
2. Search for best price (hotel/travel)
3. Check hotel reviews
4. Compare options (flights, hotels, etc.)
5. Research flights

RETAIL PERSPECTIVE

The Effect That Voice Will Have on Retail

Gwen Morrison and Manolo Almagro

Retail is a here-and-now, spur-of-the-moment tactile type of industry. But you are wrong if you think that voice won't disrupt retail-related industries beyond searching for the nearest location, product informa-tion, and shipment news. In fact, voice will disrupt retail in many ways. To help get a handle on it, we con-tacted Gwen Morrison, former CEO of WPP's Global Retail Practice and Partner, Candezant Advisory, and Manolo Almagro, managing partner, Q Division. Both Gwen and Manolo are recognized leaders in retail innovation. Gwen's career, for instance, is focused on the intersection of retail, brand activation, engage-ment, and innovation. As CEO of WPP's Global Retail Practice, she spent over fifteen years helping clients and agencies navigate the dynamic retail environment across the world with a focus on shopper behav-ior, technology transformation, format development, and corporate responsibility. She's worked with major international brands across CPG, retail, banking, and automotive. She has led industry research in emerging markets, written for business publications such as HBR and Brandweek, and serves on the edi-torial board of the Journal of Brand Strategy. *A frequent speaker at international conferences, including the National Retail Federation, CES, and Retail Leaders Forum in Sydney, Gwen also guest lectures at UC Berkeley, Northwestern University, and the University of Arizona. As a partner with Candezant Advisory, she consults several retail tech start-up companies and is an ambassador of Open Voice Network, where she is a senior advisor and cochair of the OVN Commerce Community. Meanwhile, Manolo Almagro is a twenty-five-plus-year veteran in retail technology and leads Q Division, a global team of business man-agement consultants, transformative tech, and digital commerce experts who help companies choose the strategies and technology to accelerate their digital transformation. Manolo shares his insights as an industry speaker and commentator for such global trade events as CES, Aviation World, Infocom, MWC Barcelona, Euroshop, and NRF. Among his technical achievements, Manolo is a named inventor on retail software patent US #6038545 and was recognized by Infocom/AVIXA as an inaugural Emerging Trend Fellow. Here is what they have to say:*

The year 2020 was the year in which every consumer digital behavior accelerated five-plus years forward—every digital behavior, that is, except voice commerce. During the COVID pandemic, we watched e-commerce explode, as people were forced into the digital channels as the only way to shop for their essentials. But voice shopping didn't take off. According to a December 2020 eMar-keter survey, "More than half of US adults said they have never shopped for goods via voice—and have no interest in trying voice shopping. In fact, just 9% of US adults have ever shopped via voice, and only 2% have done so regularly."[a]

The main reason voice is taking off for search of basic information such as news and weather but lagging in the commerce sector is the lack of visual context. Without an integrated screen, voice-enabled devices continue to be command led versus inspiration led. Visual platforms such as Pinterest increased in popularity during the pandemic. They provided ideas including how to beautify a home office or how to occupy at-home children.

Humanizing Voice Experiences at Retail

For voice to finally succeed at retail, the digital experience must become more natural and humanized. Consider this example of a future fashion/apparel use case illustrating voice UX as a more natural extension of how people shop:

- Mary is deciding what she'll wear to a party. She starts to explore the possibilities with a voice-enabled shopping assistant that already knows her tastes and preferences. This system is already linked to her preferred stores and payment systems.
- Mary's chosen style assistant is embedded into a device that is both conversational and visual. As she talks to the style assistant, recommendations can be displayed on a large screen, projected into a room, sent to a mobile device, or delivered through AR glasses or VR headset.
- From her home, Mary describes the upcoming event, indicates the type of look she is after, or refers to "the look" her favorite celebrity or fashion influencer posted. The voice assistant selects images of outfits and presents them via the visual interface.
- When Mary sees something that she likes, she asks for the "runway view." Using Mary's personal 3D avatar and personalized POVs—the mixed reality fashion show begins, set to Mary's favorite streaming music playlists. Once she picks her outfits, they're shipped to her within hours in a branded package that feels as special as what's in the box.

Compare this experience with what happens today with a desktop search. Most online shopping is currently directed toward replenishment items and basics. Through the pandemic many other categories experienced gains. But while apparel is becoming more shoppable with integration of video and chat, the high rate of returns points to fundamental barriers. When a shopper enters a brick-and-mortar store, the architectural design, lighting, and visual merchandising create a transition for the shopper's mindset. Our colleagues at the renowned retail design firm, Fitch, describe the ideal retail environment as one that facilitates three universal "mind states" that characterize shoppers around the world: dreaming, exploring, and locating.

In the dreaming state, shoppers haven't yet defined what they want, but are seeking inspiration and experience. Think of entering a Selfridges or Bergdorf Goodman and moving through all the theatrical displays. This is where shopping is both entertaining and inspiring. Exploring is when the shopper transitions to a focus on a category or brand. The shopper is looking for something, yet they are open to ideas and suggestions. In the locating mind state, shoppers want to easily find an item and are buckling down to the work of comparing prices comparisons and determining sizes.

In the current state of voice commerce, the locating function is being deployed in online shopping. Retailers in the United States and Europe are piloting the use of wayfinding for third-party "pickers" and for helping store employees restock inventory. Large-format retailers such as those in the home improvement category have identified how integration of voice can have benefits for both shoppers and employees. A voice request to either a kiosk or mobile app can make products easier to find—resulting in reduced friction, added value, and a more pleasant shopping experience. These are the three criteria that must be met to deploy voice, or any technology, to retail.

Voice, the Future of Customer Service, Loyalty, and Payments

The impact of voice at retail goes beyond just making it easier or more fun to shop. Voice tech will be used to gain a deeper understanding of consumer sentiment and emotions as part of the overall customer journey. Voice analytics will detect customer emotions—analyzing tone of voice and speech patterns and processing millions of customer conversations into real-time sentiment analysis. This data will allow the voice assistants to detect the customer's emotional state and simulate the appropriate human empathy response. If a customer is getting frustrated, then the voice AI can take a more empathetic and nurturing tone or even transfer the interaction to an actual human for resolution.

Advancements in such technologies as AI, speech to text, natural language processing, and machine learning will supercharge voice assistants' delivery of empathetic customer experiences with the ability to process millions of customer engagements, uncovering unmet customer needs, finding the most effective ways to convert customers, and predicting what types of pricing deals and promotional offers will encourage customers to increase their basket or average check sizes.

The next natural evolution of voice commerce experiences will be in the use of voice biometrics to authenticate payments. Paying via voice is fast, frictionless, and secure. Use-case implications are very simple, consumer voice prints will be validated at the beginning of every shopping experience, ensuring a seamless commerce conversation with the voice assistant, and ending with a simple confirmation that the sale will be charged to the owner of the account.

Voice will give a boost to the shopping experience from the dreaming to the exploring to the locating to the paying—but it will also provide valuable intel on the customer's state of mind along the path to purchase. With that insight, there's a chance to enrich every touchpoint along the way.

[a] Sara Lebow, "The Majority of US Adults Have No Interest in Voice Shopping," Insider Intelligence, published March 18, 2021, https://www.insiderintelligence.com/content/majority-of-us-adults-have-no-interest-Voice-shopping.

 EXTENDED CASE STUDY

Mercedes Benz In-Car Experience

The automotive industry is one category that can immediately take advantage of the functional benefits voice assistants can offer. Not only is hands free and eyes free convenient, an in-car voice assistant can contribute to safety while enhancing the driving experience. Mercedes-Benz recognized this opportunity to revolutionize the in-car experience and in 2019, launched the "Hey Mercedes" voice assistant as part of the Mercedes-Benz User Experience (MBUX) technology.[a] Initially available in the A-class model, the system is activated with the keyword phrase "Hey Mercedes."[b] It enabled customers to control a range of functions, from cabin temperature to radio to the navigation system, all through simple, intuitive voice commands for the first time in Mercedes cars.[c]

To ensure that the voice assistant supported Mercedes-Benz's overarching goal of providing the most comfortable and safe driving experience possible, the team had a lofty goal for the voice assistant: it had to allow customers to ask it for anything the same way they would to anyone else in the car. Making that possible meant designing a voice assistant that didn't rely on rigid (and unfortunately, unnatural) commands and understood the various accents, dialects, and phrases from all the regions where the cars were available. The result was a voice assistant that could recognize a passenger saying, "Hey Mercedes, I'm hot" and know that it meant to turn on the air conditioning. Says Ben Boeser, director of Open Innovation, Mercedes-Benz R&D North America, "To really tweak the voice assistant in a way to understand different accents from different nationalities was something we didn't anticipate in the beginning but became quite core to a seamless customer experience."[d]

While controlling in-car functionality and navigation were important features of the voice assistant, it was equally important that Mercedes-Benz customers could ask about things beyond the car such as weather updates, sports scores, or just general information. Partnering with the company SoundHound and its Houndify hybrid engine and domain libraries, Mercedes-Benz was able to create a voice assistant that had speed and accuracy in cloud-based recognition and responses and could also understand context (location or prior queries). This enabled the team to create a truly conversational voice assistant that would give the weather for the current location when asked if an umbrella was needed that day or look up and share a stock price when asked.

"That's what's really useful for our customers, to not only be able to control your car, but ask for anything. Mercedes and Houndify will change the way people talk to their cars, forever!" said Juergen Scherder, Sr., manager, Speech and Digital Assistants, Mercedes-Benz R&D North America.[e]

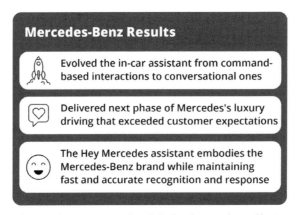

Mercedes-Benz Results

- Evolved the in-car assistant from command-based interactions to conversational ones
- Delivered next phase of Mercedes's luxury driving that exceeded customer expectations
- The Hey Mercedes assistant embodies the Mercedes-Benz brand while maintaining fast and accurate recognition and response

Figure 10.1. As a result of their pioneering efforts, Mercedes-Benz decided to extend their exclusive voice experience to the majority of their product line.

While Mercedes-Benz gives top priority to its customers, it also places priority on its brand. So it wouldn't be enough to have a voice assistant that performed well—it also needed to embody the Mercedes-Benz brand values at every level. This meant thinking through and then delivering on what it meant to integrate the brand values into the voice assistant's personality, tone, and humor (although, if you ask her to tell a joke, she will respond that she can't because her engineers are German[f]).

In addition to the A-Class, the Hey Mercedes voice assistant has been added to additional models and in 2020 and 2021 was available in the CLA, E-class, GLA, GLB, GLC, GLE, and GLS models. Mercedes-Benz continues to evolve and innovate the voice assistant and at the 2022 CES Show introduced a new version of the assistant in its VISION EQXX, a research prototype car featuring an electric drivetrain and advanced software.[g]

[a] Bud Smail Motorcars, LTD, "MBUX 'Hey Mercedes' Voice Assistant," published June 29, 2020, accessed February 3, 2022, https://www.smailmercedesbenz.com/blog/mercedes-benz-mbux-hey-mercedes-Voice-assistant/.

[b] Mercedes-Benz, "Mercedes-Benz User Experience: Revolution in the Cockpit," published October 2018, accessed February 3, 2022, https://group.mercedes-benz.com/innovation/case/connectivity/mbux-2.html.

[c] Andre Berton, "MBUX Voice Assistant: It Understands You Perfectly," Mercedes-Benz Group, published December 18, 2018, accessed February 3, 2022, https://group.mercedes-benz.com/magazine/technology-innovation/mbux-Voice-assistant-hey-mercedes.html.

[d] Karen Scates, "How Mercedes Benz's MBUX Voice Control Revolutionizes the User Experience," SoundHound, published June 17, 2020, accessed February 14, 2023, https://www.soundhound.com/voice-ai-blog/how-mercedes-benzs-mbux-voice-control-revolutionizes-the-user-experience/.

[e] Scates, "How Mercedes Benz's MBUX Voice Control Revolutionizes the User Experience."

[f] SoundHound Team, "The New Mercedes-Benz Infotainment System MBUX—Powered by Houndify," SoundHound, published September 14, 2018, accessed February 3, 2022, https://Voices.soundhound.com/the-new-mercedes-benz-infotainment-system-mbux-powered-by-houndify-9ab78a6f6fa4/.

[g] Ezra Dyer, "Watch as We Show How Hey Mercedes Voice Assistant Gives Your Car Attitude," *Car and Driver*, published March 23, 2020, accessed February 3, 2022, https://www.caranddriver.com/news/a31806187/hey-mercedes-digital-assistant-mbux/#; and PYMNTS, "In-Car Voice Makes Itself Heard at CES," published January 4, 2022, accessed February 3, 2022, https://www.pymnts.com/commerce-connected/2022/in-car-Voice-makes-itself-heard-at-ces/.

Voice for Today and for the Future

As we showed in the early chapters, voice technology is becoming increasingly interwoven into the fabric of our customers' lives—from search to product support to the presentation of unique experiences. It has quickly evolved from being something novel to an indispensable part of your customers' lives because it makes their lives easier and their experiences better. We outlined, in chapter 4, a strategic path to adoption and a view of the current voice user base that shows many people have already traveled far down the adoption path. As a result, marketers must now move from rushing to create branded voice applications to be the first brands in this channel, to fully capitalizing on the value of voice's ability to engage prospects and satisfy customers.

As we write this final, short chapter, we are reminded of the Gartner Hype Cycle, particularly the cycles for emerging technologies and another one for artificial intelligence. For those of you who don't know the Gartner Hype Cycle, there are five key phases along their path: (1) Innovation Trigger (an event that gets people talking); (2) Peak of Inflated Expectations (with lots of media coverage, but no proof of success); (3) Trough of Disillusionment (when the hype doesn't pay off); (4) Slope of Enlightenment; and (5) Plateau of Productivity.[1] It's designed to help businesses understand if the hype is real as well as when it's time to adopt the innovation.

Most of the news we hear in the consumer press about technology happens early in the hype cycle, particularly when the innovation is in the Peak of Inflated Expectations. Because of the recent layoffs at Amazon and Google, marketers might perceive that voice has been overhyped, which means that it's entering Gartner's Trough of Disillusionment.

While there has been some debate, we see that voice technology has begun to emerge from this gloomy phase in the Gartner Hype Cycle—or as Ahmed Bouzid said on the VUX World podcast, voice is "trying to move from hype to value."[2] Although its capabilities may have been overhyped in the past, voice technology has progressed significantly and is now delivering real value to businesses and consumers. Voice has come a long way from its initial inception and the initial hype.

In the past, voice technology, like voice assistants, were primarily used for simple tasks, such as answering basic questions or providing directions. It has made significant progress in its ability to understand and respond to human language, and voice applications are increasingly being used in various industries, such as customer service, health care, and banking, among others. With advancements in natural language processing and machine learning, voice technology can now handle more complex tasks, such as making reservations, scheduling appointments, and even diagnosing medical conditions. Based on the technological developments and user trends, we believe that voice technology has entered the Slope of Enlightenment, if we are to keep with Gartner's phases. And by the time you're reading this book, voice technology might already be in the Plateau of Productivity phase, which means that the field has matured, usage is widespread, and the benefits to marketers and consumers have become widely recognized.

At the same time, we believe that we are now witnessing a new hype cycle for conversational AI fueled by the exploding interest in large language models (LLMs) like ChatGPT and Lambda and their ability to generate conversational responses to prompts, which can make them seem very humanlike. This has led to their use in a wide range of applications, including chatbots and virtual assistants. But it's important to note that LLMs are just one component of conversational AI and their role in generating hype is only a small part of the larger trend toward the adoption of conversational interfaces.

Conversational AI encompasses a broad range of technologies and approaches, including rule-based "if-then" chatbots, intent-based "query" chatbots, voice assistants, and more. The interest and media hype around conversational AI is driven not just by technology, but also by a broader cultural shift toward more natural and intuitive human–computer interactions. Businesses and customers are increasingly expecting personalized, convenient, and natural language interactions with technology, which has been the driver of the development and adoption of conversational AI.

The trend toward voice technology and conversational AI adoption is driven by a range of factors, including their widening relevance and value to marketers and customers. But regardless of how sophisticated the methods by which brands deliver their experiences and services, the information customers need to make decisions will remain at the heart of their success.

We outlined the approaches, strategies, and processes you can take with voice so you can ensure the experience helps your brand and business by assisting, engaging, and at times, entertaining your prospects and customers. It includes a review of the ethical considerations so your brand's voice program does the right thing. We also showed how you can establish the goals and KPIs that align with your overall marketing objectives. We proposed ways to create an approach to identifying and developing the content to fuel your voice marketing program and to analyze the results of your voice program so you can tweak and refine your content to ensure that it performs at the optimal level. Finally, we included case studies and a variety of diverse perspectives to help you stretch the boundaries of your own voice program so you can truly delight and bring joy to your prospects and customers.

While the frameworks we shared in this book have been explained in the context of voice, they also can be applied to other emerging channels and technologies because these channels will go through the same path to adoption. Imagine how AR/VR, the metaverse, conversational search, and even new technology that has not yet been invented will change the way you will interact with your audience. But reaching your prospects and customers through these new channels all boils down to putting into action the process and considerations we outlined here.

You now know what to do. To bend a phrase from Nike, now you just need to do it. And we know you're eager to get started, which is why we kept this chapter short. You now have the tools. And as data throughout this book and other studies have shown, now is the time to get started, as there is a customer demand for voice-driven innovation across customer and brand experiences.

Before we leave you, we have one simple request. We would love to hear your success stories with integrating voice capabilities into your marketing programs and branded customer experiences, especially if they were inspired by ideas in this book. It's all we ask. And please reach out with any questions that could help you along the way. We're easy to find. And we're invested in your success!

Glossary

Amazon Alexa: Also known simply as Alexa, is the virtual assistant developed by Amazon that is available via the Alexa and Echo family of devices: Dot, Look, Plus, Show, and Speaker. The Amazon Alexa app can also be used via smartphone.

Artificial Intelligence (AI): The simulation of human intelligence processes by computer systems, including machine learning, natural language processing, and problem solving.

ASR: Automatic speech recognition technology that can recognize and transcribe spoken words into text.

Audio Branding: The use of sound elements such as music, sound effects, and voice to create a distinctive brand identity and emotional connection with the audience.

Audio Logo: A brief audio clip that represents a brand and is used for audio branding purposes.

Audio UX: Audio UX is the specific focus on strategically crafted alerts and signals that incorporate a brand into the user experience. When done well, audio UX can highlight a brand's essence while guiding the user through functions.

Automated Telephone Attendants (ATAs): Interactive voice response (IVR) systems that use prerecorded audio messages and voice recognition to interact with callers and provide assistance.

Automatic Dialog Evaluation: A process to evaluate the quality of a voice or chatbot interaction.

Biometric Speaker Recognition: The process of using voice biometrics to identify an individual.

Bixby: Samsung's proprietary voice assistant.

Capsules: A term used in the context of voice assistants to describe single-purpose voice applications that can be launched and executed using voice commands.

Chatbots: Computer programs that use artificial intelligence to simulate human conversation through text or voice-based interactions.

Context Awareness: The ability of AI to understand context and adapt the response.

Conversational AI: A type of artificial intelligence that uses natural language processing and machine learning to enable humanlike communication between machines and humans.

Dialog Management: The ability of conversational AI to manage a conversation with a user, understanding context and responding accordingly.

Emotion Detection: The ability of AI to detect and interpret human emotions through voice and language cues.

First-Party Voice Apps (1P Apps): Voice applications developed by the manufacturer of the voice assistant, such as Amazon Alexa Skills or Google Assistant Actions.

Google Assistant: The virtual assistant developed by Google that is primarily available on mobile and smart home devices such as Pixel Android phones and Google's Home Hub.

Google Home: A voice-activated speaker and home assistant developed by Google.

Google Voice Actions: Like Alexa Skills, Actions were applications that enabled users to extend the functionality of the Google Assistant, which powers the Google Home. The range of actions extended from a quick command such as turning on a light or playing music to a longer conversation such as playing a game. Google sunsetted Google Voice Actions in June 2023, encouraging developers to integrate voice into their websites and mobile apps.

Hearables: Headphones or in-ear devices that deliver voice experiences without a screen.

In-Car Assistant: A voice assistant integrated into a car's infotainment system.

Intent: The user's goal or objective expressed through a voice command.

Intent Recognition: The ability of AI to accurately recognize the user's intended action or request.

Invocation Marketing: The use of voice commands and conversational interfaces to trigger a branded voice application, a marketing message, or a promotional experience.

Keyword Spotting: A process that enables the identification of specific keywords or phrases in a voice conversation.

Large Language Models (LLMs): A class of artificial intelligence models that are designed to process and understand human language. These models are built using deep learning techniques and trained on large amounts of data, enabling them to generate humanlike responses to text-based queries.

Lilt: A small upward or downward pitch variation in speech that can convey different emotions or meanings.

Machine Learning: A type of artificial intelligence that enables machines to learn from data and improve performance on a specific task without being explicitly programmed.

Metaverse: A collective virtual shared space that is created by the convergence of physical and virtual reality.

Micro Melody: A short, composed sound that serves as a signal that a device has been turned or off, a connection has been made, an error has occurred, or an action has been completed. These prompts can also be used to remind the user to take the next action and provide other types of audio feedback. These composed and recorded sounds could be shorter than a second.

Multimodal: Smart devices that have a speaker and a screen, allowing for multiple modalities of user experience. An example of a multimodal device is the Amazon Echo Show.

Multimodal Interaction: The integration of multiple modes of communication (e.g., voice and touch) to improve the user experience.

Natural Language Generation (NLG): The natural language processing task of generating natural language from a machine representation system. Essentially the reverse of NLU, this is the process that translates data back into a written narrative that becomes the spoken response back to a user.

Natural Language Processing (NLP): A brand of artificial intelligence that enables machines to understand, interpret, and respond to human language.

Natural Language Understanding (NLU): The aspect of NLP that gives AI the ability to understand the meaning of human language.

Neural Networks: A machine learning approach modeled after the structure of the human brain, used to solve complex tasks such as speech recognition and natural language understanding.

Polly Voice: Amazon's text-to-speech technology that converts written text into lifelike speech.

Rhythmic Quality: The pattern of rhythm and cadence in speech that contributes to its emotional impact and overall meaning.

Sentiment Analysis: The process of analyzing voice data to determine the mood or sentiment of the user.

Siri: Apple's proprietary voice assistant that uses natural language processing and voice recognition to interact with users and perform tasks.

Siri Shortcuts: A feature in Siri that allows users to create custom voice commands for specific actions or sequences of actions.

Skills: Amazon Alexa Skills are voice-driven capabilities that are used to enhance and personalize Alexa devices that enable users to do anything from play a game, get information, or even read a story. There are tens of thousands of skills available, but it's also possible to create your own skill for your own need.

Smart Display: Smart speakers that come with touchscreens.

Smart Speaker: A type of speaker and voice command device with an integrated virtual assistant that offers interactive actions and hands-free activation with the help of one "wake word."

Sonic Branding: Sonic branding is how your brand sounds to the world. Similar to the way that logos and colors provide visual brand cues, sonic or audio branding provides musical and vocal brand cues. A sonic identity builds a stronger, more coherent brand that helps a brand stand out and be understood. See Audio Branding.

Sonic Signals: Short pings, beeps, and thoughtfully composed sounds that act as audio prompts, reassurances, and reminders. See Micro Melody.

Speech Recognition: The ability of machines to recognize and interpret spoken language.

Speech Synthesis Markup Language (SSML): A language used to control the voice and intonation of a text-to-speech (TTS) system.

Speech to Text (STT): A technology that can convert spoken words to text.

Synthetic Voice: A computer-generated voice that simulates human speech.

Text to Dialog (TTD): A system that utilizes conversational AI to translate written text to conversational language.

Text to Speech (TTS): A technology that converts written text into spoken words.

Third-Party Voice Apps: Voice applications developed by third-party developers that can be used with a voice assistant, such as Alexa Skills or Google Assistant Actions.

Timbre: The tonal quality and character of a voice that distinguishes it from other voices.

Virtual Assistant: An AI-powered program that can perform tasks or services for an individual through natural language commands.

Voice: An umbrella term for any interaction that allows a person to control a computer or device by simply talking to it.

Voice Analytics: The process of analyzing voice data to gain insights into customer behavior.

Voice Application: Also known as a voice app, refers to a software application that is designed to operate on a voice-enabled device, such as a smart speaker, smartphone, or smartwatch, and is primarily controlled by voice commands.

Voice Assistant: A digital assistant that uses voice recognition, speech synthesis, and natural language processing (NLP) to provide a service through a particular application.

Voice Authentication: A technology that uses voice biometrics to authenticate a user's identity.

Voice Branding: The process of creating a unique brand voice and personality for a voice assistant.

Voice Commerce: The use of voice technology to enable customers to purchase products and services using voice commands.

Voice-Enabled Customer Relationship Management (CRM): The use of voice technology to improve customer service and engagement, including voice-activated chatbots and virtual assistants.

Voice Experience: The overall user experience of interacting with a voice assistant or other voice-enabled device or application.

Voice First: A design approach that prioritizes voice interaction as the primary method of interacting with a device or application.

Voice Marketing: The use of voice technology to create and deliver marketing messages and campaigns to consumers, including through voice assistants and other voice-enabled devices.

Voice Only: Voice-enabled devices that have voice as the only input and output. An example of a voice-only device is the Amazon Echo Dot.

Voice Personalization: The use of voice technology to provide personalized recommendations and experiences.

Voice Search: The category of searches conducted by speaking questions or commands to smart speakers, mobile phones, or other voice-enabled devices.

Voice SEO: A set of techniques used to optimize content for voice search.

Voice Technology: Technology that enables machines to recognize and respond to spoken commands and questions.

Voice UX: Voice user experience that aims to improve user interaction with voice assistants.

Wake-Up Word Accuracy: The ability of a device to accurately recognize a wake-up word or phrase.

Wake Word: A specific word or phrase used to activate a virtual assistant or voice-activated device.

Notes

Chapter 1: Marketing Over Voice Applications

1. Margaret Joy, "Auto Attendant: What It Is and Why You Use It Every Day," *Onsip*, accessed February 20, 2023, https://www.onsip.com/voip-resources/voip-fundamentals/auto-attendant-what-it-is-and-why-you-use-it-every-day.

2. IBM.com, "What Is Artificial Intelligence (AI)?" published June 3, 2020, accessed March 29, 2022, https://www.ibm.com/cloud/learn/what-is-artificial-intelligence; and IBM.com, "What Is Conversational AI?" published August 31, 2020, https://www.ibm.com/cloud/learn/conversational-ai.

3. Google Assistant, "Conversational Actions Sunset Overview," accessed December 28, 2022, https://developers.google.com/assistant/ca-sunset.

4. Pymnts.com, "Amazon Puts Alexa Under Microscope in Cost-Cutting Review," published November 10, 2022, https://www.pymnts.com/news/retail/2022/amazon-puts-alexa-under-microscope-in-cost-cutting-review/.

5. Vixen Labs, "Voice Consumer Index 2022," published June 2022, accessed January 23, 2023, https://vixenlabs.co/research/voice-consumer-index-2022.

6. Federica Laricchia, "Smart Speaker Household Penetration Rate in the United States from 2014 to 2025," Statista, published February 14, 2022, https://www.statista.com/statistics/1022847/united-states-smart-speaker-household-penetration/.

7. https://martech.org/roughly-1-in-4-u-s-adults-now-owns-a-smart-speaker-according-to-new-report/ All I could find was this but the data is different than what you've wrote.

8. Natalie Gagliordi, "Smart Speakers Are Now the Fastest-Growing Consumer Technology," ZDNET, accessed January 26, 2023, https://www.zdnet.com/article/smart-speakers-are-now-the-fastest-growing-consumer-technology/.

9. Greg Sterling, "Google Says 20 Percent of Mobile Queries Are Voice Searches," *Search Engine Land*, published March 18, 2016, https://searchengineland.com/google-reveals-20-percent-queries-voice-queries-249917.

10. Swadhin Agrawal, "70+ New Voice Search Statistics, Trends & Facts for 2022," DigitalGYD, published March 25, 2022, https://www.digitalgyd.com/voice-search-statistics/#:~:text=25%25%20of%20queries%20on%20desktops,average%20for%20text%2Dbased%20queries.

11. DBS Interactive, "Voice Search Statistics and Emerging Trends," accessed May 2, 2023, https://www.dbswebsite.com/blog/trends-in-voice-search/.

12. Vixen Labs, "Voice Consumer Index 2022," published June 2022, accessed January 23, 2023, https://vixenlabs.co/research/voice-consumer-index-2022.

13. Thomas C. Redman, "Bad Data Costs the U.S. $3 Trillion per Year," *Harvard Business Review*, published September 22, 2016, accessed January 24, 2023, https://hbr.org/2016/09/bad-data-costs-the-u-s-3-trillion-per-year.

Chapter 2: Branding in a Voice-First World

1. Stefan Heini, *Building Relationships with Stakeholders in Corporate Branding* (Munich, Germany: GRIN Verlag, 2014).

2. Laurence Minsky and Ilan Geva, *Global Brand Management: A Guide to Developing, Building and Managing an International Brand* (London: Kogan Page, 2020).

3. Minsky and Geva, *Global Brand Management*.

4. Tiahn Wetzler, "The Advantages of a Mobile-First Strategy: Everything You Need to Know," Adjust, published March 26, 2021, accessed January 1, 2022, https://www.adjust.com/blog/the-advantages-of-a-mobile-first-strategy/.

5. A. Brad Schwartz, "The Infamous 'War of the Worlds' Radio Broadcast Was a Magnificent Fluke," *Smithsonian Magazine*, published May 6, 2015, accessed January 1, 2022, https://www.smithsonianmag.com/history/infamous-war-worlds-radio-broadcast-was-magnificent-fluke-180955180/.

6. Vixen Labs, "Voice Consumer Index 2022," published June 2022, accessed January 23, 2023, https://vixenlabs.co/research/voice-consumer-index-2022.

7. Eric Hall Schwartz, "New Voice App Takes Kids on Lucky Charms Branded Audio Adventure," Voicebot.ai, published September 16, 2020, accessed January 8, 2022, https://voicebot.ai/2020/09/16/new-voice-app-take-kids-on-lucky-charms-branded-audio-adventure/.

8. Schwartz, "New Voice App Takes Kids on Lucky Charms Branded Audio Adventure."

Chapter 3: Audio Branding and Its Importance

1. Marie Charlotte Götting, "U.S. Podcasting Industry—Statistics & Facts," Statista, published January 19, 2023, accessed January 23, 2023, https://www.statista.com/topics/3170/podcasting/#topicOverview.

2. Marie Charlotte Götting, "U.S. Radio Industry—Statistics & Facts," Statista, published January 6, 2023, accessed January 23, 2023, https://www.statista.com/topics/1330/radio/#topicOverview.

3. Vixen Labs, "Voice Consumer Index 2022," published June 2022, accessed January 23, 2023, https://vixenlabs.co/research/voice-consumer-index-2022.

4. Sara Lebow, "The Majority of US Adults Have No Interest in Voice Shopping," *eMarketer*, published March 18, 2021, accessed November 6, 2021, https://www.emarketer.com/content/majority-of-us-adults-have-no-interest-voice-shopping?ecid=NL1014.

5. Pymnts.com, "New PYMNTS Data Show Voice-Enabled Commerce Is a Business Winner for 40 Pct of Consumers, published August 15, 2021, accessed June 30, 2022, https://www.pymnts.com/news/payment-methods/2021/hed-new-pymnts-data-show-voice-enabled-commerce-is-a-business-winner-for-40pct-of-consumers/.

6. Susan Westwater and Scot Westwater, "Voice Consumer Index 2021 Executive Summary," Vixen Labs, published June 2021, accessed September 7, 2022, https://vixenlabs.co/wp-content/uploads/2022/08/VCI2021_ExecutiveSummary_VixenLabs.pdf

7. Vixen Labs, "Voice Consumer Index 2022."

8. Sheila Shayon, "Visa Engages the Senses with Sonic Branding," BrandKnew, published December 13, 2017, accessed September 7, 2020, https://www.brandknewmag.com/visa-engages-the-senses-with-sonic-branding/.

9. MarcomCentral, "The Importance of Building Trust with Brand Consistency," published January 14, 2020, accessed January 1, 2021, https://marcom.com/build-trust-brand-consistency/#:~:text=Brand%20consistency%20is%0a%20driving%20factor%20in%20building,always%2%200strive%20to%20live%20up%20to%20customer%20expectations.

10. Cathy Applefeld Olson, "How Shell Is Winning at the Sonic Branding Game," *Forbes*, published January 14, 2021, accessed January 27, 2023, https://www.forbes.com/sites/cathyolson/2021/01/14/how-shell-is-winning-at-the-sonic-branding-game/?sh=393c11f53803.

11. Ipsos, "The Power of You: Why Distinctive Brand Assets Are a Driving Force of Creative Effectiveness," published February 13, 2020, accessed February 3, 2021, https://www.ipsos.com/en/power-you-why-distinctive-brand-assets-are-driving-force-creative-effectiveness.

12. Ipsos, "The Power Of You."

13. Ibid.

14. Oliver Skinner, "Sonic Logos: A Master Class to Designing Your Brand Soundscape," Voices, published March 3, 2020, accessed January 24, 2021, https://www.voices.com/blog/sonic-logos.

15. Franchise Help, "We'll Leave the Light On for You: Motel 6's Advertising Success," accessed September 6, 2020, https://www.franchisehelp.com/franchisee-resource-center/motel-6-well-leave-the-light-on-for-you-advertising-success/.

16. Jay Peters, "The Mac's Iconic Startup Chime Is Back in macOS Big Sur," *The Verge*, published June 23, 2020, https://www.theverge.com/2020/6/23/21300545/apple-mac-macos-big-sur-startup-chime-sound-back-return.

17. Ronald Van Haaften, "2.1.2.2 Branding Principles," Rovaha, accessed December 20, 2021, https://www.van-haaften.nl/branding/corporate-branding/121-branding-principles.

Chapter 4: Understanding the Audience for Voice

1. Wayne W. LaMorte, "Diffusion of Innovation Theory," Boston University School of Public Health, https://sphweb.bumc.bu.edu/otlt/mph-modules/sb/behavioralchangetheories/BehavioralChangeTheories4.html.

2. Everett M. Rogers, *Diffusion of Innovations* (fifth ed.) (Free Press, 2003).

3. Vixen Labs, "Voice Consumer Index 2022," published June 2022, accessed January 23, 2023, https://vixenlabs.co/research/voice-consumer-index-2022.

4. Meghan Tocci, "Smartphone History and Evolution," SimpleTexting, published August 19, 2019, updated January 13, 2023, accessed February 20, 2023, https://simpletexting.com/where-have-we-come-since-the-first-smartphone/.

5. Bret Kinsella, "U.S. Smart Speaker Growth Flat Lined in 2020," Voicebot.ai, published April 14, 2021, accessed February 20, 2023, https://voicebot.ai/2021/04/14/u-s-smart-speaker-growth-flat-lined-in-2020/.

6. Kinsella, Bret, "Smartphone Voice Assistant Consumer Adoption Report Executive Summary," Voicebot.ai, Published November 2020, accessed September 2022, https://research.voicebot.ai/report-list/smartphone-voice-assistant-consumer-adoption-report-2020/.

7. Vixen Labs, "Voice Consumer Index 2022."

8. Ibid.

9. Ibid.

10. Ibid.

11. Mintel Store, "US Smart Homes Market Report 2021," accessed May 4, 2023, https://store.mintel.com/report/us-smart-homes-market-report-2021.

12. Mintel Store, "US Home Entertainment Technology: Hardware and Services Market Report 2021," accessed May 5, 2023, https://store.mintel.com/report/us-home-entertainment-technology-hardware-services-market-report.

13. National Public Media, "The Smart Audio Report," published June 2022, https://www.nationalpublicmedia.com/insights/reports/smart-audio-report/.

14. Mintel Store, "US Smart Homes Market Report 2021."

15. Paul Thagard, "What Is Trust? Trust Is an Emotional Brain State, Not Just an Expectation of Behavior," *Psychology Today*, published October 9, 2018, accessed November 23, 2021, https://www.psychologytoday.com/us/blog/hot-thought/201810/what-is-trust.

16. Roy J. Lewicki and Edward C. Tomlinson, "Trust and Trust Building," in *Beyond Intractability*, ed. Guy Burgess and Heidi Burgess, Conflict Information Consortium, University of Colorado,

Boulder, published December 2003, accessed November 23, 2021, http://www.beyondintractability.org/essay/trust-building.

17. Lewicki and Tomlinson, "Trust and Trust Building."

18. Susan Westwater and Scot Westwater, *Voice Strategy: Creating Useful and Usable Voice Experiences* (Independent, 2019).

19. Internet Encyclopedia of Philosophy, "Theory of Mind," accessed February 13, 2023, https://iep.utm.edu/theomind/.

Chapter 5: Data Privacy and Ethical Considerations

1. Vixen Labs, "Voice Consumer Index 2021," accessed May 5, 2023, https://vixenlabs.co/voice-consumer-index.

2. Amazon, "Policy Testing," accessed January 15, 2022, https://developer.amazon.com/en-US/docs/alexa/custom-skills/policy-testing-for-an-alexa-skill.html.

3. Steve Symanovich, "Privacy vs. Security: What's the Difference?" Norton, updated January 18, 2021, https://us.norton.com/internetsecurity-privacy-privacy-vs-security-whats-the-difference.html.

4. Laurence Minsky, Ben DiSanti, and Joseph Carson, "When It Comes to Cyber Security, a Step Ahead Is a Step Out of Harm's Way," *The European Business Review*, published November 10, 2017, accessed February 20, 2023, https://www.europeanbusinessreview.com/when-it-comes-to-cyber-security-a-step-ahead-is-a-step-out-of-harms-way/.

5. Minsky, DiSanti, and Carson, "When It Comes to Cyber Security, a Step Ahead Is a Step Out of Harm's Way."

6. Laurence Minsky and Keith Quesenberry, "Hunter or Hunted? How Digital Media and GDPR Increases Importance of Inbound B2B Sales," *The European Business Review*, published January 30, 2018, accessed: February 17, 2023, https://www.europeanbusinessreview.com/hunter-or-hunted-how-digital-media-and-gdpr-increases-importance-of-inbound-b2b-sales/.

7. Emily Mullin, "Voice Analysis Tech Could Diagnose Disease," *MIT Technology Review*, published January 19, 2017, accessed January 12, 2022, https://www.technologyreview.com/2017/01/19/154498/voice-analysis-tech-could-diagnose-disease/.

8. Brian Chevalier, "Diagnosing Disease with Speech Analytics," *Speech Technology*, published August 5, 2019, accessed January 12, 2022, https://www.speechtechmag.com/Articles/ReadArticle.aspx?ArticleID=133289.

9. PYMNTS, "Two-Factor Voice Authentication: Now We're Talking," published October 30, 2017, accessed February 17, 2023, https://www.pymnts.com/voice-activation/2017/two-factor-voice-authentication-as-biometrics-in-retail/.

10. Robert Zafft, *The Right Way to Win: Making Business Ethics Work in the Real World* (Lanham, MD: Rowman & Littlefield, 2020), 9.

11. Megan Specia, "Siri and Alexa Reinforce Gender Bias, U.N. Finds," *The New York Times*, published May 22, 2019, accessed January 12, 2022, https://www.nytimes.com/2019/05/22/world/siri-alexa-ai-gender-bias.html.

Chapter 6: Goals and KPIs for Voice Marketing

1. Amazon, "Chompers," accessed February 20, 2023, https://www.amazon.com/Gimlet-Media-Chompers/dp/B079WCGTKX/ref=sr_1_1?crid=8G5JYADMSW0C&keywords=chompers&qid=1664221035&s=digital-skills&sprefix=chompers%2Calexa-skills%2C80&sr=1-1.

2. Vixen Labs, "Voice Consumer Index 2022," published June 2022, accessed January 23, 2023, https://vixenlabs.co/research/voice-consumer-index-2022.

3. Vixen Labs, "Voice Consumer Index 2022."

Chapter 7: Developing Marketing Content for Voice

1. Bret Kinsella, "Voice Assistants Alexa, Bixby, Google Assistant and Siri Rely on Wikipedia and Yelp to Answer Many Common Questions about Brands," Voicebot.ai, published July 11, 2019, accessed February 20, 2023, https://voicebot.ai/2019/07/11/voice-assistants-alexa-bixby-google-assistant-and-siri-rely-on-wikipedia-and-yelp-to-answer-many-common-questions-about-brands/.

2. Laurence Minsky and William Rosen, *The Activation Imperative: How to Build Brands and Business by Inspiring Action* (Rowman & Littlefield Publishers, 2016).

Chapter 8: The Advantage of Marketing the Voice Experience

1. Scot Westwater and Susan Westwater, "2021 Voice Consumer Index," Vixen Labs, published June 30, 2021, accessed June 30, 2021, https://vixenlabs.co/voice-consumer-index.

2. Westwater and Westwater, "2021 Voice Consumer Index."

3. Steve Olenski, "Behold the Business Value of Omni-Channel Orchestration," September 6, 2017.

4. Olenski, "Behold the Business Value of Omni-Channel Orchestration."

5. Amazon, "Food Network Kitchen."

6. Headspace, "Headspace on Google Assistant."

Chapter 9: Analyzing, Maintaining, and Refining a Voice Strategy

1. Scot Westwater and Susan Westwater, "2021 Voice Consumer Index White Paper," Vixen Labs, published June 30, 2021, accessed June 30, 2021, https://vixenlabs.co/voice-consumer-index.

Chapter 10: Voice Implementations Across Industries

1. Vixen Labs, "Voice Consumer Index 2022," published June 2022, accessed January 23, 2023, https://vixenlabs.co/research/voice-consumer-index-2022.

2. Vixen Labs, "Voice Consumer Index 2022."

3. Ibid.

4. Ibid.

5. Ibid.

6. Ibid.

7. Ibid.

Chapter 11: Voice for Today and for the Future

1. Gartner, "Gartner Hype Cycle," accessed February 20, 2023, https://www.gartner.com/en/research/methodologies/gartner-hype-cycle.

2. Kane Simms, "Does Voice First Suck? And Is It Stuck? With Bret Kinsella, John Kelvie and Ahmed Bouzid," VUX, published February 8, 2021, accessed February 20, 2023, https://vux.world/does-voice-first-suck-and-is-it-stuck/.

Further Reading

The AI Marketing Canvas: A Five-Stage Road Map to Implementing Artificial Intelligence in Marketing, Raj Venkatesan and Jim Lecinski

Audio Branding: Using Sound to Build Your Brand, Laurence Minsky and Colleen Fahey

Conversational Design, Erika Hall

Conversations with Things: UX Design for Chat and Voice, Diana Deibel and Rebecca Evanhoe

Designing Connected Content: Plan and Model Digital Products for Today and Tomorrow (Voices That Matter), Carrie Hane and Mike Atherton

Designing Voice User Interfaces: Principles of Conversational Experiences, Cathy Pearl

Emotionally Engaged Digital Assistant: Humanizing Design and Technology, Shyamala Prayaga

Elements of Voice First Style, Ahmed Bouzid and Weiye Ma

Marketing Artificial Intelligence: AI, Marketing, and the Future of Business, Paul Roetzer and Mike Kaput

Voice Strategy: Creating Useful and Usable Voice Experiences, Susan Westwater and Scot Westwater

Writing Is Designing: Words and the User Experience, Michael J. Metts and Andy Welfle

Acknowledgments

We couldn't have done it alone—even with a team of four authors. It truly takes a community to birth a book on such a breakthrough business topic.

The authors would like to thank our community of support, including Manolo Almagro, Danny Bernstein, Jude R. Bettridge, Crystal Branson, Michael Brazeal, Donald Buckley, Suze Cooper, Marcella David, Nikayla Edmondson, Jason Fields, Eric Freedman, Robin Keira, Steve Keller, Roger Kibbe, Kwang-Wu Kim, Sirish Kondabolu, Philip Kotler, Natalie Mandziuk, Erin McCarthy, Gwen Morrison, Peg Murphy, Yu Ozaki, Romina Pankoke, Madison Potter, James Poulter, Shyamala Prayaga, Rhonda Present, Paul Roetzer, David Roth, Craig Sigele, Arlie Sims, Charles Spence, Jon Stein, Kalinda Ukanwa, and Sarah Andrew Wilson, among others.

We'd also like to thank Jon Stine for his contributions to the voice AI industry.

Finally, the authors would like to acknowledge and thank the late Bud Frankel. If it weren't for Frankel and Company, which he founded, the authors would not have known each other.

Index

accessibility, 9–10, 34, 49, 82; descriptions and, 129–30
accountability, in AI, 75
accuracy, wake-up word, 16, 88–89, 185
The Activation Imperative (Rosen and Minsky), 115
active listening, 57–58
activities, of users, 66, *67–68*, 94, 144–45
adaptation, 41, 43
added value, 61, 172
the Adopter (phase), 64
adoption, 9–10, 33, 161, 163; of innovations, 62–65; path to, 62, *63*, 64, 99–100, 177, 179; privacy and trust and, 64, 69–70
advantages, competitive, 12–13, 138–39
advertisements, *42*; copy for, 112, 131, 134; voice-enhanced, 100
age, of users, *66*, 80–81
agenda, learning, 147–49
AI. *See* artificial intelligence
Alexa. *See* Amazon Alexa
algorithms, 13, 72–75
Allstate, Alexa Skills and, 106, *107*, 108
Almagro, Manolo, 171–73
Amazon, 80; Show, 22–23
Amazon Alexa, 11, 33, 66, 131, 138–39, 181; invocation of, 133; Skills of, 5, 25, 120, 158, 183
analysis, of sentiment, 142, 144, 162–63, 173, 183
analytics, voice, 184; tracking of, 148; value and, 147–49
ANI. *See* artificial narrow intelligence
anthropomorphism, 104
APIs. *See* application programming interfaces
App Actions, of Google Assistant, 5, 60
Apple, 5, 48. *See also* Siri
appliances, smart, 80, 136–37
application programming interfaces (APIs), 35, 156–57, 161

applications (apps): of Food Network, 130; Headspace, 130–31; mobile, 34; voice, 4–5, *107*, 182, 184
apps. *See* applications
archetypes, 46
artificial intelligence (AI), 105, 142; accountability in, 75; bias in, 72–75; context awareness of, 137, 181; conversational, 3, *4*, 30, 36, 178, 182; disruption of, 13–15
artificial narrow intelligence (ANI), 13–14
AR/VR. *See* augmented reality/virtual reality
ASR. *See* automatic speech recognition
assets, brand, 41–42, 45–46
assistants: custom, 33–36; Google and, 17–18, 66, 131, 182; in-car, 1, 7, 53, 137, 182; virtual, 178, 184; voice, 5, 53, 65, 184
ATAs. *See* automated telephone attendants
atmospherics, 28
attention, audio branding and, 41–42
audience, intended, 128–29. *See also* users
audio: information delivery and, 111–13; logo in, 181; style guide for, 50–51
audio branding, 49–50, 181; attention and, 41–42; consistency in, 28, 41, 77, 117; music in, 43–44; visual branding compared to, 21–22, 40–42, 52
audio classification, 74
audit: of algorithms, 74–75; brand, 29; of content, 115
auditory pitch, 54
augmented reality/virtual reality (AR/VR), 63–64, 137, 179
Austin, Lucie, 138
authentication, voice, 6, 82, 87, 184; biometrics and, 89, 173
automated telephone attendants (ATAs), 3, 181
automatic dialog evaluation, 181
automatic speech recognition (ASR), 72–73, 75, 181

About the Authors

Laurence Minsky, professor, Communication Department, School of Media Arts, Columbia College Chicago, serves as a creative and strategic marketing consultant for leading agencies, corporations, and nonprofits across the globe in addition to his academic responsibilities. He is coauthor of *Global Brand Management: A Guide to Developing, Building, and Managing an International Brand*; *Audio Branding: Using Sound to Build Your Brand*; and *The Activation Imperative: How to Build Brands and Business by Inspiring Action*, the executive editor of *The Get a Job Workshop: How to Find Your Way to a Creative Career in Advertising, Branding, Collateral, Digital, Experiential and More*, and the author of *How to Succeed in Advertising When All You Have Is Talent* (second edition), among others. He has also been published by *Harvard Business Review*, the *European Business Review*, *Journal of Healthcare Management Standards*, *MarketingProfs*, and elsewhere; has been quoted in *The New York Times*, *Chicago Tribune*, *Chicago Sun-Times*, *San Diego Union Tribune*, *The Telegraph*, *Exame* (Brazil's largest business magazine), *Crain's Chicago Business*, and other publications; and is a frequent presenter at conferences and workshops, including at Chicago Ideas Week, The Voice Summit, The One Club for Art & Copy, American Marketing Association's Chicago BrandSmart Conference, RealtivityFest, Direct Marketing Association of Kansas City, ANA (Association of National Advertisers), and more. Finally, Laurence is an award-winning creative with more than 125 industry accolades to date, has served on the juries of leading industry award shows, and has created marketing and communication solutions for many blue-chip clients across the globe.

Susan Westwater, cofounder and CEO of Pragmatic Digital, advises the world's leading brands on how to capitalize on the incredible opportunity voice and conversational AI represent. She combines the strategic marketing and brand knowledge she gained from over twenty years at top-tier agencies such as Leo Burnett and working in corporate to help clients expand their brands into conversational experiences to solve marketing and customer experience problems. Susan has presented numerous talks, workshops, articles, research papers, and books focused on the role voice, conversational AI, and other emerging technologies like the metaverse play in marketing and business strategy. She is an ambassador of the Open Voice Network, an instructor at the AI Academy for Marketers, and a chapter lead for Women in Voice. Susan is coauthor of *Voice Strategy: Creating Useful and Usable Voice Experiences* (which was a #1 release on Amazon) and has been published in the *Journal of Digital and Social Media Marketing* and the *Journal of Brand Strategy*. She was recognized as Top Voice Influencer in Voicebot's Top 68 Leaders in Voice 2020 and has been featured in the Voicebot.ai Annual Trend Wrap-Up for the past three years. Her client experience includes

Canadian Tire, The Coca-Cola Company, Danone, Kaiser Permanente, The Kraft Heinz Company, Nestlé, Shell, United Airlines, USPS, Visa USA, and more.

Scot Westwater, cofounder and CCO of Pragmatic Digital, helps leading companies improve their marketing and customer experiences through voice and conversational AI. He leverages more than twenty-five years of design, UX, and digital strategy to create effective voice experiences. Along with his wife, Susan, he cowrote *Voice Strategy: Creating Useful and Usable Voice Experiences.* He has spoken at industry events like SEMrush World Marketing Day, Project Voice, VOICE Global, and VOICE22. In addition, he enjoys giving guest lectures for master's level marketing and HCI classes. He's an ambassador for the Open Voice Network and an instructor for the Marketing AI Institute. Scot was recognized in Voicebot's Top 68 Leaders in Voice 2020 and was recently included in Sound Hound's "Top 40 Voice AI Influencers to Follow on Twitter." His clients past and present include Abbvie, Abbot Nutrition, the AARP Foundation Baxter, Crate and Barrel, Pfizer, Planterra Foods, Sixième Son, Swag Ball, and Walgreens, among others.

Colleen Fahey, US managing director, Sixième Son, is a creative executive with deep expertise in branding and multi-touchpoint marketing. Colleen opened Sixième Son, the world's leading sonic branding agency, in North America in 2012 and has led the firm into categories as diverse as financial services, health care, baby products, heavy industry, footwear, and food. Recognizing the strong connection between voice activation and sonic branding, she joined the Open Voice Network (since then, Sixième Son has created their sonic brand) and helped establish the Chicago chapter of Women in Voice. Prior to launching Sixième Son, USA, Colleen was EVP, executive creative director at Frankel (now called Arc Worldwide), where, early in her career, she led the creative team that brought the Happy Meal from an occasional promotion to a permanent product. After Frankel's purchase by Publicis, she worked with Publicis Groupe to help leading brands in the United States, Europe, Latin America, and Asia to bring their clients nontraditional approaches to marketing. Coauthor of *Audio Branding: Using Sound to Build Your Brand*, she has also been published by the *Harvard Business Review* and *The European Business Review*, among many others. She's a sought-after speaker and will willingly hop on a stage to share her excitement about the magic of sound.